McGraw Hill Companies
2460 Kerper Blvd.
Dubuque, Iowa 52001

Customized

FUNDAMENTALS OF DIGITAL LOGIC WITH VHDL DESIGN

Stephen Brown and Zvonko Vranesic
Department of Electrical and Computer Engineering
University of Toronto

The McGraw-Hill Companies, Inc
Primis Custom Publishing

*New York St. Louis San Francisco Auckland Bogota
Caracas Lisbon London Madrid Mexico Milan Montreal
New Delhi Paris San Juan Singapore Sydney Tokyo Toronto*

McGraw-Hill

A Division of The McGraw-Hill Companies

Customized Fundamentals of Digital Logic with VHDL Design

This book contains selected material from *Fundamentals of Digital Logic with VHDL
Design, First Edition*, by Stephen Brown and Zvonko Vranesic, Copyright © 2000 by
The McGraw-Hill Companies, Inc. Reprinted with permission of the publisher.

10 QDB QDB 15 14 13 12 11

ISBN-13: 978-0-07-241044-0
ISBN-10: 0-07-241044-2

Printer/Binder: Quad/Graphics Dubuque

Contents

1

DESIGN CONCEPTS

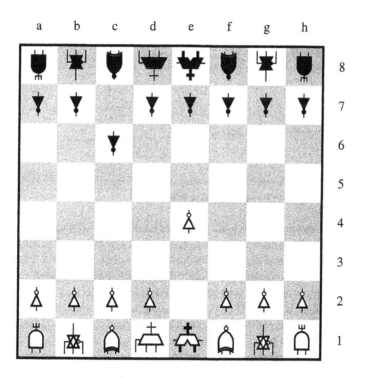

1. e2–e4, c7–c6

This book is about logic circuits—the circuits from which computers are built. Proper understanding of logic circuits is vital for today's electrical and computer engineers. These circuits are the key ingredient of computers and are also used in many other applications. They are found in commonly used products, such as digital watches, various household appliances, CD players, and electronic games, as well as in large systems, such as the equipment for telephone and television networks.

The material in this book will introduce the reader to the many issues involved in the design of logic circuits. It explains the key ideas with simple examples and shows how complex circuits can be derived from elementary ones. We cover the classical theory used in the design of logic circuits in great depth because it provides the reader with an intuitive understanding of the nature of such circuits. But throughout the book we also illustrate the modern way of designing logic circuits, using sophisticated *computer aided design (CAD)* software tools. The CAD methodology adopted in the book is based on the industry-standard design language called VHDL. Design with VHDL is first introduced in Chapter 2, and usage of VHDL and CAD tools is an integral part of each chapter in the book.

Logic circuits are implemented electronically, using transistors on an integrated circuit chip. With modern technology it is possible to fabricate chips that contain tens of millions of transistors, as in the case of computer processors. The basic building blocks for such circuits are easy to understand, but there is nothing simple about a circuit that contains tens of millions of transistors. The complexity that comes with the large size of logic circuits can be handled successfully only by using highly organized design techniques. We introduce these techniques in this chapter, but first we briefly describe the hardware technology used to build logic circuits.

1.1 DIGITAL HARDWARE

Logic circuits are used to build computer hardware, as well as many other types of products. All such products are broadly classified as *digital hardware*. The reason that the name *digital* is used will become clear later in the book—it derives from the way in which information is represented in computers, as electronic signals that correspond to digits of information.

The technology used to build digital hardware has evolved dramatically over the past four decades. Until the 1960s logic circuits were constructed with bulky components, such as transistors and resistors that came as individual parts. The advent of integrated circuits made it possible to place a number of transistors, and thus an entire circuit, on a single chip. In the beginning these circuits had only a few transistors, but as the technology improved they became larger. Integrated circuit chips are manufactured on a silicon wafer, such as the one shown in Figure 1.1. The wafer is cut to produce the individual chips, which are then placed inside a special type of chip package. By 1970 it was possible to implement all circuitry needed to realize a microprocessor on a single chip. Although early microprocessors had modest computing capability by today's standards, they opened the door for the information processing revolution by providing the means for implementation of affordable personal computers. About 30 years ago Gordon Moore, chairman of Intel Corporation, observed that integrated circuit technology was progressing at an astounding rate, doubling the number of transistors that could be placed on a chip every 1.5 to 2 years.

Figure 1.1   A silicon wafer (courtesy of Altera Corp.).

This phenomenon, informally known as *Moore's law*, continues to the present day. Thus in the early 1990s microprocessors could be manufactured with a few million transistors, and by the late 1990s it has become possible to fabricate chips that contain more than 10 million transistors.

Moore's law is expected to continue to hold true for at least the next decade. A consortium of integrated circuit manufacturers called the Semiconductor Industry Association (SIA) produces an estimate of how the technology is expected to evolve. Known as the *SIA Roadmap* [1], this estimate predicts the minimum size of a transistor that can be fabricated on an integrated circuit chip. The size of a transistor is measured by a parameter called its *gate length*, which we will discuss in Chapter 3. A sample of the SIA Roadmap is given in Table 1.1. In 1999 the minimum possible gate length that can be reliably manufactured is $0.14~\mu$m. The first row of the table indicates that the minimum gate length is expected to reduce steadily to about $0.035~\mu$m by the year 2012. The size of a transistor determines how many transistors can be placed in a given amount of chip area, with the current maximum being about 14 million transistors per cm^2. This number is expected to grow to 100 million transistors by the year 2012. The largest chip size is expected to be about 1300 mm^2 at that time; thus chips with up to 1.3 billion transistors will be possible! There is no doubt that this technology will have a huge impact on all aspects of people's lives.

The designer of digital hardware may be faced with designing logic circuits that can be implemented on a single chip or, more likely, designing circuits that involve a number of chips placed on a *printed circuit board (PCB)*. Frequently, some of the logic circuits can be realized in existing chips that are readily available. This situation simplifies the design task and shortens the time needed to develop the final product. Before we discuss the design

Table 1.1   A sample of the SIA Roadmap

	Year					
	1999	**2001**	**2003**	**2006**	**2009**	**2012**
Transistor gate length	$0.14~\mu$m	$0.12~\mu$m	$0.10~\mu$m	$0.07~\mu$m	$0.05~\mu$m	$0.035~\mu$m
Transistors per cm^2	14 million	16 million	24 million	40 million	64 million	100 million
Chip size	800 mm^2	850 mm^2	900 mm^2	1000 mm^2	1100 mm^2	1300 mm^2

process in more detail, we should introduce the different types of integrated circuit chips that may be used.

There exists a large variety of chips that implement various functions that are useful in the design of digital hardware. The chips range from very simple chips with low functionality to extremely complex chips. For example, a digital hardware product may require a microprocessor to perform some arithmetic operations, memory chips to provide storage capability, and interface chips that allow easy connection to input and output devices. Such chips are available from various vendors.

For most digital hardware products, it is also necessary to design and build some logic circuits from scratch. For implementing these circuits, three main types of chips may be used: standard chips, programmable logic devices, and custom chips. These are discussed next.

1.1.1 STANDARD CHIPS

Numerous chips are available that realize some commonly used logic circuits. We will refer to these as *standard chips*, because they usually conform to an agreed-upon standard in terms of functionality and physical configuration. Each standard chip contains a small amount of circuitry (usually involving fewer than 100 transistors) and performs a simple function. To build a logic circuit, the designer chooses the chips that perform whatever functions are needed and then defines how these chips should be interconnected to realize a larger logic circuit.

Standard chips were popular for building logic circuits until the early 1980s. However, as integrated circuit technology improved, it became inefficient to use valuable space on PCBs for chips with low functionality. Another drawback of standard chips is that the functionality of each chip is fixed and cannot be changed.

1.1.2 PROGRAMMABLE LOGIC DEVICES

In contrast to standard chips that have fixed functionality, it is possible to construct chips that contain circuitry that can be configured by the user to implement a wide range of different logic circuits. These chips have a very general structure and include a collec-

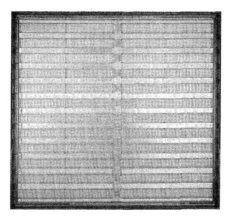

Figure 1.2   A field-programmable gate array chip (courtesy of Altera Corp.).

tion of *programmable switches* that allow the internal circuitry in the chip to be configured in many different ways. The designer can implement whatever functions are needed for a particular application by choosing an appropriate configuration of the switches. The switches are programmed by the end user, rather than when the chip is manufactured. Such chips are known as *programmable logic devices (PLDs)*. We will introduce them in Chapter 3.

Most types of PLDs can be programmed multiple times. This capability is advantageous because a designer who is developing a prototype of a product can program a PLD to perform some function, but later, when the prototype hardware is being tested, can make corrections by reprogramming the PLD. Reprogramming might be necessary, for instance, if a designed function is not quite as intended or if new functions are needed that were not contemplated in the original design.

PLDs are available in a wide range of sizes. They can be used to realize much larger logic circuits than a typical standard chip can realize. Because of their size and the fact that they can be tailored to meet the requirements of a specific application, PLDs are widely used today. One of the most sophisticated types of PLD is known as a *field-programmable gate array (FPGA)*. FPGAs that contain more than 100 million transistors will soon be available [2,3]. A photograph of an FPGA chip that has 10 million transistors is shown in Figure 1.2. The chip consists of a large number of small logic circuit elements, which can be connected together using the programmable switches. The logic circuit elements are arranged in a regular two-dimensional structure.

1.1.3 CUSTOM-DESIGNED CHIPS

PLDs are available as off-the-shelf components that can be purchased from different suppliers. Because they are programmable, they can be used to implement most logic circuits found in digital hardware. However, PLDs also have a drawback in that the programmable switches consume valuable chip area and limit the speed of operation of implemented circuits. Thus in some cases PLDs may not meet the desired performance or cost objectives. In such situations it is possible to design a chip from scratch; namely, the logic circuitry that must be included on the chip is designed first and then an appropriate technology is chosen to implement the chip. Finally, the chip is manufactured by a company that has the fabrication facilities. This approach is known as *custom* or *semi-custom design*, and such chips are called *custom* or *semi-custom chips*. Such chips are intended for use in specific applications and are sometimes called *application-specific integrated circuits (ASICs)*.

The main advantage of a custom chip is that its design can be optimized for a specific task; hence it usually leads to better performance. It is possible to include a larger amount of logic circuitry in a custom chip than would be possible in other types of chips. The cost of producing such chips is high, but if they are used in a product that is sold in large quantities, then the cost per chip, amortized over the total number of chips fabricated, may be lower than the total cost of off-the-shelf chips that would be needed to implement the same function(s). Moreover, if a single chip can be used instead of multiple chips to achieve the same goal, then a smaller area is needed on a PCB that houses the chips in the final product. This results in a further reduction in cost.

A disadvantage of the custom-design approach is that manufacturing a custom chip often takes a considerable amount of time, on the order of months. In contrast, if a PLD can be used instead, then the chips are programmed by the end user and no manufacturing delays are involved.

1.2 THE DESIGN PROCESS

The availability of computer-based tools has greatly influenced the design process in a wide variety of design environments. For example, designing an automobile is similar in the general approach to designing a furnace or a computer. Certain steps in the development cycle must be performed if the final product is to meet the specified objectives. We will start by introducing a typical development cycle in the most general terms. Then we will focus on the particular aspects that pertain to the design of logic circuits.

The flowchart in Figure 1.3 depicts a typical development process. We assume that the process is to develop a product that meets certain expectations. The most obvious requirements are that the product must function properly, that it must meet an expected level of performance, and that its cost should not exceed a given target.

The process begins with the definition of product specifications. The essential features of the product are identified, and an acceptable method of evaluating the implemented features in the final product is established. The specifications must be tight enough to ensure that the developed product will meet the general expectations, but should not be unnecessarily constraining (that is, the specifications should not prevent design choices that may lead to unforeseen advantages).

From a complete set of specifications, it is necessary to define the general structure of an initial design of the product. This step is difficult to automate. It is usually performed by a human designer because there is no clear-cut strategy for developing a product's overall structure—it requires considerable design experience and intuition.

After the general structure is established, CAD tools are used to work out the details. Many types of CAD tools are available, ranging from those that help with the design

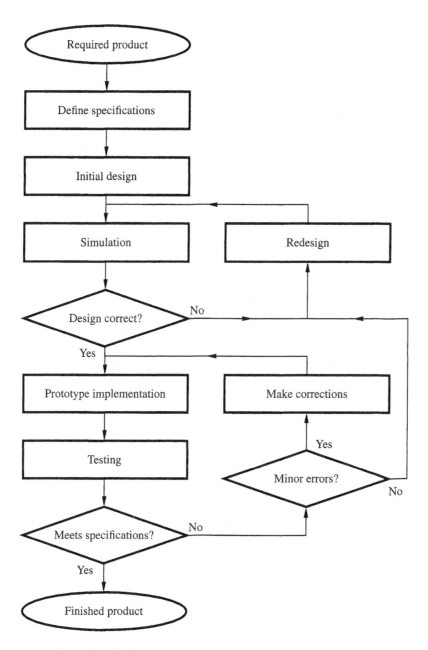

Figure 1.3   The development process.

of individual parts of the system to those that allow the entire system's structure to be represented in a computer. When the initial design is finished, the results must be verified against the original specifications. Traditionally, before the advent of CAD tools, this step involved constructing a physical model of the designed product, usually including just the key parts. Today it is seldom necessary to build a physical model. CAD tools enable designers to simulate the behavior of incredibly complex products, and such simulations are used to determine whether the obtained design meets the required specifications. If errors are found, then appropriate changes are made and the verification of the new design is repeated through simulation. Although some design flaws may escape detection via simulation, usually all but the most subtle problems are discovered in this way.

When the simulation indicates that the design is correct, a complete physical prototype of the product is constructed. The prototype is thoroughly tested for conformance with the specifications. Any errors revealed in the testing must be fixed. The errors may be minor, and often they can be eliminated by making small corrections directly on the prototype of the product. In case of large errors, it is necessary to redesign the product and repeat the steps explained above. When the prototype passes all the tests, then the product is deemed to be successfully designed and it can go into production.

1.3   DESIGN OF DIGITAL HARDWARE

Our previous discussion of the development process is relevant in a most general way. The steps outlined in Figure 1.3 are fully applicable in the development of digital hardware. Before we discuss the complete sequence of steps in this development environment, we should emphasize the iterative nature of the design process.

1.3.1   BASIC DESIGN LOOP

Any design process comprises a basic sequence of tasks that are performed in various situations. This sequence is presented in Figure 1.4. Assuming that we have an initial concept about what should be achieved in the design process, the first step is to generate an initial design. This step often requires a lot of manual effort because most designs have some specific goals that can be reached only through the designer's knowledge, skill, and intuition. The next step is the simulation of the design at hand. There exist excellent CAD tools to assist in this step. To carry out the simulation successfully, it is necessary to have adequate input conditions that can be applied to the design that is being simulated and later to the final product that has to be tested. Applying these input conditions, the simulator tries to verify that the designed product will perform as required under the original product specifications. If the simulation reveals some errors, then the design must be changed to overcome the problems. The redesigned version is again simulated to determine whether the errors have disappeared. This loop is repeated until the simulation indicates a successful design. A prudent designer expends considerable effort to remedy errors during simulation because errors are typically much harder to fix if they are discovered late in the design process. Even so, some errors may not be detected during simulation, in which case they have to be dealt with in later stages of the development cycle.

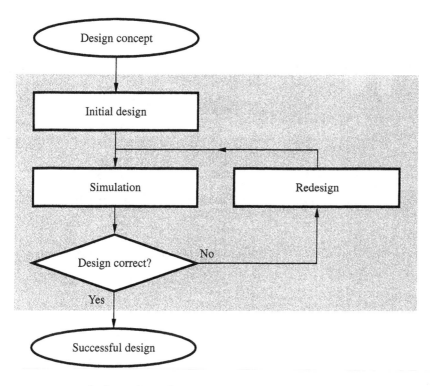

Figure 1.4   The basic design loop.

1.3.2 DESIGN OF A DIGITAL HARDWARE UNIT

Digital hardware products usually involve one or more PCBs that contain many chips and other components. Development of such products starts with the definition of the overall structure. Then the required integrated circuit chips are selected, and the PCBs that house and connect the chips together are designed. If the selected chips include PLDs or custom chips, then these chips must be designed before the PCB-level design is undertaken. Since the complexity of circuits implemented on individual chips and on the circuit boards is usually very high, it is essential to make use of good CAD tools.

An example of a PCB is given in Figure 1.5. The PCB is a part of a large computer system designed at the University of Toronto. This computer, called *NUMAchine* [4,5], is a *multiprocessor*, which means that it contains many processors that can be used together to work on a particular task. The PCB in the figure contains one processor chip and various memory and support chips. Complex logic circuits are needed to form the interface between the processor and the rest of the system. A number of PLDs are used to implement these logic circuits.

To illustrate the complete development cycle in more detail, we will consider the steps needed to produce a digital hardware unit that can be implemented on a PCB. This hardware

Figure 1.5   A printed circuit board.

could be viewed as a very complex logic circuit that performs the functions defined by the product specifications. Figure 1.6 shows the design flow, assuming that we have a design concept that defines the expected behavior and characteristics of this large circuit.

An orderly way of dealing with the complexity involved is to partition the circuit into smaller blocks and then to design each block separately. Breaking down a large task into more manageable smaller parts is known as the divide-and-conquer approach. The design of each block follows the procedure outlined in Figure 1.4. The circuitry in each block is defined, and the chips needed to implement it are chosen. The operation of this circuitry is simulated, and any necessary corrections are made.

Having successfully designed all blocks, the interconnection between the blocks must be defined, which effectively combines these blocks into a single large circuit. Now it is necessary to simulate this complete circuit and correct any errors. Depending on the errors encountered, it may be necessary to go back to the previous steps as indicated by the paths A, B, and C in the flowchart. Some errors may be caused by incorrect connections

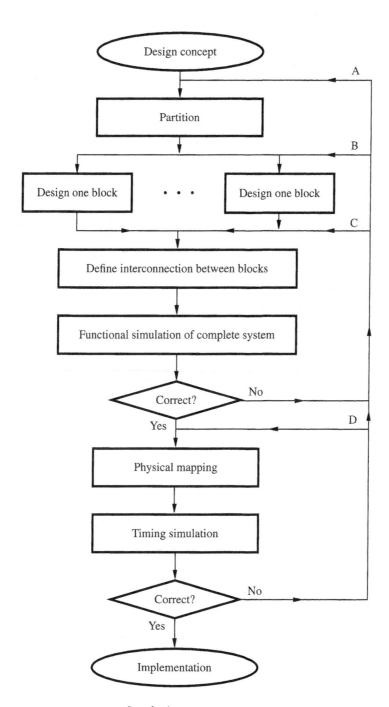

Figure 1.6 Design flow for logic circuits.

between the blocks, in which case these connections have to be redefined, following path C. Some blocks may not have been designed correctly, in which case path B is followed and the erroneous blocks are redesigned. Another possibility is that the very first step of partitioning the overall large circuit into blocks was not done well, in which case path A is followed. This may happen, for example, if none of the blocks implement some functionality needed in the complete circuit.

Successful completion of functional simulation suggests that the designed circuit will correctly perform all of its functions. The next step is to decide how to realize this circuit on a PCB. The physical location of each chip on the board has to be determined, and the wiring pattern needed to make connections between the chips has to be defined. We refer to this step as the *physical design* of the PCB. CAD tools are relied on heavily to perform this task automatically.

Once the placement of chips and the actual wire connections on the PCB have been established, it is desirable to see how this physical layout will affect the performance of the circuit on the finished board. It is reasonable to assume that if the previous functional simulation indicated that all functions will be performed correctly, then the CAD tools used in the physical design step will ensure that the required functional behavior will not be corrupted by placing the chips on the board and wiring them together to realize the final circuit. However, even though the functional behavior may be correct, the realized circuit may operate more slowly than desired and thus lead to inadequate performance. This condition occurs because the physical wiring on the PCB involves metal traces that present resistance and capacitance to electrical signals and thus may have a significant impact on the speed of operation. To distinguish between simulation that considers only the functionality of the circuit and simulation that also considers timing behavior, it is customary to use the terms *functional simulation* and *timing simulation*. A timing simulation may reveal potential performance problems, which can then be corrected by using the CAD tools to make changes in the physical design of the PCB.

Having completed the design process, the designed circuit is ready for physical implementation. The steps needed to implement a prototype board are indicated in Figure 1.7. A first version of the board is built and tested. Most minor errors that are detected can usually be corrected by making changes directly on the prototype board. This may involve changes in wiring or perhaps reprogramming some PLDs. Larger problems require a more substantial redesign. Depending on the nature of the problem, the designer may have to return to any of the points A, B, C, or D in the design process of Figure 1.6.

We have described the development process where the final circuit is implemented using many chips on a PCB. The material presented in this book is directly applicable to this type of design problem. However, for practical reasons the design examples that appear in the book are relatively small and can be realized in a single integrated circuit, either a custom-designed chip or a PLD. All the steps in Figure 1.6 are relevant in this case as well, with the understanding that the circuit blocks to be designed are on a smaller scale.

1.4 LOGIC CIRCUIT DESIGN IN THIS BOOK

In this book we use PLDs extensively to illustrate many aspects of logic circuit design. We selected this technology because it is widely used in real digital hardware products

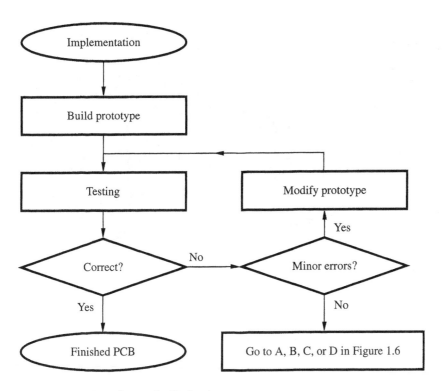

Figure 1.7   Completion of PCB development.

and because the chips are user programmable. PLD technology is particularly well suited for educational purposes because many readers have access to facilities for programming PLDs, which enables the reader to actually implement the sample circuits. To illustrate practical design issues, in this book we use two types of PLDs—they are the two types of devices that are widely used in digital hardware products today. One type is known as *complex programmable logic devices* (CPLDs) and the other as *field-programmable gate arrays* (FPGAs). These chips are introduced in Chapter 3.

We will illustrate the automated design of logic circuits using a sophisticated CAD system from Altera Corporation, one of the world's leading suppliers of PLDs. The system is called *MAX+plusII*. This industrial-quality software supports all phases of the design cycle and is powerful and easy to use. To allow the reader to obtain hands-on experience with the CAD tools, a CD-ROM containing the MAX+plusII software accompanies the book. The software is easily installed on a suitable personal computer, and we provide a sequence of complete step-by-step tutorials to illustrate the proper use of the CAD tools in concert with the book.

For educational purposes Altera provides a laboratory development PCB, which is called the UP-1 board. This PCB, shown in Figure 1.8, contains both a CPLD and an FPGA chip and has an interface for connecting the board to a personal computer. Logic circuits can be designed on the computer using MAX+plusII and then *downloaded* into the PLDs, thus realizing the designed circuit. The reader is encouraged to obtain the board from Altera,

Figure 1.8   The Altera UP-1 laboratory development board.

which can be done by accessing the University Program part of Altera's Web site. All the examples of logic circuits presented in this book can be implemented on the UP-1 board.

1.5 THEORY AND PRACTICE

Modern design of logic circuits depends heavily on CAD tools, but the discipline of logic design evolved long before CAD tools were invented. This chronology is quite obvious because the very first computers were built with logic circuits, and there certainly were no computers available on which to design them!

Numerous manual design techniques have been developed to deal with logic circuits. Boolean algebra, which we will introduce in Chapter 2, was adopted as a mathematical means for representing such circuits. An enormous amount of "theory" was developed, showing how certain design issues may be treated. To be successful, a designer had to apply this knowledge in practice.

CAD tools not only made it possible to design incredibly complex circuits but also made the design work much simpler in general. They perform many tasks automatically, which may suggest that today's designer need not understand the theoretical concepts used in the tasks performed by CAD tools. An obvious question would then be, Why should one study the theory that is no longer needed for manual design? Why not simply learn how to use the CAD tools?

There are three big reasons for learning the relevant theory. First, although the CAD tools perform the automatic tasks of optimizing a logic circuit to meet particular design objectives, the designer has to give the original description of the logic circuit. If the designer specifies a circuit that has inherently bad properties, then the final circuit will also be of poor quality. Second, the algebraic rules and theorems for design and manipulation of logic circuits are directly implemented in today's CAD tools. It is not possible for a user of the tools to understand what the tools do without grasping the underlying theory. Third, CAD tools offer many optional processing steps that a user can invoke when working on a design. The designer chooses which options to use by examining the resulting circuit produced by the CAD tools and deciding whether it meets the required objectives. The only way that the designer can know whether or not to apply a particular option in a given situation is to know what the CAD tools will do if that option is invoked—again, this implies that the designer must be familiar with the underlying theory. We discuss the classical logic circuit theory extensively in this book, because it is not possible to become an effective logic circuit designer without understanding the fundamental concepts.

On a final note, there is another good reason to learn some logic circuit theory even if it were not required for CAD tools. Simply put, it is interesting and intellectually challenging. In the modern world filled with sophisticated automatic machinery, it is tempting to rely on tools as a substitute for thinking. However, in logic circuit design, as in any type of design process, computer-based tools are not a substitute for human intuition and innovation. Computer-based tools can produce good digital hardware designs only when employed by a designer who thoroughly understands the nature of logic circuits.

REFERENCES

1. Semiconductor Industry Association, "National Technology Roadmap for Semi-conductors," http://www.semichips.org/

2. Altera Corporation, "APEX 20K Advance Information Brief," http://www.altera.com

3. Xilinx Corporation, "Virtex Field Programmable Gate Arrays," http://www.xilinx.com

4. S. Brown, N. Manjikian, Z. Vranesic, S. Caranci, A. Grbic, R. Grindley, M. Gusat, K. Loveless, Z. Zilic, and S. Srbljic, "Experience in Designing a Large-Scale Multiprocessor Using Field-Programmable Devices and Advanced CAD Tools," 33rd IEEE Design Automation Conference, Las Vegas, June 1996.

5. A. Grbic, S. Brown, S. Caranci, R. Grindley, M. Gusat, G. Lemieux, K. Loveless, N. Manjikian, S. Srbljic, M. Stumm, Z. Vranesic, and Z. Zilic, "The Design and Implementation of the NUMAchine Multiprocessor," IEEE Design Automation Conference, San Francisco, June 1998.

2

INTRODUCTION TO LOGIC CIRCUITS

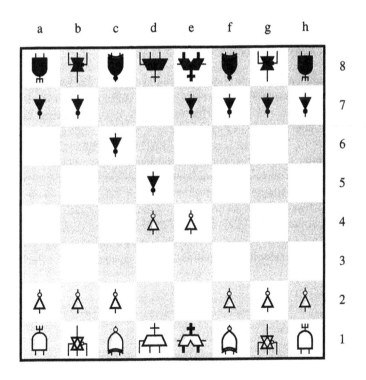

2. d2–d4, d7–d5

The study of logic circuits is motivated mostly by their use in digital computers. But such circuits also form the foundation of many other digital systems where performing arithmetic operations on numbers is not of primary interest. For example, in a myriad of control applications actions are determined by some simple logical operations on input information, without having to do extensive numerical computations.

Logic circuits perform operations on digital signals and are usually implemented as electronic circuits where the signal values are restricted to a few discrete values. In *binary* logic circuits there are only two values, 0 and 1. In *decimal* logic circuits there are 10 values, from 0 to 9. Since each signal value is naturally represented by a digit, such logic circuits are referred to as *digital circuits*. In contrast, there exist *analog circuits* where the signals may take on a continuous range of values between some minimum and maximum levels.

In this book we deal with binary circuits, which have the dominant role in digital technology. We hope to provide the reader with an understanding of how these circuits work, how are they represented in mathematical notation, and how are they designed using modern design automation techniques. We begin by introducing some basic concepts pertinent to the binary logic circuits.

2.1 VARIABLES AND FUNCTIONS

The dominance of binary circuits in digital systems is a consequence of their simplicity, which results from constraining the signals to assume only two possible values. The simplest binary element is a switch that has two states. If a given switch is controlled by an input variable x, then we will say that the switch is open if $x = 0$ and closed if $x = 1$, as illustrated in Figure 2.1a. We will use the graphical symbol in Figure 2.1b to represent such switches in the diagrams that follow. Note that the control input x is shown explicitly in the symbol. In Chapter 3 we will explain how such switches are implemented with transistors.

Consider a simple application of a switch, where the switch turns a small lightbulb on or off. This action is accomplished with the circuit in Figure 2.2a. A battery provides the power source. The lightbulb glows when sufficient current passes through its filament, which is an electrical resistance. The current flows when the switch is closed, that is, when $x = 1$. In this example the input that causes changes in the behavior of the circuit is the

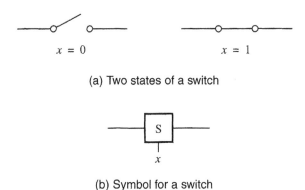

$x = 0$ $x = 1$

(a) Two states of a switch

(b) Symbol for a switch

Figure 2.1   A binary switch.

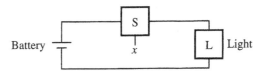

(a) Simple connection to a battery

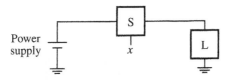

(b) Using a ground connection as the return path

Figure 2.2   A light controlled by a switch.

switch control x. The output is defined as the state (or condition) of the light L. If the light is on, we will say that $L = 1$. If the the light is off, we will say that $L = 0$. Using this convention, we can describe the state of the light L as a function of the input variable x. Since $L = 1$ if $x = 1$ and $L = 0$ if $x = 0$, we can say that

$$L(x) = x$$

This simple *logic expression* describes the output as a function of the input. We say that $L(x) = x$ is a *logic function* and that x is an *input variable*.

The circuit in Figure 2.2a can be found in an ordinary flashlight, where the switch is a simple mechanical device. In an electronic circuit the switch is implemented as a transistor and the light may be a light-emitting diode (LED). An electronic circuit is powered by a power supply of a certain voltage, perhaps 5 volts. One side of the power supply is connected to ground, as shown in Figure 2.2b. The ground connection may also be used as the return path for the current, to close the loop, which is achieved by connecting one side of the light to ground as indicated in the figure. Of course, the light can also be connected by a wire directly to the grounded side of the power supply, as in Figure 2.2a.

Consider now the possibility of using two switches to control the state of the light. Let x_1 and x_2 be the control inputs for these switches. The switches can be connected either in series or in parallel as shown in Figure 2.3. Using a series connection, the light will be turned on only if both switches are closed. If either switch is open, the light will be off. This behavior can be described by the expression

$$L(x_1, x_2) = x_1 \cdot x_2$$
$$\text{where} \quad L = 1 \text{ if } x_1 = 1 \text{ and } x_2 = 1,$$
$$L = 0 \text{ otherwise.}$$

The "$\cdot$" symbol is called the *AND operator*, and the circuit in Figure 2.3a is said to implement a *logical AND function*.

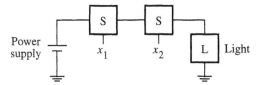

(a) The logical AND function (series connection)

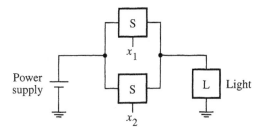

(b) The logical OR function (parallel connection)

Figure 2.3   Two basic functions.

The parallel connection of two switches is given in Figure 2.3b. In this case the light will be on if either x_1 or x_2 switch is closed. The light will also be on if both switches are closed. The light will be off only if both switches are open. This behavior can be stated as

$$L(x_1, x_2) = x_1 + x_2$$

where $L = 1$ if $x_1 = 1$ or $x_2 = 1$ or if $x_1 = x_2 = 1$,

$L = 0$ if $x_1 = x_2 = 0$.

The $+$ symbol is called the *OR operator*, and the circuit in Figure 2.3b is said to implement a *logical OR function*.

In the above expressions for AND and OR, the output $L(x_1, x_2)$ is a logic function with input variables x_1 and x_2. The AND and OR functions are two of the most important logic functions. Together with some other simple functions, they can be used as building blocks

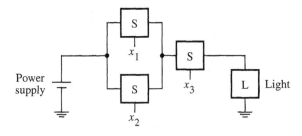

Figure 2.4   A series-parallel connection.

for the implementation of all logic circuits. Figure 2.4 illustrates how three switches can be used to control the light in a more complex way. This series-parallel connection of switches realizes the logic function

$$L(x_1, x_2, x_3) = (x_1 + x_2) \cdot x_3$$

The light is on if $x_3 = 1$ and, at the same time, at least one of the x_1 or x_2 inputs is equal to 1.

2.2 INVERSION

So far we have assumed that some positive action takes place when a switch is closed, such as turning the light on. It is equally interesting and useful to consider the possibility that a positive action takes place when a switch is opened. Suppose that we connect the light as shown in Figure 2.5. In this case the switch is connected in parallel with the light, rather than in series. Consequently, a closed switch will short-circuit the light and prevent the current from flowing through it. Note that we have included an extra resistor in this circuit to ensure that the closed switch does not short-circuit the power supply. The light will be turned on when the switch is opened. Formally, we express this functional behavior as

$$L(x) = \overline{x}$$
$$\text{where} \quad L = 1 \text{ if } x = 0,$$
$$L = 0 \text{ if } x = 1$$

The value of this function is the inverse of the value of the input variable. Instead of using the word *inverse*, it is more common to use the term *complement*. Thus we say that $L(x)$ is a complement of x in this example. Another frequently used term for the same operation is the *NOT operation*. There are several commonly used notations for indicating the complementation. In the preceding expression we placed an overbar on top of x. This notation is probably the best from the visual point of view. However, when complements are needed in expressions that are typed using a computer keyboard, which is often done when using CAD tools, it is impractical to use overbars. Instead, either an apostrophe is

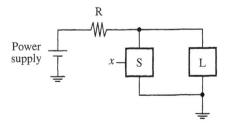

Figure 2.5   An inverting circuit.

placed after the variable, or the exclamation mark or the word NOT is placed in front of the variable to denote the complementation. Thus the following are equivalent:

$$\bar{x} = x' = !x = \text{NOT } x$$

The complement operation can be applied to a single variable or to more complex operations. For example, if

$$f(x_1, x_2) = x_1 + x_2$$

then the complement of f is

$$\bar{f}(x_1, x_2) = \overline{x_1 + x_2}$$

This expression yields the logic value 1 only when neither x_1 nor x_2 is equal to 1, that is, when $x_1 = x_2 = 0$. Again, the following notations are equivalent:

$$\overline{x_1 + x_2} = (x_1 + x_2)' = !(x_1 + x_2) = \text{NOT } (x_1 + x_2)$$

2.3 TRUTH TABLES

We have introduced the three most basic logic operations—AND, OR, and complement—by relating them to simple circuits built with switches. This approach gives these operations a certain "physical meaning." The same operations can also be defined in the form of a table, called a *truth table*, as shown in Figure 2.6. The first two columns (to the left of the heavy vertical line) give all four possible combinations of logic values that the variables x_1 and x_2 can have. The next column defines the AND operation for each combination of values of x_1 and x_2, and the last column defines the OR operation. Because we will frequently need to refer to "combinations of logic values" applied to some variables, we will adopt a shorter term, *valuation*, to denote such a combination of logic values.

The truth table is a useful aid for depicting information involving logic functions. We will use it in this book to define specific functions and to show the validity of certain functional relations. Small truth tables are easy to deal with. However, they grow exponentially in size with the number of variables. A truth table for three input variables has eight rows because there are eight possible valuations of these variables. Such a table is given in Figure 2.7, which defines three-input AND and OR functions. For four-input variables the truth table has 16 rows, and so on.

x_1	x_2	$x_1 \cdot x_2$	$x_1 + x_2$
0	0	0	0
0	1	0	1
1	0	0	1
1	1	1	1

AND   OR

Figure 2.6   A truth table for the AND and OR operations.

x_1	x_2	x_3	$x_1 \cdot x_2 \cdot x_3$	$x_1 + x_2 + x_3$
0	0	0	0	0
0	0	1	0	1
0	1	0	0	1
0	1	1	0	1
1	0	0	0	1
1	0	1	0	1
1	1	0	0	1
1	1	1	1	1

Figure 2.7   Three-input AND and OR operations.

The AND and OR operations can be extended to n variables. An AND function of variables $x_1, x_2, \cdots, x_n$ has the value 1 only if all n variables are equal to 1. An OR function of variables $x_1, x_2, \cdots, x_n$ has the value 1 if at least one, or more, of the variables is equal to 1.

2.4 LOGIC GATES AND NETWORKS

The three basic logic operations introduced in the previous sections can be used to implement logic functions of any complexity. A complex function may require many of these basic operations for its implementation. Each logic operation can be implemented electronically with transistors, resulting in a circuit element called a *logic gate*. A logic gate has one or more inputs and one output that is a function of its inputs. It is often convenient to describe a logic circuit by drawing a circuit diagram, or *schematic*, consisting of graphical symbols representing the logic gates. The graphical symbols for the AND, OR, and NOT gates are shown in Figure 2.8. The figure indicates on the left side how the AND and OR gates are drawn when there are only a few inputs. On the right side it shows how the symbols are augmented to accommodate a greater number of inputs. We will show how logic gates are built using transistors in Chapter 3.

A larger circuit is implemented by a *network* of gates. For example, the logic function from Figure 2.4 can be implemented by the network in Figure 2.9. The complexity of a given network has a direct impact on its cost. Because it is always desirable to reduce the cost of any manufactured product, it is important to find ways for implementing logic circuits as inexpensively as possible. We will see shortly that a given logic function can be implemented with a number of different networks. Some of these networks are simpler than others, hence searching for the solutions that entail minimum cost is prudent.

In technical jargon a network of gates is often called a *logic network* or simply a *logic circuit*. We will use these terms interchangeably.

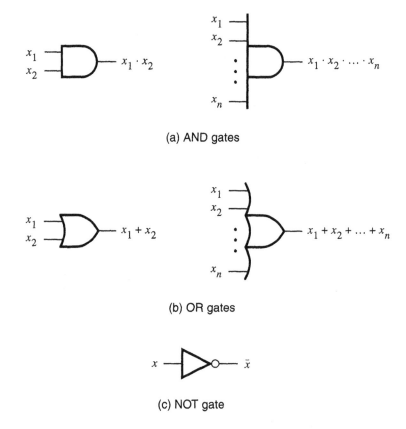

(a) AND gates

(b) OR gates

(c) NOT gate

Figure 2.8   The basic gates.

2.4.1 ANALYSIS OF A LOGIC NETWORK

A designer of digital systems is faced with two basic issues. For an existing logic network, it must be possible to determine the function performed by the network. This task is referred to as the *analysis* process. The reverse task of designing a new network that implements a desired functional behavior is referred to as the *synthesis* process. The analysis process is rather straightforward and much simpler than the synthesis process.

Figure 2.10a shows a simple network consisting of three gates. To determine its functional behavior, we can consider what happens if we apply all possible input signals to it. Suppose that we start by making $x_1 = x_2 = 0$. This forces the output of the NOT gate

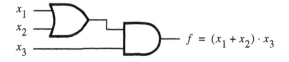

Figure 2.9   The function from Figure 2.4.

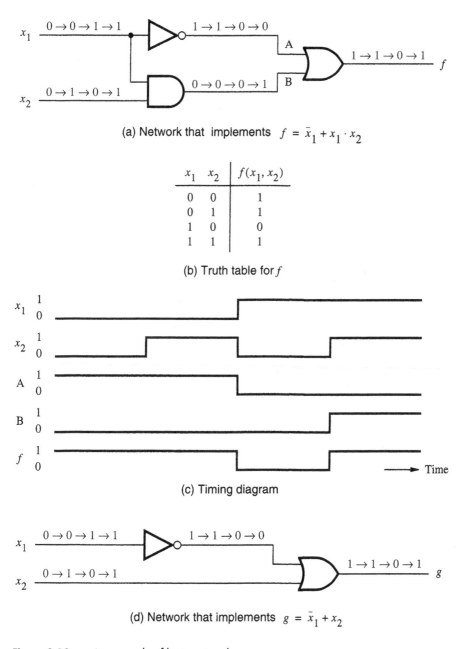

(a) Network that implements $f = \bar{x}_1 + x_1 \cdot x_2$

x_1	x_2	$f(x_1, x_2)$
0	0	1
0	1	1
1	0	0
1	1	1

(b) Truth table for f

(c) Timing diagram

(d) Network that implements $g = \bar{x}_1 + x_2$

Figure 2.10   An example of logic networks.

to be equal to 1 and the output of the AND gate to be 0. Because one of the inputs to the OR gate is 1, the output of this gate will be 1. Therefore, $f = 1$ if $x_1 = x_2 = 0$. If we let $x_1 = 0$ and $x_2 = 1$, then no change in the value of f will take place, because the outputs of the NOT and AND gates will still be 1 and 0, respectively. Next, if we apply $x_1 = 1$ and $x_2 = 0$, then the output of the NOT gate changes to 0 while the output of the AND gate remains at 0. Both inputs to the OR gate are then equal to 0; hence the value of f will be 0. Finally, let $x_1 = x_2 = 1$. Then the output of the AND gate goes to 1, which in turn causes f to be equal to 1. Our verbal explanation can be summarized in the form of the truth table shown in Figure 2.10b.

Timing Diagram

We have determined the behavior of the network in Figure 2.10a by considering the four possible valuations of the inputs x_1 and x_2. Suppose that the signals that correspond to these valuations are applied to the network in the order of our discussion; that is, $(x_1, x_2) = (0, 0)$ followed by $(0, 1)$, $(1, 0)$, and $(1, 1)$. Then changes in the signals at various points in the network would be as indicated in blue in the figure. The same information can be presented in graphical form, known as a *timing diagram*, as shown in Figure 2.10c. The time runs from left to right, and each input valuation is held for some fixed period. The figure shows the waveforms for the inputs and output of the network, as well as for the internal signals at the points labeled A and B.

Timing diagrams are used for many purposes. They depict the behavior of a logic circuit in a form that can be observed when the circuit is tested using instruments such as logic analyzers and oscilloscopes. Also, they are often generated by CAD tools to show the designer how a given circuit is expected to behave before it is actually implemented electronically. We will introduce the CAD tools later in this chapter and will make use of them throughout the book.

Functionally Equivalent Networks

Now consider the network in Figure 2.10d. Going through the same analysis procedure, we find that the output g changes in exactly the same way as f does in part (a) of the figure. Therefore, $g(x_1, x_2) = f(x_1, x_2)$, which indicates that the two networks are functionally equivalent; the output behavior of both networks is represented by the truth table in Figure 2.10b. Since both networks realize the same function, it makes sense to use the simpler one, which is less costly to implement.

In general, a logic function can be implemented with a variety of different networks, probably having different costs. This raises an important question: How does one find the best implementation for a given function? Many techniques exist for synthesizing logic functions. We will discuss the main approaches in Chapter 4. For now, we should note that some manipulation is needed to transform the more complex network in Figure 2.10a into the network in Figure 2.10d. Since $f(x_1, x_2) = \bar{x}_1 + x_1 \cdot x_2$ and $g(x_1, x_2) = \bar{x}_1 + x_2$, there must exist some rules that can be used to show the equivalence

$$\bar{x}_1 + x_1 \cdot x_2 = \bar{x}_1 + x_2$$

We have already established this equivalence through detailed analysis of the two circuits and construction of the truth table. But the same outcome can be achieved through algebraic manipulation of logic expressions. In the next section we will discuss a mathematical approach for dealing with logic functions, which provides the basis for modern design techniques.

2.5   BOOLEAN ALGEBRA

In 1849 George Boole published a scheme for the algebraic description of processes involved in logical thought and reasoning [1]. Subsequently, this scheme and its further refinements became known as *Boolean algebra*. It was almost 100 years later that this algebra found application in the engineering sense. In the late 1930s Claude Shannon showed that Boolean algebra provides an effective means of describing circuits built with switches [2]. The algebra can, therefore, be used to describe logic circuits. We will show that this algebra is a powerful tool that can be used for designing and analyzing logic circuits. The reader will come to appreciate that it provides the foundation for much of our modern digital technology.

Axioms of Boolean Algebra

Like any algebra, Boolean algebra is based on a set of rules that are derived from a small number of basic assumptions. These assumptions are called *axioms*. Let us assume that Boolean algebra B involves elements that take on one of two values, 0 and 1. Assume that the following axioms are true:

1a. $0 \cdot 0 = 0$

1b. $1 + 1 = 1$

2a. $1 \cdot 1 = 1$

2b. $0 + 0 = 0$

3a. $0 \cdot 1 = 1 \cdot 0 = 0$

3b. $1 + 0 = 0 + 1 = 1$

4a.   If $x = 0$, then $\bar{x} = 1$

4b.   If $x = 1$, then $\bar{x} = 0$

Single-Variable Theorems

From the axioms we can define some rules for dealing with single variables. These rules are often called *theorems*. If x is a variable in B, then the following theorems hold:

5a. $x \cdot 0 = 0$

5b. $x + 1 = 1$

6a. $x \cdot 1 = x$

6b. $x + 0 = x$

7a. $x \cdot x = x$

7b. $x + x = x$

8a. $x \cdot \bar{x} = 0$

8b. $x + \bar{x} = 1$

9. $\bar{\bar{x}} = x$

It is easy to prove the validity of these theorems by perfect induction, that is, by substituting the values $x = 0$ and $x = 1$ into the expressions and using the axioms given above. For example, in theorem 5a, if $x = 0$, then the theorem states that $0 \cdot 0 = 0$, which is true according to axiom $1a$. Similarly, if $x = 1$, then theorem $5a$ states that $1 \cdot 0 = 0$, which is also true according to axiom $3a$. The reader should verify that theorems $5a$ to 9 can be proven in this way.

Duality

Notice that we have listed the axioms and the single-variable theorems in pairs. This is done to reflect the important *principle of duality*. Given a logic expression, its *dual* is obtained by replacing all $+$ operators with $\cdot$ operators, and vice versa, and by replacing all 0s with 1s, and vice versa. The dual of any true statement (axiom or theorem) in Boolean algebra is also a true statement. At this point in the discussion, the reader will not appreciate why duality is a useful concept. However, this concept will become clear later in the chapter, when we will show that duality implies that at least two different ways exist to express every logic function with Boolean algebra. Often, one expression leads to a simpler physical implementation than the other and is thus preferable.

Two- and Three-Variable Properties

To enable us to deal with a number of variables, it is useful to define some two- and three-variable algebraic identities. For each identity, its dual version is also given. These identities are often referred to as *properties*. They are known by the names indicated below. If x, y, and z are the variables in B, then the following properties hold:

$10a.$	$x \cdot y = y \cdot x$	*Commutative*
$10b.$	$x + y = y + x$	
$11a.$	$x \cdot (y \cdot z) = (x \cdot y) \cdot z$	*Associative*
$11b.$	$x + (y + z) = (x + y) + z$	
$12a.$	$x \cdot (y + z) = x \cdot y + x \cdot z$	*Distributive*
$12b.$	$x + y \cdot z = (x + y) \cdot (x + z)$	
$13a.$	$x + x \cdot y = x$	*Absorption*
$13b.$	$x \cdot (x + y) = x$	
$14a.$	$x \cdot y + x \cdot \bar{y} = x$	*Combining*
$14b.$	$(x + y) \cdot (x + \bar{y}) = x$	
$15a.$	$\overline{x \cdot y} = \bar{x} + \bar{y}$	*DeMorgan's theorem*
$15b.$	$\overline{x + y} = \bar{x} \cdot \bar{y}$	
$16a.$	$x + \bar{x} \cdot y = x + y$	
$16b.$	$x \cdot (\bar{x} + y) = x \cdot y$	

Again, we can prove the validity of these properties either by perfect induction or by performing algebraic manipulation. Figure 2.11 illustrates how perfect induction can be used to prove DeMorgan's theorem, using the format of a truth table. The evaluation of left-hand and right-hand sides of the identity in $15a$ gives the same result.

We have listed a number of axioms, theorems, and properties. Not all of these are necessary to define Boolean algebra. For example, assuming that the $+$ and $\cdot$ operations are defined, it is sufficient to include theorems 5 and 8 and properties 10 and 12. These are sometimes referred to as Huntington's basic postulates [3]. The other identities can be derived from these postulates.

x	y	$x \cdot y$	$\overline{x \cdot y}$	$\overline{x}$	$\overline{y}$	$\overline{x} + \overline{y}$
0	0	0	1	1	1	1
0	1	0	1	1	0	1
1	0	0	1	0	1	1
1	1	1	0	0	0	0

$$\underbrace{\qquad\qquad}_{\text{LHS}} \qquad \underbrace{\qquad\qquad}_{\text{RHS}}$$

Figure 2.11   Proof of DeMorgan's theorem in 15a.

The preceding axioms, theorems, and properties provide the information necessary for performing algebraic manipulation of more complex expressions.

Example 2.1

Let us prove the validity of the logic equation

$$(x_1 + x_3) \cdot (\overline{x}_1 + \overline{x}_3) = x_1 \cdot \overline{x}_3 + \overline{x}_1 \cdot x_3$$

The left-hand side can be manipulated as follows. Using the distributive property, 12a, gives

$$\text{LHS} = (x_1 + x_3) \cdot \overline{x}_1 + (x_1 + x_3) \cdot \overline{x}_3$$

Applying the distributive property again yields

$$\text{LHS} = x_1 \cdot \overline{x}_1 + x_3 \cdot \overline{x}_1 + x_1 \cdot \overline{x}_3 + x_3 \cdot \overline{x}_3$$

Note that the distributive property allows ANDing the terms in parenthesis in a way analogous to multiplication in ordinary algebra. Next, according to theorem 8a, the terms $x_1 \cdot \overline{x}_1$ and $x_3 \cdot \overline{x}_3$ are both equal to 0. Therefore,

$$\text{LHS} = 0 + x_3 \cdot \overline{x}_1 + x_1 \cdot \overline{x}_3 + 0$$

From 6b it follows that

$$\text{LHS} = x_3 \cdot \overline{x}_1 + x_1 \cdot \overline{x}_3$$

Finally, using the commutative property, 10a and 10b, this becomes

$$\text{LHS} = x_1 \cdot \overline{x}_3 + \overline{x}_1 \cdot x_3$$

which is the same as the right-hand side of the initial equation.

Example 2.2

Consider the logic equation

$$x_1 \cdot \overline{x}_3 + \overline{x}_2 \cdot \overline{x}_3 + x_1 \cdot x_3 + \overline{x}_2 \cdot x_3 = \overline{x}_1 \cdot \overline{x}_2 + x_1 \cdot x_2 + x_1 \cdot \overline{x}_2$$

The left-hand side can be manipulated as follows

$$\begin{aligned}
\text{LHS} &= x_1 \cdot \overline{x}_3 + x_1 \cdot x_3 + \overline{x}_2 \cdot \overline{x}_3 + \overline{x}_2 \cdot x_3 \quad &\text{using } 10b \\
&= x_1 \cdot (\overline{x}_3 + x_3) + \overline{x}_2 \cdot (\overline{x}_3 + x_3) \quad &\text{using } 12a
\end{aligned}$$

$$= x_1 \cdot 1 + \bar{x}_2 \cdot 1 \quad \text{using } 8b$$
$$= x_1 + \bar{x}_2 \quad\quad\quad \text{using } 6a$$

The right-hand side can be manipulated as

$$\text{RHS} = \bar{x}_1 \cdot \bar{x}_2 + x_1 \cdot (x_2 + \bar{x}_2) \quad \text{using } 12a$$
$$= \bar{x}_1 \cdot \bar{x}_2 + x_1 \cdot 1 \quad\quad\quad \text{using } 8b$$
$$= \bar{x}_1 \cdot \bar{x}_2 + x_1 \quad\quad\quad\quad \text{using } 6a$$
$$= x_1 + \bar{x}_1 \cdot \bar{x}_2 \quad\quad\quad\quad \text{using } 10b$$
$$= x_1 + \bar{x}_2 \quad\quad\quad\quad\quad \text{using } 16a$$

Being able to manipulate both sides of the initial equation into identical expressions establishes the validity of the equation. Note that the same logic function is represented by either the left- or the right-hand side of the above equation; namely

$$f(x_1, x_2, x_3) = x_1 \cdot \bar{x}_3 + \bar{x}_2 \cdot \bar{x}_3 + x_1 \cdot x_3 + \bar{x}_2 \cdot x_3$$
$$= \bar{x}_1 \cdot \bar{x}_2 + x_1 \cdot x_2 + x_1 \cdot \bar{x}_2$$

As a result of manipulation, we have found a much simpler expression

$$f(x_1, x_2, x_3) = x_1 + \bar{x}_2$$

which also represents the same function. This simpler expression would result in a lower-cost logic circuit that could be used to implement the function.

Examples 2.1 and 2.2 illustrate the purpose of the axioms, theorems, and properties as a mechanism for algebraic manipulation. Even these simple examples suggest that it is impractical to deal with highly complex expressions in this way. However, these theorems and properties provide the basis for automating the synthesis of logic functions in CAD tools. To understand what can be achieved using these tools, the designer needs to be aware of the fundamental concepts.

2.5.1 THE VENN DIAGRAM

We have suggested that perfect induction can be used to verify the theorems and properties. This procedure is quite tedious and not very informative from the conceptual point of view. A simple visual aid that can be used for this purpose also exists. It is called the Venn diagram, and the reader is likely to find that it provides for a more intuitive understanding of how two expressions may be equivalent.

The Venn diagram has traditionally been used in mathematics to provide a graphical illustration of various operations and relations in the algebra of sets. A set s is a collection of elements that are said to be the members of s. In the Venn diagram the elements of a set are represented by the area enclosed by a contour such as a square, a circle, or an ellipse. For example, in a universe N of integers from 1 to 10, the set of even numbers is $E = \{2, 4, 6, 8, 10\}$. A contour representing E encloses the even numbers. The odd numbers form the complement of E; hence the area outside the contour represents $\bar{E} = \{1, 3, 5, 7, 9\}$.

Since in Boolean algebra there are only two values (elements) in the universe, $B = \{0, 1\}$, we will say that the area within a contour corresponding to a set s denotes that $s = 1$, while the area outside the contour denotes $s = 0$. In the diagram we will shade the area where $s = 1$. The concept of the Venn diagram is illustrated in Figure 2.12. The universe B is represented by a square. Then the constants 1 and 0 are represented as shown in parts (a) and (b) of the figure. A variable, say, x, is represented by a circle, such that the area inside the circle corresponds to $x = 1$, while the area outside the circle corresponds to $x = 0$. This is illustrated in part (c). An expression involving one or more variables is depicted by

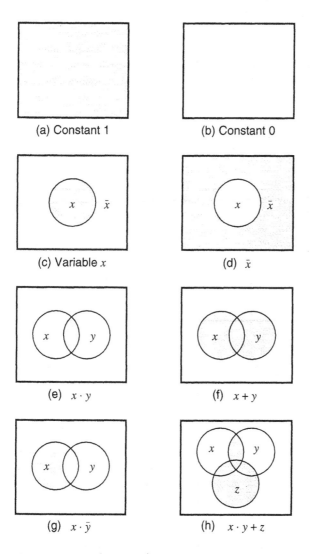

Figure 2.12   The Venn diagram representation.

shading the area where the value of the expression is equal to 1. Part (d) indicates how the complement of x is represented.

To represent two variables, x and y, we draw two overlapping circles. Then the area where the circles overlap represents the case where $x = y = 1$, namely, the AND of x and y, as shown in part (e). Since this common area consists of the intersecting portions of x and y, the AND operation is often referred to formally as the *intersection* of x and y. Part (f) illustrates the OR operation, where $x + y$ represents the total area within both circles, namely, where at least one of x or y is equal to 1. Since this combines the areas in the circles, the OR operation is formally often called the *union* of x and y.

Part (g) depicts the product term $x \cdot \bar{y}$, which is represented by the intersection of the area for x with that for $\bar{y}$. Part (h) gives a three-variable example; the expression $x \cdot y + z$ is the union of the area for z with that of the intersection of x and y.

To see how we can use Venn diagrams to verify the equivalence of two expressions, let us demonstrate the validity of the distributive property, 12a, in section 2.5. Figure 2.13 gives the construction of the left and right sides of the identity that defines the property

$$x \cdot (y + z) = x \cdot y + x \cdot z$$

Part (a) shows the area where $x = 1$. Part (b) indicates the area for $y + z$. Part (c) gives the diagram for $x \cdot (y + z)$, the intersection of shaded areas in parts (a) and (b). The right-hand

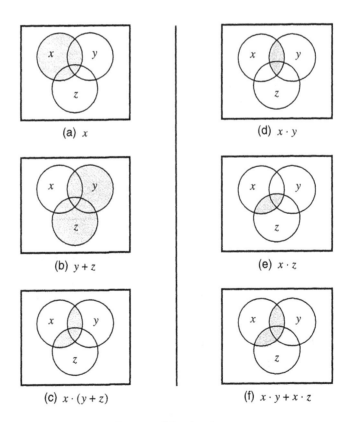

(a) x

(d) $x \cdot y$

(b) $y + z$

(e) $x \cdot z$

(c) $x \cdot (y + z)$

(f) $x \cdot y + x \cdot z$

Figure 2.13   Verification of the distributive property $x \cdot (y + z) = x \cdot y + x \cdot z$.

side is constructed in parts (d), (e), and (f). Parts (d) and (e) describe the terms $x \cdot y$ and $x \cdot z$, respectively. The union of the shaded areas in these two diagrams then corresponds to the expression $x \cdot y + x \cdot z$, as seen in part (f). Since the shaded areas in parts (c) and (f) are identical, it follows that the distributive property is valid.

As another example, consider the identity

$$x \cdot y + \bar{x} \cdot z + y \cdot z = x \cdot y + \bar{x} \cdot z$$

which is illustrated in Figure 2.14. Notice that this identity states that the term $y \cdot z$ is fully covered by the terms $x \cdot y$ and $\bar{x} \cdot z$; therefore, this term can be omitted.

The reader should use the Venn diagram to prove some other identities. It is particularly instructive to prove the validity of DeMorgan's theorem in this way.

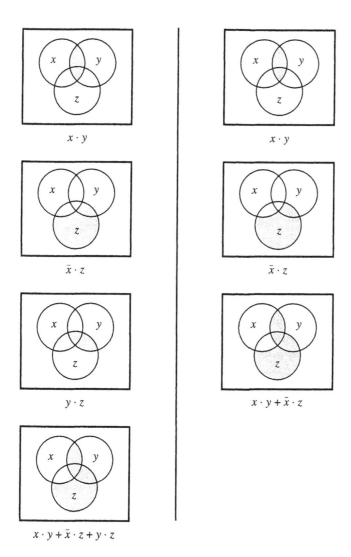

Figure 2.14 Verification of $x \cdot y + \bar{x} \cdot z + y \cdot z = x \cdot y + \bar{x} \cdot z$.

2.5.2 NOTATION AND TERMINOLOGY

Boolean algebra is based on the AND and OR operations. We have adopted the symbols
$\cdot$ and $+$ to denote these operations. These are also the standard symbols for the familiar
arithmetic multiplication and addition operations. Considerable similarity exists between
the Boolean operations and the arithmetic operations, which is the main reason why the
same symbols are used. In fact, when single digits are involved there is only one significant
difference; the result of $1 + 1$ is equal to 2 in ordinary arithmetic, whereas it is equal to 1
in Boolean algebra as defined by theorem 7b in section 2.5.

When dealing with digital circuits, most of the time the $+$ symbol obviously represents
the OR operation. However, when the task involves the design of logic circuits that perform
arithmetic operations, some confusion may develop about the use of the $+$ symbol. To
avoid such confusion, an alternative set of symbols exists for the AND and OR operations.
It is quite common to use the $\wedge$ symbol to denote the AND operation, and the $\vee$ symbol for
the OR operation. Thus, instead of $x_1 \cdot x_2$, we can write $x_1 \wedge x_2$, and instead of $x_1 + x_2$, we
can write $x_1 \vee x_2$.

Because of the similarity with the arithmetic addition and multiplication operations,
the OR and AND operations are often called the *logical sum* and *product* operations. Thus
$x_1 + x_2$ is the logical sum of x_1 and x_2, and $x_1 \cdot x_2$ is the logical product of x_1 and x_2. Instead
of saying "logical product" and "logical sum," it is customary to say simply "product" and
"sum." Thus we say that the expression

$$x_1 \cdot \overline{x}_2 \cdot x_3 + \overline{x}_1 \cdot x_4 + x_2 \cdot x_3 \cdot \overline{x}_4$$

is a sum of three product terms, whereas the expression

$$(\overline{x}_1 + x_3) \cdot (x_1 + \overline{x}_3) \cdot (\overline{x}_2 + x_3 + x_4)$$

is a product of three sum terms.

2.5.3 PRECEDENCE OF OPERATIONS

Using the three basic operations—AND, OR, and NOT—it is possible to construct an infinite
number of logic expressions. Parentheses can be used to indicate the order in which the
operations should be performed. However, to avoid an excessive use of parentheses, another
convention defines the precedence of the basic operations. It states that in the absence of
parentheses, operations in a logic expression must be performed in the order: NOT, AND,
and then OR. Thus in the expression

$$x_1 \cdot x_2 + \overline{x}_1 \cdot \overline{x}_2$$

it is first necessary to generate the complements of x_1 and x_2. Then the product terms $x_1 \cdot x_2$
and $\overline{x}_1 \cdot \overline{x}_2$ are formed, followed by the sum of the two product terms. Observe that in the
absence of this convention, we would have to use parentheses to achieve the same effect as
follows:

$$(x_1 \cdot x_2) + ((\overline{x}_1) \cdot (\overline{x}_2))$$

Finally, to simplify the appearance of logic expressions, it is customary to omit the ·
operator when there is no ambiguity. Therefore, the preceding expression can be written as

$$x_1 x_2 + \bar{x}_1 \bar{x}_2$$

We will use this style throughout the book.

2.6 Synthesis Using AND, OR, and NOT Gates

Armed with some basic ideas, we can now try to implement arbitrary functions using the
AND, OR, and NOT gates. Suppose that we wish to design a logic circuit with two inputs,
x_1 and x_2. Assume that x_1 and x_2 represent the states of two switches, either of which may
be open (0) or closed (1). The function of the circuit is to continuously monitor the state
of the switches and to produce an output logic value 1 whenever the switches (x_1, x_2) are
in states $(0, 0)$, $(0, 1)$, or $(1, 1)$. If the state of the switches is $(1, 0)$, the output should be
0. Another way of stating the required functional behavior of this circuit is that the output
must be equal to 0 if the switch x_1 is closed and x_2 is open; otherwise, the output must be
1. We can express the required behavior using a truth table, as shown in Figure 2.15.

A possible procedure for designing a logic circuit that implements the truth table is to
create a product term that has a value of 1 for each valuation for which the output function
f has to be 1. Then we can take a logical sum of these product terms to realize f. Let us
begin with the fourth row of the truth table, which corresponds to $x_1 = x_2 = 1$. The product
term that is equal to 1 for this valuation is $x_1 \cdot x_2$, which is just the AND of x_1 and x_2. Next
consider the first row of the table, for which $x_1 = x_2 = 0$. For this valuation the value 1 is
produced by the product term $\bar{x}_1 \cdot \bar{x}_2$. Similarly, the second row leads to the term $\bar{x}_1 \cdot x_2$.
Thus f may be realized as

$$f(x_1, x_2) = x_1 x_2 + \bar{x}_1 \bar{x}_2 + \bar{x}_1 x_2$$

The logic network that corresponds to this expression is shown in Figure 2.16a.

Although this network implements f correctly, it is not the simplest such network. To
find a simpler network, we can manipulate the obtained expression using the theorems and

x_1	x_2	$f(x_1, x_2)$
0	0	1
0	1	1
1	0	0
1	1	1

Figure 2.15   A function to be synthesized.

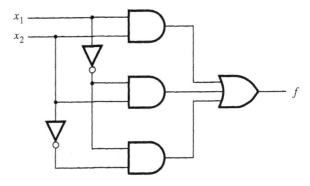

(a) Canonical sum-of-products

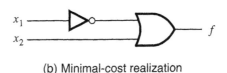

(b) Minimal-cost realization

Figure 2.16   Two implementations of the function in Figure 2.15.

properties from section 2.5. According to theorem 7b, we can replicate any term in a logical sum expression. Replicating the third product term, the above expression becomes

$$f(x_1, x_2) = x_1 x_2 + \bar{x}_1 \bar{x}_2 + \bar{x}_1 x_2 + \bar{x}_1 x_2$$

Using the commutative property 10b to interchange the second and third product terms gives

$$f(x_1, x_2) = x_1 x_2 + \bar{x}_1 x_2 + \bar{x}_1 \bar{x}_2 + \bar{x}_1 x_2$$

Now the distributive property 12a allows us to write

$$f(x_1, x_2) = (x_1 + \bar{x}_1) x_2 + \bar{x}_1 (\bar{x}_2 + x_2)$$

Applying theorem 8b we get

$$f(x_1, x_2) = 1 \cdot x_2 + \bar{x}_1 \cdot 1$$

Finally, theorem 6a leads to

$$f(x_1, x_2) = x_2 + \bar{x}_1$$

The network described by this expression is given in Figure 2.16b. Obviously, the cost of this network is much less than the cost of the network in part (a) of the figure.

This simple example illustrates two things. First, a straightforward implementation of a function can be obtained by using a product term (AND gate) for each row of the truth table for which the function is equal to 1. Each product term contains all input variables, and it is formed such that if the input variable x_i is equal to 1 in the given row, then x_i is entered in the term; if $x_i = 0$, then $\bar{x}_i$ is entered. The sum of these product terms realizes the desired function. Second, there are many different networks that can realize a given function. Some of these networks may be simpler than others. Algebraic manipulation can be used to derive simplified logic expressions and thus lower-cost networks.

The process whereby we begin with a description of the desired functional behavior and then generate a circuit that realizes this behavior is called *synthesis*. Thus we can say that we "synthesized" the networks in Figure 2.16 from the truth table in Figure 2.15. Generation of AND-OR expressions from a truth table is just one of many types of synthesis techniques that we will encounter in this book.

2.6.1 SUM-OF-PRODUCTS AND PRODUCT-OF-SUMS FORMS

Having introduced the synthesis process by means of a very simple example, we will now present it in more formal terms using the terminology that is encountered in the technical literature. We will also show how the principle of duality, which was introduced in section 2.5, applies broadly in the synthesis process.

If a function f is specified in the form of a truth table, then an expression that realizes f can be obtained by considering either the rows in the table for which $f = 1$, as we have already done, or by considering the rows for which $f = 0$, as we will explain shortly.

Minterms

For a function of n variables, a product term in which each of the n variables appears once is called a *minterm*. The variables may appear in a minterm either in uncomplemented or complemented form. For a given row of the truth table, the minterm is formed by including x_i if $x_i = 1$ and by including $\bar{x}_i$ if $x_i = 0$.

To illustrate this concept, consider the truth table in Figure 2.17. We have numbered the rows of the table from 0 to 7, so that we can refer to them easily. (The reader who is already familiar with the binary number representation will realize that the row numbers chosen are just the numbers represented by the bit patterns of variables x_1, x_2, and x_3; we will discuss number representation in Chapter 5.) The figure shows all minterms for the three-variable table. For example, in the first row the variables have the values $x_1 = x_2 = x_3 = 0$, which leads to the minterm $\bar{x}_1\bar{x}_2\bar{x}_3$. In the second row $x_1 = x_2 = 0$ and $x_3 = 1$, which gives the minterm $\bar{x}_1\bar{x}_2x_3$, and so on. To be able to refer to the individual minterms easily, it is convenient to identify each minterm by an index that corresponds to the row numbers shown in the figure. We will use the notation m_i to denote the minterm for row number i. Thus $m_0 = \bar{x}_1\bar{x}_2\bar{x}_3$, $m_1 = \bar{x}_1\bar{x}_2x_3$, and so on.

Sum-of-Products Form

A function f can be represented by an expression that is a sum of minterms, where each minterm is ANDed with the value of f for the corresponding valuation of input variables. For example, the two-variable minterms are $m_0 = \bar{x}_1\bar{x}_2$, $m_1 = \bar{x}_1x_2$, $m_2 = x_1\bar{x}_2$, and $m_3 = x_1x_2$. The function in Figure 2.15 can be represented as

Row number	x_1	x_2	x_3	Minterm	Maxterm
0	0	0	0	$m_0 = \bar{x}_1\bar{x}_2\bar{x}_3$	$M_0 = x_1 + x_2 + x_3$
1	0	0	1	$m_1 = \bar{x}_1\bar{x}_2 x_3$	$M_1 = x_1 + x_2 + \bar{x}_3$
2	0	1	0	$m_2 = \bar{x}_1 x_2\bar{x}_3$	$M_2 = x_1 + \bar{x}_2 + x_3$
3	0	1	1	$m_3 = \bar{x}_1 x_2 x_3$	$M_3 = x_1 + \bar{x}_2 + \bar{x}_3$
4	1	0	0	$m_4 = x_1\bar{x}_2\bar{x}_3$	$M_4 = \bar{x}_1 + x_2 + x_3$
5	1	0	1	$m_5 = x_1\bar{x}_2 x_3$	$M_5 = \bar{x}_1 + x_2 + \bar{x}_3$
6	1	1	0	$m_6 = x_1 x_2\bar{x}_3$	$M_6 = \bar{x}_1 + \bar{x}_2 + x_3$
7	1	1	1	$m_7 = x_1 x_2 x_3$	$M_7 = \bar{x}_1 + \bar{x}_2 + \bar{x}_3$

Figure 2.17   Three-variable minterms and maxterms.

$$f = m_0 \cdot 1 + m_1 \cdot 1 + m_2 \cdot 0 + m_3 \cdot 1$$
$$= m_0 + m_1 + m_3$$
$$= \bar{x}_1\bar{x}_2 + \bar{x}_1 x_2 + x_1 x_2$$

which is the form that we derived in the previous section using an intuitive approach. Only the minterms that correspond to the rows for which $f = 1$ appear in the resulting expression.

Any function f can be represented by a sum of minterms that correspond to the rows in the truth table for which $f = 1$. The resulting implementation is functionally correct and unique, but it is not necessarily the lowest-cost implementation of f. A logic expression consisting of product (AND) terms that are summed (ORed) is said to be of the *sum-of-products* form. If each product term is a minterm, then the expression is called a *canonical sum-of-products* for the function f. As we have seen in the example of Figure 2.16, the first step in the synthesis process is to derive a canonical sum-of-products expression for the given function. Then we can manipulate this expression, using the theorems and properties of section 2.5, with the goal of finding a functionally equivalent sum-of-products expression that has a lower cost.

As another example, consider the three-variable function $f(x_1, x_2, x_3)$, specified by the truth table in Figure 2.18. To synthesize this function, we have to include the minterms m_1, m_4, m_5, and m_6. Copying these minterms from Figure 2.17 leads to the following canonical sum-of-products expression for f

$$f(x_1, x_2, x_3) = \bar{x}_1\bar{x}_2 x_3 + x_1\bar{x}_2\bar{x}_3 + x_1\bar{x}_2 x_3 + x_1 x_2\bar{x}_3$$

This expression can be manipulated as follows

$$f = (\bar{x}_1 + x_1)\bar{x}_2 x_3 + x_1(\bar{x}_2 + x_2)\bar{x}_3$$
$$= 1 \cdot \bar{x}_2 x_3 + x_1 \cdot 1 \cdot \bar{x}_3$$
$$= \bar{x}_2 x_3 + x_1\bar{x}_3$$

This is the minimum-cost sum-of-products expression for f. It describes the circuit shown in Figure 2.19a. A good indication of the *cost* of a logic circuit is the total number of gates

Row number	x_1	x_2	x_3	$f(x_1, x_2, x_3)$
0	0	0	0	0
1	0	0	1	1
2	0	1	0	0
3	0	1	1	0
4	1	0	0	1
5	1	0	1	1
6	1	1	0	1
7	1	1	1	0

Figure 2.18   A three-variable function.

plus the total number of inputs to all gates in the circuit. Using this measure, the cost of the network in Figure 2.19a is 13, because there are five gates and eight inputs to the gates. By comparison, the network implemented on the basis of the canonical sum-of-products would have a cost of 27; from the preceding expression, the OR gate has four inputs, each of the four AND gates has three inputs, and each of the three NOT gates has one input.

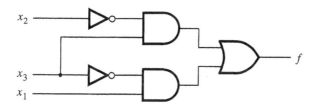

(a) A minimal sum-of-products realization

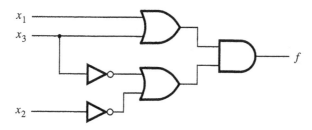

(b) A minimal product-of-sums realization

Figure 2.19   Two realizations of the function in Figure 2.18.

Minterms, with their row-number subscripts, can also be used to specify a given function in a more concise form. For example, the function in Figure 2.18 can be specified as

$$f(x_1, x_2, x_3) = \sum (m_1, m_4, m_5, m_6)$$

or even more simply as

$$f(x_1, x_2, x_3) = \sum m(1, 4, 5, 6)$$

The $\sum$ sign denotes the logical sum operation. This shorthand notation is often used in practice.

Maxterms

The principle of duality suggests that if it is possible to synthesize a function f by considering the rows in the truth table for which $f = 1$, then it should also be possible to synthesize f by considering the rows for which $f = 0$. This alternative approach uses the complements of minterms, which are called *maxterms*. All possible maxterms for three-variable functions are listed in Figure 2.17. We will refer to a maxterm M_j by the same row number as its corresponding minterm m_j as shown in the figure.

Product-of-Sums Form

If a given function f is specified by a truth table, then its complement $\bar{f}$ can be represented by a sum of minterms for which $\bar{f} = 1$, which are the rows where $f = 0$. For example, for the function in Figure 2.15

$$\bar{f}(x_1, x_2) = m_2$$
$$= x_1 \bar{x}_2$$

If we complement this expression using DeMorgan's theorem, the result is

$$\bar{\bar{f}} = f = \overline{x_1 \bar{x}_2}$$
$$= \bar{x}_1 + x_2$$

Note that we obtained this expression previously by algebraic manipulation of the canonical sum-of-products form for the function f. The key point here is that

$$f = \bar{m}_2 = M_2$$

where M_2 is the maxterm for row 2 in the truth table.

As another example, consider again the function in Figure 2.18. The complement of this function can be represented as

$$\bar{f}(x_1, x_2, x_3) = m_0 + m_2 + m_3 + m_7$$
$$= \bar{x}_1 \bar{x}_2 \bar{x}_3 + \bar{x}_1 x_2 \bar{x}_3 + \bar{x}_1 x_2 x_3 + x_1 x_2 x_3$$

Then f can be expressed as

$$f = \overline{m_0 + m_2 + m_3 + m_7}$$
$$= \bar{m}_0 \cdot \bar{m}_2 \cdot \bar{m}_3 \cdot \bar{m}_7$$

$$= M_0 \cdot M_2 \cdot M_3 \cdot M_7$$
$$= (x_1 + x_2 + x_3)(x_1 + \overline{x}_2 + x_3)(x_1 + \overline{x}_2 + \overline{x}_3)(\overline{x}_1 + \overline{x}_2 + \overline{x}_3)$$

This expression represents f as a product of maxterms.

A logic expression consisting of sum (OR) terms that are the factors of a logical product (AND) is said to be of the *product-of-sums* form. If each sum term is a maxterm, then the expression is called a *canonical product-of-sums* for the given function. Any function f can be synthesized by finding its canonical product-of-sums. This involves taking the maxterm for each row in the truth table for which $f = 0$ and forming a product of these maxterms.

Returning to the preceding example, we can attempt to reduce the complexity of the derived expression that comprises a product of maxterms. Using the commutative property 10b and the associative property 11b from section 2.5, this expression can be written as

$$f = ((x_1 + x_3) + x_2)((x_1 + x_3) + \overline{x}_2)(x_1 + (\overline{x}_2 + \overline{x}_3))(\overline{x}_1 + (\overline{x}_2 + \overline{x}_3))$$

Then, using the combining property 14b, the expression reduces to

$$f = (x_1 + x_3)(\overline{x}_2 + \overline{x}_3)$$

The corresponding network is given in Figure 2.19b. The cost of this network is 13. While this cost happens to be the same as the cost of the sum-of-products version in Figure 2.19a, the reader should not assume that the cost of a network derived in the sum-of-products form will in general be equal to the cost of a corresponding circuit derived in the product-of-sums form.

Using the shorthand notation, an alternative way of specifying our sample function is

$$f(x_1, x_2, x_3) = \Pi(M_0, M_2, M_3, M_7)$$

or more simply

$$f(x_1, x_2, x_3) = \Pi M(0, 2, 3, 7)$$

The Π sign denotes the logical product operation.

The preceding discussion has shown how logic functions can be realized in the form of logic circuits, consisting of networks of gates that implement basic functions. A given function may be realized with circuits of a different structure, which usually implies a difference in cost. An important objective for a designer is to minimize the cost of the designed circuit. We will discuss the most important techniques for finding minimum-cost implementations in Chapter 4.

2.7   DESIGN EXAMPLES

Logic circuits provide a solution to a problem. They implement functions that are needed to carry out specific tasks. Within the framework of a computer, logic circuits provide complete capability for execution of programs and processing of data. Such circuits are complex and difficult to design. But regardless of the complexity of a given circuit, a designer of logic circuits is always confronted with the same basic issues. First, it is necessary to specify the desired behavior of the circuit. Second, the circuit has to be synthesized and implemented.

Finally, the implemented circuit has to be tested to verify that it meets the specifications. The desired behavior is often initially described in words, which then must be turned into a formal specification. In this section we give two simple examples of design.

2.7.1 THREE-WAY LIGHT CONTROL

Assume that a large room has three doors and that a switch near each door controls a light in the room. It has to be possible to turn the light on or off by changing the state of any one of the switches.

As a first step, let us turn this word statement into a formal specification using a truth table. Let x_1, x_2, and x_3 be the input variables that denote the state of each switch. Assume that the light is off if all switches are open. Closing any one of the switches will turn the light on. Then turning on a second switch will have to turn off the light. Thus the light will be on if exactly one switch is closed, and it will be off if two (or no) switches are closed. If the light is off when two switches are closed, then it must be possible to turn it on by closing the third switch. If $f(x_1, x_2, x_3)$ represents the state of the light, then the required functional behavior can be specified as shown in the truth table in Figure 2.20. The canonical sum-of-products expression for the specified function is

$$f = m_1 + m_2 + m_4 + m_7$$
$$= \bar{x}_1 \bar{x}_2 x_3 + \bar{x}_1 x_2 \bar{x}_3 + x_1 \bar{x}_2 \bar{x}_3 + x_1 x_2 x_3$$

This expression cannot be simplified into a lower-cost sum-of-products expression. The resulting circuit is shown in Figure 2.21a.

An alternative realization for this function is in the product-of-sums forms. The canonical expression of this type is

$$f = M_0 \cdot M_3 \cdot M_5 \cdot M_6$$
$$= (x_1 + x_2 + x_3)(x_1 + \bar{x}_2 + \bar{x}_3)(\bar{x}_1 + x_2 + \bar{x}_3)(\bar{x}_1 + \bar{x}_2 + x_3)$$

The resulting circuit is depicted in Figure 2.21b. It has the same cost as the circuit in part (a) of the figure.

x_1	x_2	x_3	f
0	0	0	0
0	0	1	1
0	1	0	1
0	1	1	0
1	0	0	1
1	0	1	0
1	1	0	0
1	1	1	1

Figure 2.20   Truth table for the three-way light control.

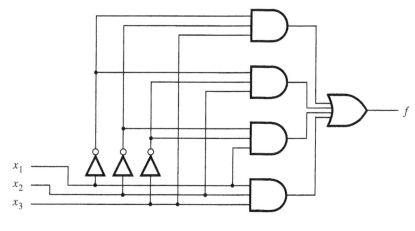

(a) Sum-of-products realization

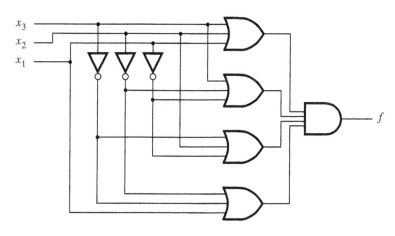

(b) Product-of-sums realization

Figure 2.21 Implementation of the function in Figure 2.20.

When the designed circuit is implemented, it can be tested by applying the various input valuations to the circuit and checking whether the output corresponds to the values specified in the truth table. A straightforward approach is to check that the correct output is produced for all eight possible input valuations.

2.7.2 MULTIPLEXER CIRCUIT

In computer systems it is often necessary to choose data from exactly one of a number of possible sources. Suppose that there are two sources of data, provided as input signals x_1 and x_2. The values of these signals change in time, perhaps at regular intervals. Thus sequences of 0s and 1s are applied on each of the inputs x_1 and x_2. We want to design a circuit that produces an output that has the same value as either x_1 or x_2, dependent on the value of a selection control signal s. Therefore, the circuit should have three inputs: x_1, x_2, and s. Assume that the output of the circuit will be the same as the value of input x_1 if $s = 0$, and it will be the same as x_2 if $s = 1$.

Based on these requirements, we can specify the desired circuit in the form of a truth table given in Figure 2.22a. From the truth table, we derive the canonical sum of products

$s\ x_1\ x_2$	$f(s, x_1, x_2)$
0 0 0	0
0 0 1	0
0 1 0	1
0 1 1	1
1 0 0	0
1 0 1	1
1 1 0	0
1 1 1	1

(a) Truth table

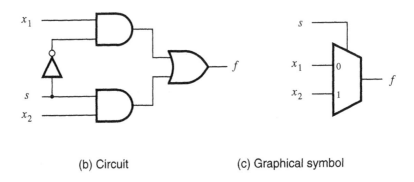

(b) Circuit   (c) Graphical symbol

s	$f(s, x_1, x_2)$
0	x_1
1	x_2

(d) More compact truth-table representation

Figure 2.22   Implementation of a multiplexer.

$$f(s, x_1, x_2) = \bar{s}x_1\bar{x}_2 + \bar{s}x_1x_2 + s\bar{x}_1x_2 + sx_1x_2$$

Using the distributive property, this expression can be written as

$$f = \bar{s}x_1(\bar{x}_2 + x_2) + s(\bar{x}_1 + x_1)x_2$$

Applying theorem 8*b* yields

$$f = \bar{s}x_1 \cdot 1 + s \cdot 1 \cdot x_2$$

Finally, theorem 6*a* gives

$$f = \bar{s}x_1 + sx_2$$

A circuit that implements this function is shown in Figure 2.22*b*. Circuits of this type are used so extensively that they are given a special name. A circuit that generates an output that exactly reflects the state of one of a number of data inputs, based on the value of one or more selection control inputs, is called a *multiplexer*. We say that a multiplexer circuit "multiplexes" input signals onto a single output.

In this example we derived a multiplexer with two data inputs, which is referred to as a "2-to-1 multiplexer." A commonly used graphical symbol for the 2-to-1 multiplexer is shown in Figure 2.22*c*. The same idea can be extended to larger circuits. A 4-to-1 multiplexer has four data inputs and one output. In this case two selection control inputs are needed to choose one of the four data inputs that is transmitted as the output signal. An 8-to-1 multiplexer needs eight data inputs and three selection control inputs, and so on.

Note that the statement "$f = x_1$ if $s = 0$, and $f = x_2$ if $s = 1$" can be presented in a more compact form of a truth table, as indicated in Figure 2.22*d*. In later chapters we will have occasion to use such representation.

We showed how a multiplexer can be built using AND, OR, and NOT gates. In Chapter 3 we will show other possibilities for constructing multiplexers. In Chapter 6 we will discuss the use of multiplexers in considerable detail.

Designers of logic circuits rely heavily on CAD tools. We want to encourage the reader to become familiar with the CAD tool support provided with this book as soon as possible. We have reached a point where an introduction to these tools is useful. The next section presents some basic concepts that are needed to use these tools. We will also introduce, in section 2.9, a special language for describing logic circuits, called VHDL. This language is used to describe the circuits as an input to the CAD tools, which then proceed to derive a suitable implementation.

2.8 INTRODUCTION TO CAD TOOLS

The preceding sections introduced a basic approach for synthesis of logic circuits. A designer could use this approach manually for small circuits. However, logic circuits found in complex systems, such as today's computers, cannot be designed manually—they are designed using sophisticated CAD tools that automatically implement the synthesis techniques.

To design a logic circuit, a number of CAD tools are needed. They are usually packaged together into a *CAD system*, which typically includes tools for the following tasks: design entry, synthesis and optimization, simulation, and physical design. We will introduce some of these tools in this section and will provide additional discussion in later chapters.

2.8.1 DESIGN ENTRY

The starting point in the process of designing a logic circuit is the conception of what the circuit is supposed to do and the formulation of its general structure. This step is done manually by the designer because it requires design experience and intuition. The rest of the design process is done with the aid of CAD tools. The first stage of this process involves entering into the CAD system a description of the circuit being designed. This stage is called *design entry*. We will describe three design entry methods: using truth tables, using schematic capture, and writing source code in a hardware description language.

Design Entry with Truth Tables

We have already seen that any logic function of a few variables can be described conveniently by a truth table. Many CAD systems allow design entry using truth tables, where the table is specified as a plain text file. Alternatively, it may also be possible to specify a truth table as a set of waveforms in a timing diagram. We illustrated the equivalence of these two ways of representing truth tables in the discussion of Figure 2.10. The CAD system provided with this book supports both methods of using truth tables for design entry. Figure 2.23 shows an example in which the *Waveform Editor* is used to draw the timing diagram in Figure 2.10. The CAD system is capable of transforming this timing diagram automatically into a network of logic gates equivalent to that shown in Figure 2.10*d*.

Because truth tables are practical only for functions with a small number of variables, this design entry method is not appropriate for large circuits. It can, however, be applied for a small logic function that is part of a larger circuit. In this case the truth table becomes a subcircuit that can be interconnected to other subcircuits and logic gates. The most commonly used type of CAD tool for interconnecting such circuit elements is called a *schematic capture* tool. The word *schematic* refers to a diagram of a circuit in which circuit elements, such as logic gates, are depicted as graphical symbols and connections between circuit elements are drawn as lines.

Schematic Capture

A schematic capture tool uses the graphics capabilities of a computer and a computer mouse to allow the user to draw a schematic diagram. To facilitate inclusion of basic gates in the schematic, the tool provides a collection of graphical symbols that represent gates

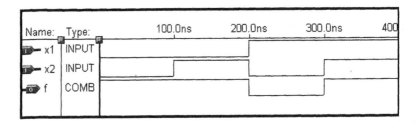

Figure 2.23   Screen capture of the Waveform Editor.

of various types with different numbers of inputs. This collection of symbols is called a *library*. The gates in the library can be imported into the user's schematic, and the tool provides a graphical way of interconnecting the gates to create a logic network.

Any subcircuits that have been previously created, using either different design entry methods or the schematic capture tool itself, can be represented as graphical symbols and included in the schematic. In practice it is common for a CAD system user to create a circuit that includes within it other smaller circuits. This methodology is known as *hierarchical design* and provides a good way of dealing with the complexities of large circuits.

Figure 2.24 gives an example of a hierarchical design created with the schematic capture tool, provided with the CAD system, called the *Graphic Editor*. The circuit includes a subcircuit represented as a rectangular graphical symbol. This subcircuit represents the logic function entered by way of the timing diagram in Figure 2.23. Note that the complete circuit implements the function $f = \overline{x}_1 + x_2\overline{x}_3$.

In comparison to design entry with truth tables, the schematic-capture facility is more amenable for dealing with larger circuits. A disadvantage of using schematic capture is that every commercial tool of this type has a unique user interface and functionality. Therefore, extensive training is often required for a designer to learn how to use such a tool, and this training must be repeated if the designer switches to another tool at a later date. Another drawback is that the graphical user interface for schematic capture becomes awkward to use when the circuit being designed is large. A useful method for dealing with large circuits is to write source code using a hardware description language to represent the circuit.

Hardware Description Languages

A *hardware description language (HDL)* is similar to a typical computer programming language except that an HDL is used to describe hardware rather than a program to be executed on a computer. Many commercial HDLs are available. Some are proprietary, meaning that they are provided by a particular company and can be used to implement circuits only in the technology provided by that company. We will not discuss the proprietary HDLs in this book. Instead, we will focus on a language that is supported by virtually all vendors that provide digital hardware technology and is officially endorsed as an *Institute of Electrical and Electronics Engineers (IEEE)* standard. The IEEE is a worldwide organization that promotes technical activities to the benefit of society in general. One of its activities involves the development of standards that define how certain technological concepts can be used in a way that is suitable for a large body of users.

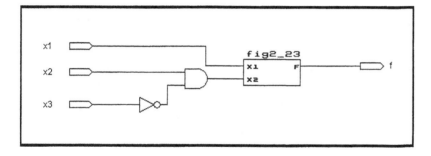

Figure 2.24   Screen capture of the Graphic Editor.

Two HDLs are IEEE standards: *VHDL (Very High Speed Integrated Circuit Hardware Description Language)* and *Verilog HDL*. Both languages are in widespread use in the industry. We use VHDL in this book because it is more popular than Verilog HDL. Although the two languages differ in many ways, the choice of using one or the other when studying logic circuits is not particularly important, because both offer similar features. Concepts illustrated in this book using VHDL can be directly applied when using Verilog HDL.

In comparison to performing schematic capture, using VHDL offers a number of advantages. Because it is supported by most companies that offer digital hardware technology, VHDL provides design *portability*. A circuit specified in VHDL can be implemented in different types of chips and with CAD tools provided by different companies, without having to change the VHDL specification. Design portability is an important advantage because digital circuit technology changes rapidly. By using a standard language, the designer can focus on the required functionality of the desired circuit without being overly concerned about the details of the technology that will eventually be used for implementation.

Design entry of a logic circuit is done by writing VHDL code. Signals in the circuit are represented as variables in the source code, and logic functions are expressed by assigning values to these variables. VHDL source code is plain text, which makes it easy for the designer to include within the code documentation that explains how the circuit works. This feature, coupled with the fact that VHDL is widely used, encourages sharing and reuse of VHDL-described circuits. This allows faster development of new products in cases where existing VHDL code can be adapted for use in the design of new circuits.

Similar to the way in which large circuits are handled in schematic capture, VHDL code can be written in a modular way that facilitates hierarchical design. Both small and large logic circuit designs can be efficiently represented in VHDL code. VHDL has been used to define circuits such as microprocessors with millions of transistors.

VHDL design entry can be combined with other methods. For example, a schematic-capture tool can be used in which a subcircuit in the schematic is described using VHDL. We will introduce VHDL in section 2.9.

2.8.2 SYNTHESIS

In section 2.4.1 we said that synthesis is the process of generating a logic circuit from a truth table. Synthesis CAD tools perform this process automatically. However, the synthesis tools also handle many other tasks. The process of *translating*, or *compiling*, VHDL code into a network of logic gates is part of synthesis.

When the VHDL code representing a circuit is passed through initial synthesis tools, the output is a lower-level description of the circuit. For simplicity we will assume that this process produces a set of logic expressions that describe the logic functions needed to realize the circuit. These expressions are then manipulated further by the synthesis tools. If the design entry is performed using schematic capture, then the synthesis tools produce a set of logic equations representing the circuit from the schematic diagram. Similarly, if truth tables are used for design entry, then the synthesis tools generate expressions for the logic functions represented by the truth tables.

Regardless of what type of design entry is used, the initial logic expressions produced by the synthesis tools are not likely to be in an optimal form. Because these expressions reflect the designer's input to the CAD tools, it is difficult for a designer to manually produce optimal results, especially for large circuits. One of the most important tasks of the synthesis tools is to manipulate the user's design to automatically produce an equivalent but better circuit. This step of synthesis is called *logic synthesis*, or *logic optimization*.

The measure of what makes one circuit better than another depends on the particular needs of a design project and the technology chosen for implementation. In section 2.6 we suggested that a good circuit might be one that has the lowest cost. There are other possible optimization goals, which are motivated by the type of hardware technology used for implementation of the circuit. We will discuss implementation technologies in Chapter 3 and return to the issue of optimization goals in Chapter 4.

After logic synthesis the optimized circuit is still represented in the form of logic equations. The final task in the synthesis process is to determine exactly how the circuit will be realized in a specific hardware technology. This task involves deciding how each logic function, represented by an expression, should be implemented using whatever physical resources are available in the technology. The task involves two steps called *technology mapping*, followed by *layout synthesis*, or *physical design*. We will discuss these steps in detail in Chapter 4.

2.8.3 FUNCTIONAL SIMULATION

Once the design entry and synthesis are complete, it is useful to verify that the designed circuit functions as expected. The tool that performs this task is called a *functional simulator*, and it uses two types of information. First, the user's initial design is represented by the logic equations generated during synthesis. Second, the user specifies valuations of the circuit's inputs that should be applied to these equations during simulation. For each valuation, the simulator evaluates the outputs produced by the equations. The output of the simulation is provided either in truth-table form or as a timing diagram. The user examines this output to verify that the circuit operates as required.

The logic equations used by the simulator are those produced by the synthesis tools before any optimizations are applied during logic synthesis. There would be no advantage in using the optimized form of the equations, because the intent is to evaluate the basic functionality of the design, which does not change as a result of optimization. The functional simulator assumes that the time needed for signals to propagate through the logic gates is negligible. In real logic gates this assumption is not realistic, regardless of the hardware technology chosen for implementation of the circuit. However, the functional simulation provides a first step in validating the basic operation of a design without concern for the effects of implementation technology. Accurate simulations that account for the timing details related to technology can be obtained by using a *timing simulator*. We will discuss timing simulation in Chapter 4.

2.8.4 SUMMARY

The CAD tools discussed in this section form a part of a CAD system. A typical design flow that the user follows is illustrated in Figure 2.25. After the design entry, initial synthesis tools perform various steps. For a function described by a truth table, the synthesis approach

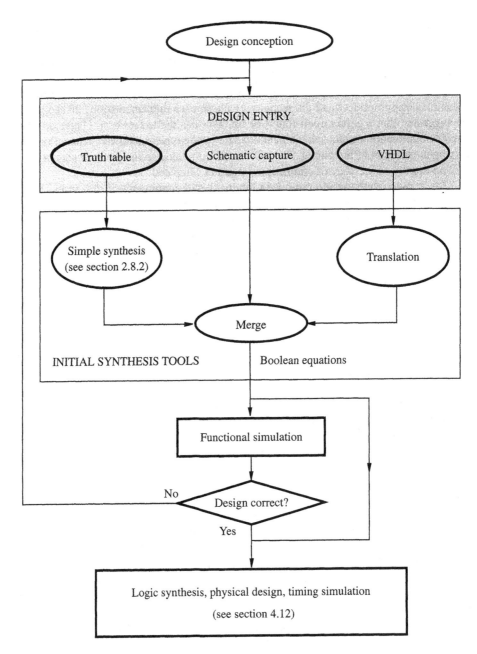

Figure 2.25   The first stages of a typical CAD system.

discussed in section 2.6 is applied to produce a logic expression for the function. For VHDL the translation process turns the VHDL source code into logic functions, which can be represented as logic expressions. As mentioned earlier, the designer can use a mixture of design entry methods. In Figure 2.25 this flexibility is reflected by the step labeled Merge, in which the components produced using any of the design entry methods are automatically merged into a single design. At this point the circuit is represented in the CAD system as a set of logic equations.

After the initial synthesis the correct operation of the designed circuit can be verified by using functional simulation. As shown in Figure 2.25, this step is not a requirement in the CAD flow and can be skipped at the designer's discretion. In practice, however, it is wise to verify that the designed circuit works as expected as early in the design process as possible. Any problems discovered during the simulation are fixed by returning to the design entry stage. Once errors are no longer apparent, the designer proceeds with the remaining tools in the CAD flow. These include logic synthesis, layout synthesis, timing simulation, and others. We have mentioned these tools only briefly thus far. The remaining CAD steps will be described in Chapter 4.

At this point the reader should have some appreciation for what is involved when using CAD tools. However, the tools can be fully appreciated only when they are used firsthand. In Appendexes B to D, we provide step-by-step tutorials that illustrate how to use the MAX+plusII CAD system, which is included with this book. The tutorial in Appendix B covers design entry with both schematic capture and VHDL, as well as functional simulation. We strongly encourage the reader to work through the hands-on material. Because the tutorial uses VHDL for design entry, we provide an introduction to VHDL in the following section.

2.10 CONCLUDING REMARKS

In this chapter we introduced the concept of logic circuits. We showed that such circuits can be implemented using logic gates and that they can be described using a mathematical model called Boolean algebra. Because practical logic circuits are often large, it is important to have good CAD tools to help the designer. This book is accompanied by the MAX+PlusII software, which is a CAD tool provided by Altera Corporation. We introduced a few basic features of this tool and urge the reader to start using this software as soon as possible.

Our discussion so far has been quite elementary. We will deal with both the logic circuits and the CAD tools in much more depth in the chapters that follow. But first, in

Chapter 3 we will examine the most important electronic technologies used to construct logic circuits. This material will give the reader an appreciation of practical constraints that a designer of logic circuits must face.

PROBLEMS

2.1 Use algebraic manipulation to prove that $x + yz = (x + y) \cdot (x + z)$. Note that this is the distributive rule, as stated in identity $12b$ in section 2.5.

2.2 Use algebraic manipulation to prove that $(x + y) \cdot (x + \bar{y}) = x$.

2.3 Use the Venn diagram to prove the identity in problem 1.

2.4 Use the Venn diagram to prove DeMorgan's theorem, as given in expressions $15a$ and $15b$ in section 2.5.

2.5 Use the Venn diagram to prove

$$(x_1 + x_2 + x_3) \cdot (x_1 + x_2 + \bar{x}_3) = x_1 + x_2$$

2.6 Determine whether or not the following expressions are valid, i.e., whether the left- and right-hand sides represent same function.
(a) $\bar{x}_1 x_3 + x_1 x_2 \bar{x}_3 + \bar{x}_1 x_2 + x_1 \bar{x}_2 = \bar{x}_2 x_3 + x_1 \bar{x}_3 + x_2 \bar{x}_3 + \bar{x}_1 x_2 x_3$
(b) $x_1 \bar{x}_3 + x_2 x_3 + \bar{x}_2 \bar{x}_3 = (x_1 + \bar{x}_2 + x_3)(x_1 + x_2 + \bar{x}_3)(\bar{x}_1 + x_2 + \bar{x}_3)$
(c) $(x_1 + x_3)(\bar{x}_1 + \bar{x}_2 + \bar{x}_3)(\bar{x}_1 + x_2) = (x_1 + x_2)(x_2 + x_3)(\bar{x}_1 + \bar{x}_3)$

2.7 Draw a timing diagram for the circuit in Figure 2.19a. Show the waveforms that can be observed on all wires in the circuit.

2.8 Repeat problem 2.7 for the circuit in Figure 2.19b.

2.9 Use algebraic manipulation to show that for three input variables x_1, x_2, and x_3

$$\sum m(1, 2, 3, 4, 5, 6, 7) = x_1 + x_2 + x_3$$

2.10 Use algebraic manipulation to show that for three input variables x_1, x_2, and x_3

$$\Pi \, M(0, 1, 2, 3, 4, 5, 6) = x_1 x_2 x_3$$

2.11 Use algebraic manipulation to find the minimum sum-of-products expression for the function $f = x_1 x_3 + x_1 \bar{x}_2 + \bar{x}_1 x_2 x_3 + \bar{x}_1 \bar{x}_2 \bar{x}_3$.

2.12 Use algebraic manipulation to find the minimum sum-of-products expression for the function $f = x_1 \bar{x}_2 \bar{x}_3 + x_1 x_2 x_4 + x_1 \bar{x}_2 x_3 \bar{x}_4$.

2.13 Use algebraic manipulation to find the minimum product-of-sums expression for the function $f = (x_1 + x_3 + x_4) \cdot (x_1 + \bar{x}_2 + x_3) \cdot (x_1 + \bar{x}_2 + \bar{x}_3 + x_4)$.

2.14 Use algebraic manipulation to find the minimum product-of-sums expression for the function $f = (x_1 + x_2 + x_3) \cdot (x_1 + \bar{x}_2 + x_3) \cdot (\bar{x}_1 + \bar{x}_2 + x_3) \cdot (x_1 + x_2 + \bar{x}_3)$.

2.15 (a) Show the location of all minterms in a three-variable Venn diagram.

(b) Show a separate Venn diagram for each product term in the function $f = x_1\bar{x}_2x_3 + x_1x_2 + \bar{x}_1x_3$. Use the Venn diagram to find the minimal sum-of-products form of f.

2.16   Represent the function in Figure 2.18 in the form of a Venn diagram and find its minimal sum-of-products form.

2.17   Figure P2.1 shows two attempts to draw a Venn diagram for four variables. For parts (a) and (b) of the figure, explain why the Venn diagram is not correct. (Hint: the Venn diagram must be able to represent all 16 minterms of the four variables.)

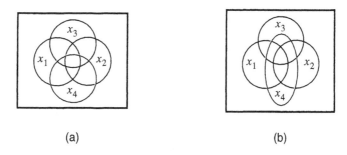

(a)   (b)

Figure P2.1   Two attempts to draw a four-variable Venn diagram.

2.18   Figure P2.2 gives a representation of a four-variable Venn diagram and shows the location of minterms m_0, m_1, and m_2. Show the location of the other minterms in the diagram. Represent the function $f = \bar{x}_1\bar{x}_2x_3\bar{x}_4 + x_1x_2x_3x_4 + \bar{x}_1x_2$ on this diagram.

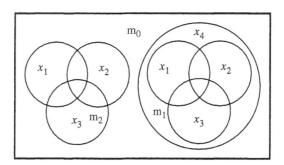

Figure P2.2   A four-variable Venn diagram.

2.19   Design the simplest sum-of-products circuit that implements the function $f(x_1, x_2, x_3) = \sum m(3, 4, 6, 7)$.

2.20   Design the simplest sum-of-products circuit that implements the function $f(x_1, x_2, x_3) = \sum m(1, 3, 4, 6, 7)$.

2.21 Design the simplest product-of-sums circuit that implements the function $f(x_1, x_2, x_3) = \Pi M\ (0, 2, 5)$.

2.22 Design the simplest product-of-sums expression for the function $f(x_1, x_2, x_3) = \Pi M\ (0, 1, 5, 7)$.

2.23 Design the simplest circuit that has three inputs, x_1, x_2, and x_3, which produces an output value of 1 whenever two or more of the input variables have the value 1; otherwise, the output has to be 0.

2.24 For the timing diagram in Figure P2.3, synthesize the function $f(x_1, x_2, x_3)$ in the simplest sum-of-products form.

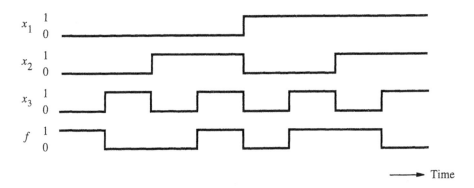

Figure P2.3   A timing diagram representing a logic function.

2.25 For the timing diagram in Figure P2.4, synthesize the function $f(x_1, x_2, x_3)$ in the simplest sum-of-products form.

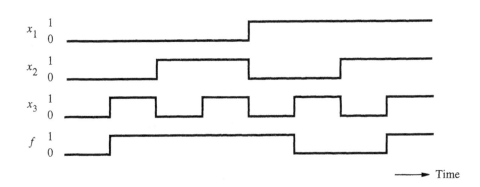

Figure P2.4   A timing diagram representing a logic function.

2.26 Design a circuit with output f and inputs x_1, x_0, y_1, and y_0. Let $X = x_1x_0$ be a number, where the four possible values of X, namely, 00, 01, 10, and 11, represent the four numbers 0, 1, 2, and 3, respectively. (We discuss representation of numbers in Chapter 5.) Similarly, let $Y = y_1y_0$ represent another number with the same four possible values. The output f should be 1 if the numbers represented by X and Y are not equal. Otherwise, f should be 0.
(a) Show the truth table for f.
(b) Synthesize the simplest possible product-of-sums expression for f.

2.27 Repeat problem 2.26 for the case where f should be 1 only if $X \geq Y$.
(a) Show the truth table for f.
(b) Show the canonical sum-of-products expression for f.
(c) Show the simplest possible sum-of-products expression for f.

2.28 (a) Use the Graphic Editor in MAX+plusII to draw schematics for the following functions

$$f_1 = x_2\bar{x}_3\bar{x}_4 + \bar{x}_1x_2x_4 + \bar{x}_1x_2x_3 + x_1x_2x_3$$
$$f_2 = x_2\bar{x}_4 + \bar{x}_1x_2 + x_2x_3$$

(b) Use functional simulation in MAX+plusII to prove that $f_1 = f_2$.

2.29 (a) Use the Graphic Editor in MAX+plusII to draw schematics for the following functions

$$f_1 = (x_1 + x_2 + \bar{x}_4) \cdot (\bar{x}_2 + x_3 + \bar{x}_4) \cdot (\bar{x}_1 + x_3 + \bar{x}_4) \cdot (\bar{x}_1 + \bar{x}_3 + \bar{x}_4)$$
$$f_2 = (x_2 + \bar{x}_4) \cdot (x_3 + \bar{x}_4) \cdot (\bar{x}_1 + \bar{x}_4)$$

(b) Use functional simulation in MAX+plusII to prove that $f_1 = f_2$.

2.30 (a) Using the Text Editor in MAX+plusII, write VHDL code to describe the following functions

$$f_1 = x_1\bar{x}_3 + x_2\bar{x}_3 + \bar{x}_3\bar{x}_4 + x_1x_2 + x_1\bar{x}_4$$
$$f_2 = (x_1 + \bar{x}_3) \cdot (x_1 + x_2 + \bar{x}_4) \cdot (x_2 + \bar{x}_3 + \bar{x}_4)$$

(b) Use functional simulation in MAX+plusII to prove that $f_1 = f_2$.

2.31 Consider the following VHDL assignment statements

```
f1 <= ((x1 AND x3) OR (NOT x1 AND NOT x3)) AND ((x2 AND x4) OR
        (NOT x2 AND NOT x4)) ;
f2 <= (x1 AND x2 AND NOT x3 AND NOT x4) OR (NOT x1 AND NOT x2 AND x3 AND x4)
        OR (x1 AND NOT x2 AND NOT x3 AND x4) OR
        (NOT x1 AND x2 AND x3 AND NOT x4) ;
```

(a) Write complete VHDL code to implement f1 and f2.
(b) Use functional simulation in MAX+plusII to prove that $f1 = \overline{f2}$.

REFERENCES

1. G. Boole, *An Investigation of the Laws of Thought*, 1854, reprinted by Dover Publications, New York, 1954.

2. C. E. Shannon, "A Symbolic Analysis of Relay and Switching Circuits," *Transactions of AIEE* 57 (1938), pp. 713–723.

3. E. V. Huntington, "Sets of Independent Postulates for the Algebra of Logic," *Transactions of the American Mathematical Society* 5 (1904), pp. 288–309.

4. Z. Navabi, *VHDL—Analysis and Modeling of Digital Systems*, 2nd ed. (McGraw-Hill: New York, 1998).

5. D. L. Perry, *VHDL*, 3rd ed. (McGraw-Hill: New York, 1998).

6. J. Bhasker, *A VHDL Primer* (Prentice-Hall: Englewood Cliffs, NJ, 1995).

7. K. Skahill, *VHDL for Programmable Logic* (Addison-Wesley: Menlo Park, CA, 1996).

8. A. Dewey, *Analysis and Design of Digital Systems with VHDL* (PWS Publishing Co.: Boston, 1997).

chapter

3

IMPLEMENTATION TECHNOLOGY

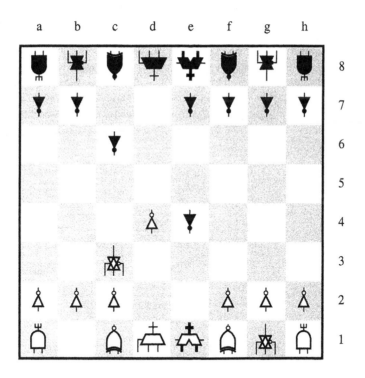

3. Nb1–c3, d5xe4

In section 1.2 we said that logic circuits are implemented using transistors and that a number of different technologies exist. We now explore technology issues in more detail.

Let us first consider how logic variables can be physically represented as signals in electronic circuits. Our discussion will be restricted to binary variables, which can take on only the values 0 and 1. In a circuit these values can be represented either as levels of voltage or current. Both alternatives are used in different technologies. We will focus on the simplest and most popular representation, using voltage levels.

The most obvious way of representing two logic values as voltage levels is to define a *threshold* voltage; any voltage below the threshold represents one logic value, and voltages above the threshold correspond to the other logic value. It is an arbitrary choice as to which logic value is associated with the low and high voltage levels. Usually, logic 0 is represented by the low voltage levels and logic 1 by the high voltages. This is known as a *positive logic* system. The opposite choice, in which the low voltage levels are used to represent logic 1 and the higher voltages are used for logic 0 is known as a *negative logic* system. In this book we use only the positive logic system, but negative logic is discussed briefly in section 3.4.

Using the positive logic system, the logic values 0 and 1 are referred to simply as "low" and "high." To implement the threshold-voltage concept, a range of low and high voltage levels is defined, as shown in Figure 3.1. The figure gives the minimum voltage, called V_{SS}, and the maximum voltage, called V_{DD}, that can exist in the circuit. We will assume that V_{SS} is 0 volts, corresponding to electrical ground, denoted *Gnd*. The voltage V_{DD} represents the power supply voltage. The most common level for V_{DD} is 5 volts, but 3.3 volts is also popular. In this chapter we will usually assume that $V_{DD} = 5$ V. Figure 3.1 indicates that voltages in the range *Gnd* to $V_{0,max}$ represent logic value 0. The name $V_{0,max}$ means the maximum voltage level that a logic circuit must recognize as low. Similarly, the range from $V_{1,min}$ to V_{DD} corresponds to logic value 1, and $V_{1,min}$ is the minimum voltage level that a logic circuit must interpret as high. The exact levels of $V_{0,max}$ and $V_{1,min}$

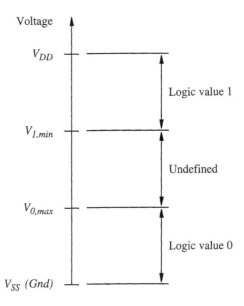

Figure 3.1   Representation of logic values by voltage levels.

depend on the particular technology used; a typical example might set $V_{0,max}$ to 40 percent of V_{DD} and $V_{1,min}$ to 60 percent of V_{DD}. The range of voltages between $V_{0,max}$ and $V_{1,min}$ is undefined. Logic signals do not normally assume voltages in this range except in transition from one logic value to the other. We will discuss the voltage levels used in logic circuits in more depth in section 3.8.3.

3.1 TRANSISTOR SWITCHES

Logic circuits are built with transistors. A full treatment of transistor behavior is beyond the scope of this text; it can be found in electronics textbooks, such as [1] and [2]. For the purpose of understanding how logic circuits are built, we can assume that a transistor operates as a simple switch. Figure 3.2a shows a switch controlled by a logic signal, x. When x is low, the switch is open, and when x is high, the switch is closed. The most popular type of transistor for implementing a simple switch is the *metal oxide semiconductor field-effect transistor (MOSFET)*. There are two different types of MOSFETs, known as *n-channel*, abbreviated *NMOS*, and *p-channel*, denoted *PMOS*.

Figure 3.2b gives a graphical symbol for an NMOS transistor. It has four electrical terminals, called the *source*, *drain*, *gate*, and *substrate*. In logic circuits the substrate (also

(a) A simple switch controlled by the input *x*

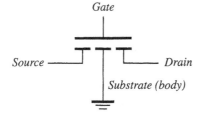

(b) NMOS transistor

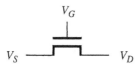

(c) Simplified symbol for an NMOS transistor

Figure 3.2 NMOS transistor as a switch.

called *body*) terminal is connected to *Gnd*. We will use the simplified graphical symbol in Figure 3.2*c*, which omits the substrate node. There is no physical difference between the source and drain terminals. They are distinguished in practice by the voltage levels applied to the transistor; by convention, the terminal with the lower voltage level is deemed to be the source.

A detailed explanation of how the transistor operates will be presented in section 3.8.1. For now it is sufficient to know that it is controlled by the voltage V_G at the gate terminal. If V_G is low, then there is no connection between the source and drain, and we say that the transistor is *turned off*. If V_G is high, then the transistor is *turned on* and acts as a closed switch that connects the source and drain terminals. In section 3.8.2 we show how to calculate the resistance between the source and drain terminals when the transistor is turned on, but for now assume that the resistance is $0 \ \Omega$.

PMOS transistors have the opposite behavior of NMOS transistors. The former are used to realize the type of switch illustrated in Figure 3.3*a*, where the switch is open when the control input *x* is high and closed when *x* is low. A symbol is shown in Figure 3.3*b*. In logic circuits the substrate of the PMOS transistor is always connected to V_{DD}, leading to the simplified symbol in Figure 3.3*c*. If V_G is high, then the PMOS transistor is turned off and acts like an open switch. When V_G is low, the transistor is turned on and acts as a closed switch that connects the source and drain. In the PMOS transistor the source is the node with the higher voltage.

$x =$ "high" $x =$ "low"

(a) A switch with the opposite behavior of Figure 3.2(*a*)

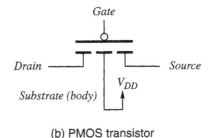

(b) PMOS transistor

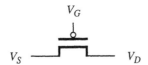

(c) Simplified symbol for an PMOS transistor

Figure 3.3   PMOS transistor as a switch.

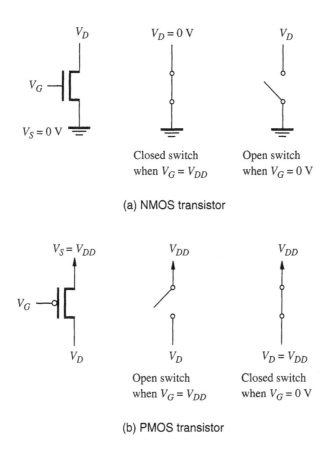

(a) NMOS transistor

(b) PMOS transistor

Figure 3.4   NMOS and PMOS transistors in logic circuits.

Figure 3.4 summarizes the typical use of NMOS and PMOS transistors in logic circuits. An NMOS transistor is turned on when its gate terminal is high, while a PMOS transistor is turned on when its gate is low. When the NMOS transistor is turned on, its drain is *pulled down* to *Gnd*, and when the PMOS transistor is turned on, its drain is *pulled up* to V_{DD}. Because of the way the transistors operate, an NMOS transistor cannot be used to pull its drain terminal completely up to V_{DD}. Similarly, a PMOS transistor cannot to pull its drain terminal completely down to *Gnd*. We discuss the operation of MOSFETs in considerable detail in section 3.8.

3.6 PROGRAMMABLE LOGIC DEVICES

The function provided by each of the 7400-series parts is fixed and cannot be tailored to suit a particular design situation. This fact, coupled with the limitation that each chip contains only a few logic gates, makes these chips inefficient for building large logic circuits. It is possible to manufacture chips that contain relatively large amounts of logic circuitry with a structure that is not fixed. Such chips were first introduced in the 1970s and are called *programmable logic devices (PLDs)*.

A PLD is a general-purpose chip for implementing logic circuitry. It contains a collection of logic circuit elements that can be customized in different ways. A PLD can be viewed as a "black box" that contains logic gates and programmable switches, as illustrated in Figure 3.24. The programmable switches allow the logic gates inside the PLD to be connected together to implement whatever logic circuit is needed.

3.6.1 PROGRAMMABLE LOGIC ARRAY (PLA)

Several types of PLDs are commercially available. The first developed was the *programmable logic array (PLA)*. The general structure of a PLA is depicted in Figure 3.25. Based on the idea that logic functions can be realized in sum-of-products form, a PLA

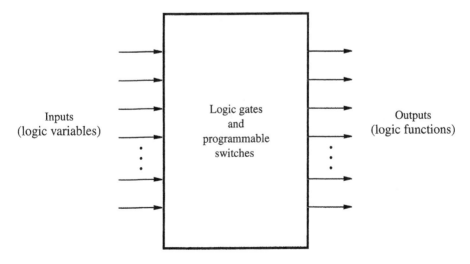

Figure 3.24   Programmable logic device as a black box.

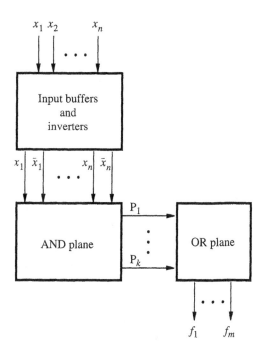

Figure 3.25   General structure of a PLA.

comprises a collection of AND gates that feeds a set of OR gates. As shown in the figure, the PLA's inputs $x_1, \ldots, x_n$ pass through a set of buffers (which provide both the true value and complement of each input) into a circuit block called an *AND plane*, or *AND array*. The AND plane produces a set of product terms $P_1, \ldots, P_k$. Each of these terms can be configured to implement any AND function of $x_1, \ldots, x_n$. The product terms serve as the inputs to an *OR plane*, which produces the outputs $f_1, \ldots, f_m$. Each output can be configured to realize any sum of $P_1, \ldots, P_k$ and hence any sum-of-products function of the PLA inputs.

A more detailed diagram of a small PLA is given in Figure 3.26, which shows a PLA with three inputs, four product terms, and two outputs. Each AND gate in the AND plane has six inputs, corresponding to the true and complemented versions of the three input signals. Each connection to an AND gate is programmable; a signal that is connected to an AND gate is indicated with a wavy line, and a signal that is not connected to the gate is shown with a broken line. The circuitry is designed such that any unconnected AND-gate inputs do not affect the output of the AND gate. In commercially available PLAs, several methods of realizing the programmable connections exist. Detailed explanation of how a PLA can be built using transistors is given in section 3.10.

In Figure 3.26 the AND gate that produces P_1 is shown connected to the inputs x_1 and x_2. Hence $P_1 = x_1 x_2$. Similarly, $P_2 = x_1 \bar{x}_3$, $P_3 = \bar{x}_1 \bar{x}_2 x_3$, and $P_4 = x_1 x_3$. Programmable connections also exist for the OR plane. Output f_1 is connected to product terms P_1, P_2, and P_3. It therefore realizes the function $f_1 = x_1 x_2 + x_1 \bar{x}_3 + \bar{x}_1 \bar{x}_2 x_3$. Similarly, output

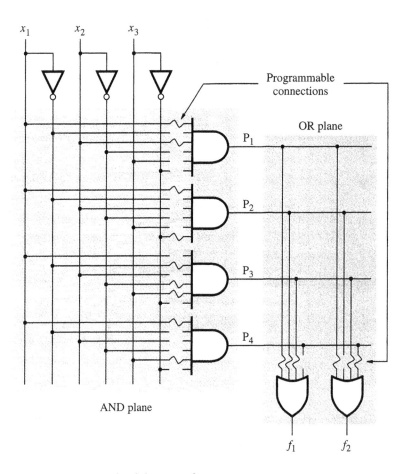

Figure 3.26 Gate-level diagram of a PLA.

$f_2 = x_1x_2 + \overline{x}_1\overline{x}_2x_3 + x_1x_3$. Although Figure 3.26 depicts the PLA programmed to implement the functions described above, by programming the AND and OR planes differently, each of the outputs f_1 and f_2 could implement various functions of x_1, x_2, and x_3. The only constraint on the functions that can be implemented is the size of the AND plane because it produces only four product terms. Commercially available PLAs come in larger sizes than we have shown here. Typical parameters are 16 inputs, 32 product terms, and eight outputs.

Although Figure 3.26 illustrates clearly the functional structure of a PLA, this style of drawing is awkward for larger chips. Instead, it has become customary in technical literature to use the style shown in Figure 3.27. Each AND gate is depicted as a single horizontal line attached to an AND-gate symbol. The possible inputs to the AND gate are drawn as vertical lines that cross the horizontal line. At any crossing of a vertical and horizontal line, a programmable connection, indicated by an X, can be made. Figure 3.27 shows the programmable connections needed to implement the product terms in Figure 3.26. Each OR gate is drawn in a similar manner, with a vertical line attached to an OR-gate symbol.

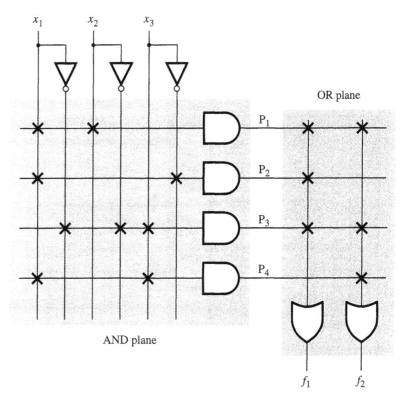

Figure 3.27   Customary schematic for the PLA in Figure 3.26.

The AND-gate outputs cross these lines, and corresponding programmable connections can be formed. The figure illustrates the programmable connections that produce the functions f_1 and f_2 from Figure 3.26.

The PLA is efficient in terms of the area needed for its implementation on an integrated circuit chip. For this reason, PLAs are often included as part of larger chips, such as microprocessors. In this case a PLA is created so that the connections to the AND and OR gates are fixed, rather than programmable. In section 3.10 we will show that both fixed and programmable PLAs can be created with similar structures.

3.11   CONCLUDING REMARKS

We have described the most important concepts that are needed to understand how logic gates are built using transistors. Our discussions of transistor fabrication, voltage levels, propagation delays, power dissipation, and the like are meant to give the reader an appreciation of the practical issues that have to be considered when designing and using logic circuits.

We have introduced several types of integrated circuit chips. Each type of chip is appropriate for specific types of applications. The standard chips, such as the 7400 series, contain only a few simple gates and are rarely used today. Exceptions to this are the buffer chips, which are employed in digital circuits that must drive large capacitive loads at high speeds. The various types of PLDs are widely used in many types of applications. Simple PLDs, like PLAs and PALs, are appropriate for implementation of small logic circuits. The SPLDs offer low cost and high speed. CPLDs can be used for the same applications as SPLDs, but CPLDs are also well suited for implementation of larger circuits of more than 20,000 gates. Many of the applications that can be targeted to CPLDs can alternatively be realized with FPGAs. Which of these two types of chips are used in a specific design situation depends on many factors. For some types of circuits, CPLDs provide slightly faster speeds than FPGAs do, but FPGAs can support larger circuits. Following the trend of putting as much circuitry as possible into a single chip, CPLDs and FPGAs are much more widely used than SPLDs. Most digital designs created in the industry today contain some type of PLD.

The gate-array, standard-cell, and custom-chip technologies are used in cases where PLDs are not appropriate. Typical applications are those that entail very large circuits, where the designed product is expected to sell in large volume.

The next chapter examines the issue of optimization of logic functions. Some of the techniques discussed are appropriate for use in the synthesis of logic circuits regardless of what type of technology is used for implementation. Other techniques are suitable for synthesizing circuits so that they can be implemented in chips with specific types of resources. We will show that when synthesizing a logic function to create a circuit, the optimization methods used depend, at least in part, on which type of chip is being used.

PROBLEMS

3.1   Consider the circuit shown in Figure P3.1.

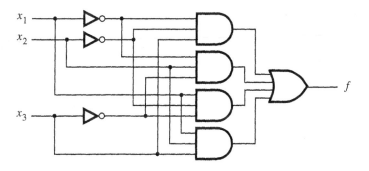

Figure P3.1   A sum-of-products CMOS circuit.

(a) Show the truth table for the logic function f.

(b) If each gate in the circuit is implemented as a CMOS gate, how many transistors are needed?

3.2   (a) Show that the circuit in Figure P3.2 is functionally equivalent to the circuit in Figure P3.1.

(b) How many transistors are needed to build this CMOS circuit?

3.3   (a) Show that the circuit in Figure P3.3 is functionally equivalent to the circuit in Figure P3.2.

(b) How many transistors are needed to build this CMOS circuit if each XOR gate is implemented using the circuit in Figure 3.61d?

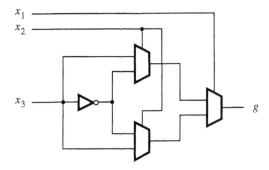

Figure P3.2   A CMOS circuit built with multiplexers.

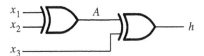

Figure P3.3   Circuit for problem 3.3.

3.4 In section 3.8.8 we said that a six-input CMOS AND gate can be constructed using 2 three-input AND gates and a two-input AND gate. This approach requires 22 transistors. Show how you can use only CMOS NAND and NOR gates to build the six-input AND gate and then calculate the number of transistors needed. (Hint: use DeMorgan's theorem.)

3.5 Repeat problem 3.4 for an eight-input CMOS OR gate.

3.6 (a) Give the truth table for the CMOS circuit in Figure P3.4.
(b) Derive a canonical sum-of-products expression for the truth table from part (a). How many transistors are needed to build a circuit representing the canonical form if only AND, OR, and NOT gates are used?

3.7 (a) Give the truth table for the CMOS circuit in Figure P3.5.
(b) Derive the simplest sum-of-products expression for the truth table in part (a). How many transistors are needed to build the sum-of-products circuit using CMOS AND, OR, and NOT gates?

3.8 Figure P3.6 shows half of a CMOS circuit. Derive the other half that contains the PMOS transistors.

3.9 Figure P3.7 shows half of a CMOS circuit. Derive the other half that contains the NMOS transistors.

3.10 Derive a CMOS complex gate for the logic function $f(x_1, x_2, x_3, x_4) = \sum m(0, 1, 2, 4, 5, 6, 8, 9, 10)$.

3.11 Derive a CMOS complex gate for the logic function $f(x_1, x_2, x_3, x_4) = \sum m(0, 1, 2, 4, 6, 8, 10, 12, 14)$.

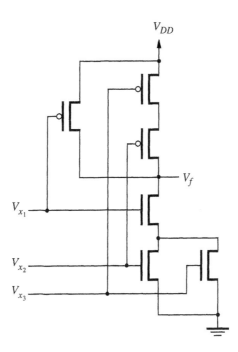

Figure P3.4   A three-input CMOS circuit.

3.12 Derive a CMOS complex gate for the logic function $f = xy + xz$. Use as few transistors as possible (Hint: consider $\overline{f}$).

3.13 Derive a CMOS complex gate for the logic function $f = xy + xz + yz$. Use as few transistors as possible (Hint: consider $\overline{f}$).

3.14 For an NMOS transistor, assume that $k'_n = 20\ \mu A/V^2$, $W/L = 2.5\ \mu m/0.5\ \mu m$, $V_{GS} = 5$ V, and $V_T = 1$ V. Calculate
(a) I_D when $V_{DS} = 5$ V.
(b) I_D when $V_{DS} = 0.2$ V.

3.15 For a PMOS transistor, assume that $k'_p = 10\ \mu A/V^2$, $W/L = 2.5\ \mu m/0.5\ \mu m$, $V_{GS} = -5$ V, and $V_T = -1$ V. Calculate
(a) I_D when $V_{DS} = -5$ V.
(b) I_D when $V_{DS} = -0.2$ V.

3.16 For an NMOS transistor, assume that $k'_n = 20\ \mu A/V^2$, $W/L = 5.0\ \mu m/0.5\ \mu m$, $V_{GS} = 5$ V, and $V_T = 1$ V. For small V_{DS}, calculate R_{DS}.

3.17 For an NMOS transistor, assume that $k'_n = 40\ \mu A/V^2$, $W/L = 3.5\ \mu m/0.35\ \mu m$, $V_{GS} = 3.3$ V, and $V_T = 0.66$ V. For small V_{DS}, calculate R_{DS}.

3.18 For a PMOS transistor, assume that $k'_p = 10\ \mu A/V^2$, $W/L = 5.0\ \mu m/0.5\ \mu m$, $V_{GS} = -5$ V, and $V_T = -1$ V. For $V_{DS} = -4.8$ V, calculate R_{DS}.

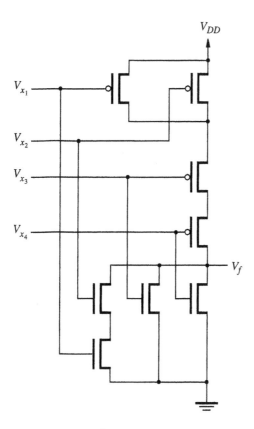

Figure P3.5   A four-input CMOS circuit.

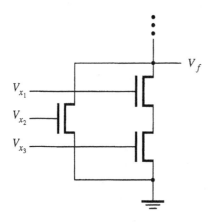

Figure P3.6   The PDN in a CMOS circuit.

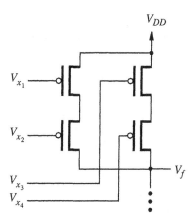

Figure P3.7   The PUN in a CMOS circuit.

3.19   For a PMOS transistor, assume that $k_p' = 16~\mu A/V^2$, $W/L = 3.5~\mu m/0.35~\mu m$, $V_{GS} = -3.3$ V, and $V_T = -0.66$ V. For $V_{DS} = -3.2$ V, calculate R_{DS}.

3.20   In the original NMOS technology, the pull-up device was an *n*-channel MOSFET. But most integrated circuits fabricated today use CMOS technology. Hence it is convenient to implement the pull-up resistor using a PMOS transistor, as shown in Figure P3.8. Such a circuit is referred to as a *pseudo-NMOS* circuit. The pull-up device is called a "weak" PMOS transistor because it has a small W/L ratio.

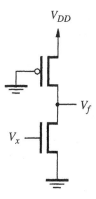

Figure P3.8   The pseudo-NMOS inverter.

When $V_x = V_{DD}$, V_f has a low value. The NMOS transistor is operating in the triode region, while the PMOS transistor limits the current flow because it is operating in the saturation region. The current through the NMOS and PMOS transistors has to be equal and is given by equations 3.1 and 3.2. Show that the low-output voltage, $V_f = V_{OL}$ is given by

$$V_f = (V_{DD} - V_T)\left[1 - \sqrt{1 - \frac{k_p}{k_n}}\right]$$

where k_p and k_n, called the *gain factors*, depend on the sizes of the PMOS and NMOS transistors, respectively. They are defined by $k_p = k'_p W_p/L_p$ and $k_n = k'_n W_n/L_n$.

3.21 For the circuit in Figure P3.8, assume the values $k'_n = 60 \ \mu A/V^2$, $k'_p = 0.4 k'_n$, $W_n/L_n = 2.0 \ \mu m/0.5 \ \mu m$, $W_p/L_p = 0.5 \ \mu m/0.5 \ \mu m$, $V_{DD} = 5$ V, and $V_T = 1$ V. When $V_x = V_{DD}$, calculate (*a*) through (*e*).
(a) The static current I_{stat}.
(b) The on-resistance of the NMOS transistor.
(c) V_{OL}.
(d) The static power dissipated in the inverter.
(e) The on-resistance of the PMOS transistor.
(f) Assume that the inverter is used to drive a capacitive load of 70 fF. Using equation 3.4, calculate the low-to-high and high-to-low propagation delays.

3.22 Repeat problem 3.21 assuming that the size of the PMOS transistor is changed to $W_p/L_p = 2.0 \ \mu m/0.5 \ \mu m$.

3.23 Figure P3.8 shows that in the pseudo-NMOS technology, the pull-up device is implemented using a PMOS transistor. Repeat problem 3.21 for a NAND gate built with pseudo-NMOS technology. Assume that both of the NMOS transistors in the gate have the same parameters, as given in problem 3.21.

3.24 Repeat problem 3.23 for a pseudo-NMOS NOR gate.

3.25 (a) For $V_{IH} = 4$ V, $V_{OH} = 4.5$ V, $V_{IL} = 1$ V, $V_{OL} = 0.3$ V, and $V_{DD} = 5$ V, calculate the noise margins NM_H and NM_L.
(b) Consider an eight-input NAND gate built using NMOS technology. If the voltage drop across each transistor is 0.1 V, what is V_{OL}? What is the corresponding NM_L using the other parameters from part (*a*)?

3.26 Under steady-state conditions for an n-input CMOS NAND gate, what are the voltage levels of V_{OL} and V_{OH}? Explain.

3.27 For a CMOS inverter, assume that the load capacitance is $C = 150$ fF and $V_{DD} = 5$ V. The inverter is cycled through the low and high voltage levels at an average rate of $f = 75$ MHz.
(a) Calculate the dynamic power dissipated in the inverter.
(b) For a chip that contains the equivalent of 250,000 inverters, calculate the total dynamic power dissipated if 20 percent of the gates change values at any given time.

3.28 Repeat problem 3.27 for $C = 120$ fF, $V_{DD} = 3.3$ V, and $f = 125$ MHz.

3.29 In a CMOS inverter, assume that $k'_n = 20 \ \mu A/V^2$, $k'_p = 0.4 \times k'_n$, $W_n/L_n = 5.0 \ \mu m/0.5 \ \mu m$, $W_p/L_p = 5.0 \ \mu m/0.5 \ \mu m$, and $V_{DD} = 5$ V. The inverter drives a load capacitance of 150 fF.

(a) Find the high-to-low propagation delay.

(b) Find the low-to-high propagation delay.

(c) What should be the dimensions of the PMOS transistor such that the low-to-high and high-to-low propagation delays are equal? Ignore the effect of the PMOS transistor's size on the load capacitance of the inverter.

3.30 Repeat problem 3.29 for the parameters $k'_n = 40\ \mu A/V^2$, $k'_p = 0.4 \times k'_n$, $W_n/L_n = W_p/L_p = 3.5\ \mu m/0.35\ \mu m$, and $V_{DD} = 3.3$ V.

3.31 In a CMOS inverter, assume that $W_n/L_n = 2$ and $W_p/L_p = 4$. For a CMOS NAND gate, calculate the required W/L ratios of the NMOS and PMOS transistors such that the available current in the gate to drive the output both low and high is equal to that in the inverter.

3.32 Repeat problem 3.31 for a CMOS NOR gate.

3.33 Repeat problem 3.31 for the CMOS complex gate in Figure 3.16. The transistor sizes should be chosen so that in the worst case the available current is at least as large as in the inverter.

3.34 Repeat problem 3.31 for the CMOS complex gate in Figure 3.17.

3.35 In Figure 3.69 we showed a solution to the static power dissipation problem when NMOS pass transistors are used. Assume that the PMOS pull-up transistor is removed from this circuit. Assume the parameters $k'_n = 60\ \mu A/V^2$, $k'_p = 0.5 \times k'_n$, $W_n/L_n = 2.0\ \mu m/0.5\ \mu m$, $W_p/L_p = 4.0\ \mu m/0.5\ \mu m$, $V_{DD} = 5$ V, and $V_T = 1$ V. For $V_B = 3.5$ V, calculate (a) through (d).

(a) The static current I_{stat}.

(b) The voltage V_f at the output of the inverter.

(c) The static power dissipation in the inverter.

(d) If a chip contains 250,000 inverters used in this manner, find the total static power dissipation.

3.36 Using the style of drawing in Figure 3.66, draw a picture of a PLA programmed to implement $f_1(x_1, x_2, x_3) = \sum m(1, 2, 4, 7)$. The PLA should have the inputs $x_1, \ldots, x_3$; the product terms $P_1, \ldots, P_4$; and the outputs f_1 and f_2.

3.37 Using the style of drawing in Figure 3.66, draw a picture of a PLA programmed to implement $f_1(x_1, x_2, x_3) = \sum m(0, 3, 5, 6)$. The PLA should have the inputs $x_1, \ldots, x_3$; the product terms $P_1, \ldots, P_4$; and the outputs f_1 and f_2.

3.38 Show how function f_1 from problem 3.36 can be realized in a PLA of the type shown in Figure 3.65. Draw a picture of such a PLA programmed to implement f_1. The PLA should have the inputs $x_1, \ldots, x_3$; the sum terms $S_1, \ldots, S_4$; and the outputs f_1 and f_2.

3.39 Show how function f_1 from problem 3.37 can be realized in a PLA of the type shown in Figure 3.65. Draw a picture of such a PLA programmed to implement f_1. The PLA should have the inputs $x_1, \ldots, x_3$; the sum terms $S_1, \ldots, S_4$; and the outputs f_1 and f_2.

3.40 Repeat problem 3.38 using the style of PLA drawing shown in Figure 3.63.

3.41 Repeat problem 3.39 using the style of PLA drawing shown in Figure 3.63.

3.42 Given that f_1 is implemented as described in problem 3.36, list all of the other possible logic functions that can be realized using output f_2 in the PLA.

3.43   Given that f_1 is implemented as described in problem 3.37, list all of the other possible logic
functions that can be realized using output f_2 in the PLA.

3.44   Consider the function $f(x_1, x_2, x_3) = x_1\bar{x}_2 + x_1x_3 + x_2\bar{x}_3$. Show a circuit using 5 two-input
lookup-tables (LUTs) to implement this expression. As shown in Figure 3.39, give the truth
table implemented in each LUT. You do not need to show the wires in the FPGA.

3.45   Consider the function $f(x_1, x_2, x_3) = \sum m(2, 3, 4, 6, 7)$. Show how it can be realized using
2 two-input LUTs. As shown in Figure 3.39, give the truth table implemented in each LUT.
You do not need to show the wires in the FPGA.

3.46   Given the function $f = x_1x_2x_4 + x_2x_3\bar{x}_4 + \bar{x}_1\bar{x}_2\bar{x}_3$, a straightforward implementation in an
FPGA with three-input LUTs requires four LUTs. Show how it can be done using only 3
three-input LUTs. Label the output of each LUT with an expression representing the logic
function that it implements.

3.47   For f in problem 3.46, show a circuit of two-input LUTs that realizes the function. You
are to use exactly 7 two-input LUTs. Label the output of each LUT with an expression
representing the logic function that it implements.

3.48   Figure 3.39 shows an FPGA programmed to implement a function. The figure shows one
pin used for function f and several pins that are unused. Without changing the programming
of any switch that is turned *on* in the FPGA in the figure, list four other logic functions, in
addition to f, that can be implemented on the unused pins.

3.49   Assume that a gate array contains the type of logic cell depicted in Figure P3.9. The inputs
$in_1, \cdots, in_7$ can be connected to either 1 or 0, or to any logic signal.

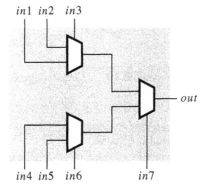

Figure P3.9   A gate-array logic cell.

(a) Show how the logic cell can be used to realize $f = x_1x_2 + x_3$.
(b) Show how the logic cell can be used to realize $f = x_1x_3 + x_2x_3$.

3.50   Assume that a gate array exists in which the logic cell used is a three-input NAND gate.
The inputs to each NAND gate can be connected to either 1 or 0, or to any logic signal. Show

how the following logic functions can be realized in the gate array. (Hint: use DeMorgan's theorem.)

(a) $f = x_1x_2 + x_3$.

(b) $f = x_1x_2x_4 + x_2x_3\bar{x}_4 + \bar{x}_1$.

3.51   Write VHDL code to represent the function $f = x_2\bar{x}_3\bar{x}_4 + \bar{x}_1x_2x_4 + \bar{x}_1x_2x_3 + x_1x_2x_3$.

(a) Use MAX+plusII to implement f in a MAX 7000 CPLD. Show the logic expression generated for f in the Compiler Report file. Use timing simulation to determine the time needed for a change in inputs x_1, x_2, or x_3 to propagate to the output f.

(b) Repeat part (a) using a FLEX 10K FPGA for implementation of the circuit.

3.52   Repeat problem 3.51 for the function $f = (x_1 + x_2 + \bar{x}_4) \cdot (\bar{x}_2 + x_3 + \bar{x}_4) \cdot (\bar{x}_1 + x_3 + \bar{x}_4) \cdot (\bar{x}_1 + \bar{x}_3 + \bar{x}_4)$.

3.53   Repeat problem 3.51 for the function $f(x_1, ..., x_7) = x_1x_3\bar{x}_6 + x_1x_4x_5\bar{x}_6 + x_2x_3x_7 + x_2x_4x_5x_7$.

3.54   What logic gate is realized by the circuit in Figure P3.10? Does this circuit suffer from any major drawbacks?

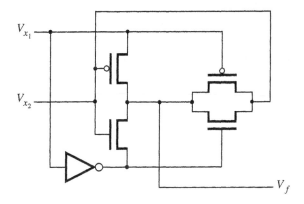

Figure P3.10   Circuit for problem 3.54.

3.55   What logic gate is realized by the circuit in Figure P3.11? Does this circuit suffer from any major drawbacks?

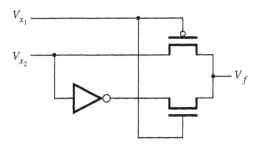

Figure P3.11   Circuit for problem 3.55.

REFERENCES

1. A. S. Sedra and K. C. Smith, *Microelectronic Circuits*, 4th ed. (Oxford University Press: New York, 1998).

2. J. M. Rabaey, *Digital Integrated Circuits*, (Prentice-Hall, 1996).

3. Texas Instruments, *Logic Products Selection Guide and Databook CD-ROM*, 1997.

4. National Semiconductor, *VHC/VHCT Advanced CMOS Logic Databook*, 1993.

5. Motorola, *CMOS Logic Databook*, 1996.

6. Toshiba America Electronic Components, *TC74VHC/VHCT Series CMOS Logic Databook*, 1994.

7. Integrated Devices Technology, *High Performance Logic Databook*, 1994.

8. J. F. Wakerly, *Digital Design Principles and Practices* (Prentice-Hall: Englewood Cliffs, NJ, 1990).

9. M. M. Mano, *Digital Design* (Prentice-Hall: Englewood Cliffs, NJ, 1991).

10. R. H. Katz, *Contemporary Logic Design* (Benjamin/Cummings: Redwood City, CA, 1994).

11. J. P. Hayes, *Introduction to Logic Design* (Addison-Wesley: Reading, MA, 1993).

12. D. D. Gajski, *Principles of Digital Design* (Prentice-Hall: Upper Saddle River, NJ, 1997).

4

OPTIMIZED IMPLEMENTATION OF LOGIC FUNCTIONS

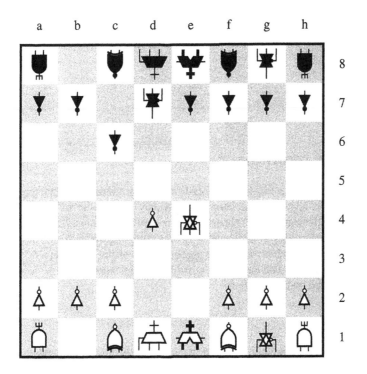

4. Nc3xe4, Nb8–d7

In Chapter 2 we showed that algebraic manipulation can be used to find the lowest-cost implementations of logic functions. The purpose of that chapter was to introduce the basic concepts in the synthesis process. The reader is probably convinced that it is easy to derive a straightforward realization of a logic function in a canonical form, but it is not at all obvious how to choose and apply the theorems and properties of section 2.5 to find a minimum-cost circuit. Indeed, the algebraic manipulation is rather tedious and quite impractical for functions of many variables.

If CAD tools are used to design logic circuits, the task of minimizing the cost of implementation does not fall to the designer; the tools perform the necessary optimizations automatically. Even so, it is essential to know something about this process. Most CAD tools have many features and options that are under control of the user. To know when and how to apply these options, the user must have an understanding of what the tools do.

In this chapter we will introduce some of the optimization techniques implemented in CAD tools and show how these techniques can be automated. As a first step we will discuss a graphical approach, known as the Karnaugh map, which provides a neat way to manually derive minimum-cost implementations of simple logic functions. Although it is not suitable for implementation in CAD tools, it illustrates a number of key concepts. We will show how both two-level and multilevel circuits can be designed. Then we will describe a cubical representation for logic functions, which is suitable for use in CAD tools. We will also continue our discussion of the VHDL language and CAD tools.

4.1 KARNAUGH MAP

In section 2.6 we saw that the key to finding a minimum-cost expression for a given logic function is to reduce the number of product (or sum) terms needed in the expression, by applying the combining property 14a (or 14b) as judiciously as possible. The Karnaugh map approach provides a systematic way of performing this optimization. To understand how it works, it is useful to review the algebraic approach from Chapter 2. Consider the function f in Figure 4.1. The canonical sum-of-products expression for f consists of minterms m_0, m_2, m_4, m_5, and m_6, so that

$$f = \bar{x}_1\bar{x}_2\bar{x}_3 + \bar{x}_1x_2\bar{x}_3 + x_1\bar{x}_2\bar{x}_3 + x_1\bar{x}_2x_3 + x_1x_2\bar{x}_3$$

The combining property 14a allows us to replace two minterms that differ in the value of only one variable with a single product term that does not include that variable at all. For example, both m_0 and m_2 include $\bar{x}_1$ and $\bar{x}_3$, but they differ in the value of x_2 because m_0 includes $\bar{x}_2$ while m_2 includes x_2. Thus

$$\bar{x}_1\bar{x}_2\bar{x}_3 + \bar{x}_1x_2\bar{x}_3 = \bar{x}_1(\bar{x}_2 + x_2)\bar{x}_3$$
$$= \bar{x}_1 \cdot 1 \cdot \bar{x}_3$$
$$= \bar{x}_1\bar{x}_3$$

Row number	x_1	x_2	x_3	f
0	0	0	0	1
1	0	0	1	0
2	0	1	0	1
3	0	1	1	0
4	1	0	0	1
5	1	0	1	1
6	1	1	0	1
7	1	1	1	0

Figure 4.1   The function $f(x_1, x_2, x_3) = \sum m(0, 2, 4, 5, 6)$.

Hence m_0 and m_2 can be replaced by the single product term $\bar{x}_1\bar{x}_3$. Similarly, m_4 and m_6 differ only in the value of x_2 and can be combined using

$$x_1\bar{x}_2\bar{x}_3 + x_1x_2\bar{x}_3 = x_1(\bar{x}_2 + x_2)\bar{x}_3$$
$$= x_1 \cdot 1 \cdot \bar{x}_3$$
$$= x_1\bar{x}_3$$

Now the two newly generated terms, $\bar{x}_1\bar{x}_3$ and $x_1\bar{x}_3$, can be combined further as

$$\bar{x}_1\bar{x}_3 + x_1\bar{x}_3 = (\bar{x}_1 + x_1)\bar{x}_3$$
$$= 1 \cdot \bar{x}_3$$
$$= \bar{x}_3$$

These optimization steps indicate that we can replace the four minterms m_0, m_2, m_4, and m_6 with the single product term $\bar{x}_3$. In other words, the minterms m_0, m_2, m_4, and m_6 are all *included* in the term $\bar{x}_3$. The remaining minterm in f is m_5. It can be combined with m_4, which gives

$$x_1\bar{x}_2\bar{x}_3 + x_1\bar{x}_2x_3 = x_1\bar{x}_2$$

Recall that theorem 7b in section 2.5 indicates that

$$m_4 = m_4 + m_4$$

which means that we can use the minterm m_4 twice—to combine with minterms m_0, m_2, and m_6 to yield the term $\bar{x}_3$ as explained above and also to combine with m_5 to yield the term $x_1\bar{x}_2$.

We have now accounted for all the minterms in f; hence all five input valuations for which $f = 1$ are covered by the minimum-cost expression

$$f = \bar{x}_3 + x_1\bar{x}_2$$

The expression has the product term $\bar{x}_3$ because $f = 1$ when $x_3 = 0$ regardless of the values of x_1 and x_2. The four minterms m_0, m_2, m_4, and m_6 represent all possible minterms for which $x_3 = 0$; they include all four valuations, 00, 01, 10, and 11, of variables x_1 and x_2. Thus if $x_3 = 0$, then it is guaranteed that $f = 1$. This may not be easy to see directly from the truth table in Figure 4.1, but it is obvious if we write the corresponding valuations grouped together:

	x_1	x_2	x_3
m_0	0	0	0
m_2	0	1	0
m_4	1	0	0
m_6	1	1	0

In a similar way, if we look at m_4 and m_5 as a group of two

	x_1	x_2	x_3
m_4	1	0	0
m_5	1	0	1

it is clear that when $x_1 = 1$ and $x_2 = 0$, then $f = 1$ regardless of the value of x_3.

The preceding discussion suggests that it would be advantageous to devise a method that allows easy discovery of groups of minterms for which $f = 1$ that can be combined into single terms. The Karnaugh map is a useful vehicle for this purpose.

The *Karnaugh map* [1] is an alternative to the truth-table form for representing a function. The map consists of *cells* that correspond to the rows of the truth table. Consider the two-variable example in Figure 4.2. Part (*a*) depicts the truth-table form, where each of the four rows is identified by a minterm. Part (*b*) shows the Karnaugh map, which has four cells. The columns of the map are labeled by the value of x_1, and the rows are labeled by x_2. This labeling leads to the locations of minterms as shown in the figure. Compared to the truth table, the advantage of the Karnaugh map is that it allows easy recognition of minterms that can be combined using property 14*a* from section 2.5. Minterms in any two cells that are adjacent, either in the same row or the same column, can be combined. For example, the minterms m_2 and m_3 can be combined as

$$m_2 + m_3 = x_1\bar{x}_2 + x_1x_2$$
$$= x_1(\bar{x}_2 + x_2)$$
$$= x_1 \cdot 1$$
$$= x_1$$

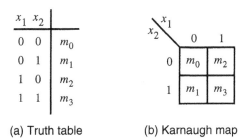

(a) Truth table   (b) Karnaugh map

Figure 4.2   Location of two-variable minterms.

The Karnaugh map is not just useful for combining pairs of minterms. As we will see in several larger examples, the Karnaugh map can be used directly to derive a minimum-cost circuit for a logic function.

Two-Variable Map

A Karnaugh map for a two-variable function is given in Figure 4.3. It corresponds to the function f of Figure 2.15. The value of f for each valuation of the variables x_1 and x_2 is indicated in the corresponding cell of the map. Because a 1 appears in both cells of the bottom row and these cells are adjacent, there exists a single product term that can cause f to be equal to 1 when the input variables have the values that correspond to either of these cells. To indicate this fact, we have circled the cell entries in the map. Rather than using the combining property formally, we can derive the product term intuitively. Both of the cells are identified by $x_2 = 1$, but $x_1 = 0$ for the left cell and $x_1 = 1$ for the right cell. Thus if $x_2 = 1$, then $f = 1$ regardless of whether x_1 is equal to 0 or 1. The product term representing the two cells is simply x_2.

Similarly, $f = 1$ for both cells in the first column. These cells are identified by $x_1 = 0$. Therefore, they lead to the product term $\bar{x}_1$. Since this takes care of all instances where $f = 1$, it follows that the minimum-cost realization of the function is

$$f = x_2 + \bar{x}_1$$

Evidently, to find a minimum-cost implementation of a given function, it is necessary to find the smallest number of product terms that produce a value of 1 for all cases where

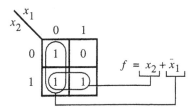

Figure 4.3   The function of Figure 2.15.

$f = 1$. Moreover, the cost of these product terms should be as low as possible. Note that a product term that covers two adjacent cells is cheaper to implement than a term that covers only a single cell. For our example once the two cells in the bottom row have been covered by the product term x_2, only one cell (top left) remains. Although it could be covered by the term $\bar{x}_1\bar{x}_2$, it is better to combine the two cells in the left column to produce the product term $\bar{x}_1$ because this term is cheaper to implement.

Three-Variable Map

A three-variable Karnaugh map is constructed by placing 2 two-variable maps side by side. Figure 4.4 shows the map and indicates the locations of minterms in it. In this case each valuation of x_1 and x_2 identifies a column in the map, while the value of x_3 distinguishes the two rows. To ensure that minterms in the adjacent cells in the map can always be combined into a single product term, the adjacent cells must differ in the value of only one variable. Thus the columns are identified by the sequence of (x_1, x_2) values of 00, 01, 11, and 10, rather than the more obvious 00, 01, 10, and 11. This makes the second and third columns different only in variable x_1. Also, the first and the fourth columns differ only in variable x_1, which means that these columns can be considered as being adjacent. The reader may find it useful to visualize the map as a rectangle folded into a cylinder where the left and the right edges in Figure 4.4b are made to touch. (A sequence of codes, or valuations, where consecutive codes differ in one variable only is known as the *Gray code*. This code is used for a variety of purposes, some of which will be encountered later in the book.)

Figure 4.5a represents the function of Figure 2.18 in Karnaugh-map form. To synthesize this function, it is necessary to cover the four 1s in the map as efficiently as possible. It is not difficult to see that two product terms suffice. The first covers the 1s in the top row, which are represented by the term $x_1\bar{x}_3$. The second term is $\bar{x}_2 x_3$, which covers the 1s in the bottom row. Hence the function is implemented as

$$f = x_1\bar{x}_3 + \bar{x}_2 x_3$$

which describes the circuit obtained in Figure 2.19a.

x_1 x_2 x_3	
0 0 0	m_0
0 0 1	m_1
0 1 0	m_2
0 1 1	m_3
1 0 0	m_4
1 0 1	m_5
1 1 0	m_6
1 1 1	m_7

(a) Truth table

x_3 \\ $x_1 x_2$	00	01	11	10
0	m_0	m_2	m_6	m_4
1	m_1	m_3	m_7	m_5

(b) Karnaugh map

Figure 4.4   Location of three-variable minterms.

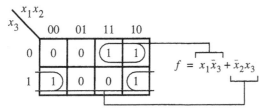

(a) The function of Figure 2.18

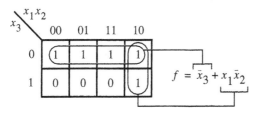

(b) The function of Figure 4.1

Figure 4.5 Examples of three-variable Karnaugh maps.

In a three-variable map it is possible to combine cells to produce product terms that correspond to a single cell, two adjacent cells, or a group of four adjacent cells. Realization of a group of four adjacent cells using a single product term is illustrated in Figure 4.5b, using the function from Figure 4.1. The four cells in the top row correspond to the (x_1, x_2, x_3) valuations 000, 010, 110, and 100. As we discussed before, this indicates that if $x_3 = 0$, then $f = 1$ for all four possible valuations of x_1 and x_2, which means that the only requirement is that $x_3 = 0$. Therefore, the product term $\bar{x}_3$ represents these four cells. The remaining 1, corresponding to minterm m_5, is best covered by the term $x_1\bar{x}_2$, obtained by combining the two cells in the right-most column. The complete realization of f is

$$f = \bar{x}_3 + x_1\bar{x}_2$$

It is also possible to have a group of eight 1s in a three-variable map. This is the trivial case where $f = 1$ for all valuations of input variables; in other words, f is equal to the constant 1.

The Karnaugh map provides a simple mechanism for generating the product terms that should be used to implement a given function. A product term must include only those variables that have the same value for all cells in the group represented by this term. If the variable is equal to 1 in the group, it appears uncomplemented in the product term; if it is equal to 0, it appears complemented. Each variable that is sometimes 1 and sometimes 0 in the group does not appear in the product term.

Four-Variable Map

A four-variable map is constructed by placing 2 three-variable maps together to create four rows in the same fashion as we used 2 two-variable maps to form the four columns in a three-variable map. Figure 4.6 shows the structure of the four-variable map and the location of minterms. We have included in this figure another frequently used way of designating the rows and columns. As shown in blue, it is sufficient to indicate the rows and columns for which a given variable is equal to 1. Thus $x_1 = 1$ for the two right-most columns, $x_2 = 1$ for the two middle columns, $x_3 = 1$ for the bottom two rows, and $x_4 = 1$ for the two middle rows.

Figure 4.7 gives four examples of four-variable functions. The function f_1 has a group of four 1s in adjacent cells in the bottom two rows, for which $x_2 = 0$ and $x_3 = 1$—they are represented by the product term $\bar{x}_2 x_3$. This leaves the two 1s in the second row to be covered, which can be accomplished with the term $x_1 \bar{x}_3 x_4$. Hence the minimum-cost implementation of the function is

$$f_1 = \bar{x}_2 x_3 + x_1 \bar{x}_3 x_4$$

The function f_2 includes a group of eight 1s that can be implemented by a single term, x_3. Again, the reader should note that if the remaining two 1s were implemented separately, the result would be the product term $x_1 \bar{x}_3 x_4$. Implementing these 1s as a part of a group of four 1s, as shown in the figure, gives the less expensive product term $x_1 x_4$.

Just as the left and the right edges of the map are adjacent in terms of the assignment of the variables, so are the top and the bottom edges. Indeed, the four corners of the map are adjacent to each other and thus can form a group of four 1s, which may be implemented by the product term $\bar{x}_2 \bar{x}_4$. This case is depicted by the function f_3. In addition to this group of 1s, there are four other 1s that must be covered to implement f_3. This can be done as shown in the figure.

In all examples that we have considered so far, a unique solution exists that leads to a minimum-cost circuit. The function f_4 provides an example where there is some choice. The groups of four 1s in the top-left and bottom-right corners of the map are realized by the terms $\bar{x}_1 \bar{x}_3$ and $x_1 x_3$, respectively. This leaves the two 1s that correspond to the term $x_1 x_2 \bar{x}_3$. But these two 1s can be realized more economically by treating them as a part of a group of four 1s. They can be included in two different groups of four, as shown in the figure. One

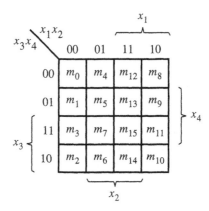

Figure 4.6   A four-variable Karnaugh map.

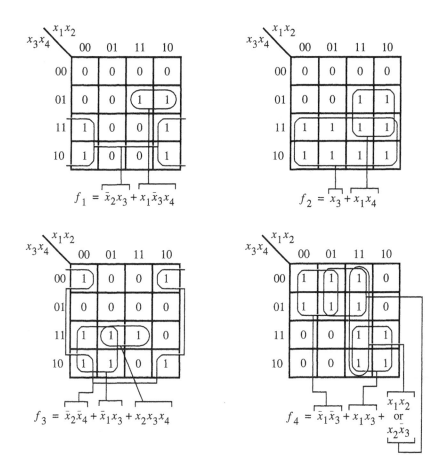

Figure 4.7   Examples of four-variable Karnaugh maps.

choice leads to the product term x_1x_2, and the other leads to $x_2\bar{x}_3$. Both of these terms have the same cost; hence it does not matter which one is chosen in the final circuit. Note that the complement of x_3 in the term $x_2\bar{x}_3$ does not imply an increased cost in comparison with x_1x_2, because this complement must be generated anyway to produce the term $\bar{x}_1\bar{x}_3$, which is included in the implementation.

Five-Variable Map

We can use 2 four-variable maps to construct a five-variable map. It is easy to imagine a structure where one map is directly behind the other, and they are distinguished by $x_5 = 0$ for one map and $x_5 = 1$ for the other map. Since such a structure is awkward to draw, we can simply place the two maps side by side as shown in Figure 4.8. For the logic function given in this example, two groups of four 1s appear in the same place in both four-variable maps; hence their realization does not depend on the value of x_5. The same is true for the two groups of two 1s in the second row. The 1 in the top-right corner appears only in the

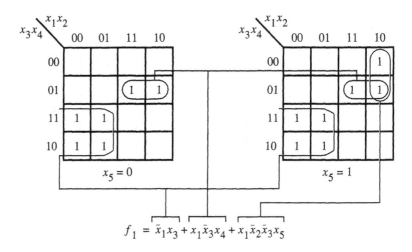

Figure 4.8   A five-variable Karnaugh map.

right map, where $x_5 = 1$; it is a part of the group of two 1s realized by the term $x_1 \bar{x}_2 \bar{x}_3 x_5$. Note that in this map we left blank those cells for which $f = 0$, to make the figure more readable. We will do likewise in a number of maps that follow.

Using a five-variable map is obviously more awkward than using maps with fewer variables. Extending the Karnaugh map concept to more variables is not useful from the practical point of view. This is not troublesome, because practical synthesis of logic functions is done with CAD tools that perform the necessary minimization automatically. Although Karnaugh maps are occasionally useful for designing small logic circuits, our main reason for introducing the Karnaugh maps is to provide a simple vehicle for illustrating the ideas involved in the minimization process.

4.2 STRATEGY FOR MINIMIZATION

For the examples in the preceding section, we used an intuitive approach to decide how the 1s in a Karnaugh map should be grouped together to obtain the minimum-cost implementation of a given function. Our intuitive strategy was to find as few as possible and as large as possible groups of 1s that cover all cases where the function has a value of 1. Each group of 1s has to comprise cells that can be represented by a single product term. The larger the group of 1s, the fewer the number of variables in the corresponding product term. This approach worked well because the Karnaugh maps in our examples were small. For larger logic functions, which have many variables, such intuitive approach is unsuitable. Instead, we must have an organized method for deriving a minimum-cost implementation. In this section we will introduce a possible method, which is similar to the techniques that are automated in CAD tools. To illustrate the main ideas, we will use Karnaugh maps. Later, in section 4.9, we will describe a different way of representing logic functions, which is used in CAD tools.

4.2.1 TERMINOLOGY

A huge amount of research work has gone into the development of techniques for synthesis of logic functions. The results of this research have been published in numerous papers. To facilitate the presentation of the results, certain terminology has evolved that avoids the need for using highly descriptive phrases. We define some of this terminology in the following paragraphs because it is useful for describing the minimization process.

Literal

A given product term consists of some number of variables, each of which may appear either in uncomplemented or complemented form. Each appearance of a variable, either uncomplemented or complemented, is called a *literal*. For example, the product term $x_1\bar{x}_2x_3$ has three literals, and the term $\bar{x}_1x_3\bar{x}_4x_6$ has four literals.

Implicant

A product term that indicates the input valuation(s) for which a given function is equal to 1 is called an *implicant* of the function. The most basic implicants are the minterms, which we introduced in section 2.6.1. For an n-variable function, a minterm is an implicant that consists of n literals.

Consider the three-variable function in Figure 4.9. There are 11 possible implicants for this function. This includes the five minterms: $\bar{x}_1\bar{x}_2\bar{x}_3$, $\bar{x}_1\bar{x}_2x_3$, $\bar{x}_1x_2\bar{x}_3$, $\bar{x}_1x_2x_3$, and $x_1x_2x_3$. Then there are the implicants that correspond to all possible pairs of minterms that can be combined, namely, $\bar{x}_1\bar{x}_2$ (m_0 and m_1), $\bar{x}_1\bar{x}_3$ (m_0 and m_2), $\bar{x}_1x_3$ (m_1 and m_3), $\bar{x}_1x_2$ (m_2 and m_3), and x_2x_3 (m_3 and m_7). Finally, there is one implicant that covers a group of four minterms, which consists of a single literal $\bar{x}_1$.

Prime Implicant

An implicant is called a *prime implicant* if it cannot be combined into another implicant that has fewer literals. Another way of stating this definition is to say that it is impossible to delete any literal in a prime implicant and still have a valid implicant.

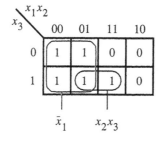

Figure 4.9 Three-variable function $f(x_1, x_2, x_3) = \sum m(0, 1, 2, 3, 7)$.

In Figure 4.9 there are two prime implicants: $\bar{x}_1$ and x_2x_3. It is not possible to delete a literal in either of them. Doing so for $\bar{x}_1$ would make it disappear. For x_2x_3, deleting a literal would leave either x_2 or x_3. But x_2 is not an implicant because it includes the valuation $(x_1, x_2, x_3) = 110$ for which $f = 0$, and x_3 is not an implicant because it includes $(x_1, x_2, x_3) = 101$ for which $f = 0$.

Cover

A collection of implicants that account for all valuations for which a given function is equal to 1 is called a *cover* of that function. A number of different covers exist for most functions. Obviously, a set of all minterms for which $f = 1$ is a cover. It is also apparent that a set of all prime implicants is a cover.

A cover defines a particular implementation of the function. In Figure 4.9 a cover consisting of minterms leads to the expression

$$f = \bar{x}_1\bar{x}_2\bar{x}_3 + \bar{x}_1\bar{x}_2x_3 + \bar{x}_1x_2\bar{x}_3 + \bar{x}_1x_2x_3 + x_1x_2x_3$$

Another valid cover is given by the expression

$$f = \bar{x}_1\bar{x}_2 + \bar{x}_1x_2 + x_2x_3$$

The cover comprising the prime implicants is

$$f = \bar{x}_1 + x_2x_3$$

While all of these expressions represent the function f correctly, the cover consisting of prime implicants leads to the lowest-cost implementation.

Cost

In Chapter 2 we suggested that a good indication of the cost of a logic circuit is the number of gates plus the total number of inputs to all gates in the circuit. We will use this definition of cost throughout the book. But we will assume that primary inputs, namely, the input variables, are available in both true and complemented forms at zero cost. Thus the expression

$$f = x_1\bar{x}_2 + x_3\bar{x}_4$$

has a cost of nine because it can be implemented using two AND gates and one OR gate, with six inputs to the AND and OR gates.

If an inversion is needed inside a circuit, then the corresponding NOT gate and its input are included in the cost. For example, the expression

$$g = \overline{x_1\bar{x}_2 + x_3}(\bar{x}_4 + x_5)$$

is implemented using two AND gates, two OR gates, and one NOT gate to complement $(x_1\bar{x}_2 + x_3)$, with nine inputs. Hence the total cost is 14.

4.2.2 MINIMIZATION PROCEDURE

We have seen that it is possible to implement a given logic function with various circuits. These circuits may have different structures and different costs. When designing a logic circuit, there are usually certain criteria that must be met. One such criterion is likely to be the cost of the circuit, which we considered in the previous discussion. In general, the larger the circuit, the more important the cost issue becomes. In this section we will assume that the main objective is to obtain a minimum-cost circuit.

Having said that cost is the primary concern, we should note that other optimization criteria may be more appropriate in some cases. For instance, in Chapter 3 we described several types of programmable-logic devices (PLDs) that have a predefined basic structure and can be programmed to realize a variety of different circuits. For such devices the main objective is to design a particular circuit so that it will fit into the target device. Whether or not this circuit has the minimum cost is not important if it can be realized successfully on the device. A CAD tool intended for design with a specific device in mind will automatically perform optimizations that are suitable for that device. We will show in section 4.7 that the way in which a circuit should be optimized may be different for different types of devices.

In the previous subsection we concluded that the lowest-cost implementation is achieved when the cover of a given function consists of prime implicants. The question then is how to determine the minimum-cost subset of prime implicants that will cover the function. Some prime implicants may have to be included in the cover, while for others there may be a choice. If a prime implicant includes a minterm for which $f = 1$ that is not included in any other prime implicant, then it must be included in the cover and is called an *essential prime implicant*. In the example in Figure 4.9, both prime implicants are essential. The term x_2x_3 is the only prime implicant that covers the minterm m_7, and $\bar{x}_1$ is the only one that covers the minterms m_0, m_1, and m_2. Notice that the minterm m_3 is covered by both of these prime implicants. The minimum-cost realization of the function is

$$f = \bar{x}_1 + x_2x_3$$

We will now present several examples in which there is a choice as to which prime implicants to include in the final cover. Consider the four-variable function in Figure 4.10. There are five prime implicants: $\bar{x}_1x_3$, $\bar{x}_2x_3$, $x_3\bar{x}_4$, $\bar{x}_1x_2x_4$, and $x_2\bar{x}_3x_4$. The essential ones

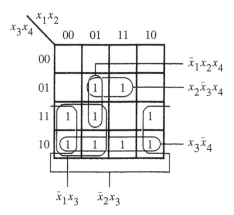

Figure 4.10 Four-variable function $f(x_1, \ldots, x_4) =$
$\sum m(2, 3, 5, 6, 7, 10, 11, 13, 14)$.

(highlighted in blue) are $\bar{x}_2 x_3$ (because of m_{11}), $x_3 \bar{x}_4$ (because of m_{14}), and $x_2 \bar{x}_3 x_4$ (because of m_{13}). They must be included in the cover. These three prime implicants cover all minterms for which $f = 1$ except m_7. It is clear that m_7 can be covered by either $\bar{x}_1 x_3$ or $\bar{x}_1 x_2 x_4$. Because $\bar{x}_1 x_3$ has a lower cost, it is chosen for the cover. Therefore, the minimum-cost realization is

$$f = \bar{x}_2 x_3 + x_3 \bar{x}_4 + x_2 \bar{x}_3 x_4 + \bar{x}_1 x_3$$

From the preceding discussion, the process of finding a minimum-cost circuit involves the following steps:

1. Generate all prime implicants for the given function f.

2. Find the set of essential prime implicants.

3. If the set of essential prime implicants covers all valuations for which $f = 1$, then this set is the desired cover of f. Otherwise, determine the nonessential prime implicants that should be added to form a complete minimum-cost cover.

The choice of nonessential prime implicants to be included in the cover is governed by the cost considerations. This choice is often not obvious. Indeed, for large functions there may exist many possibilities, and some *heuristic* approach (i.e., an approach that considers only a subset of possibilities but gives good results most of the time) has to be used. One such approach is to arbitrarily select one nonessential prime implicant and include it in the cover and then determine the rest of the cover. Next, another cover is determined assuming that this prime implicant is not in the cover. The costs of the resulting covers are compared, and the less-expensive cover is chosen for implementation.

We can illustrate the process by using the function in Figure 4.11. Of the six prime implicants, only $\bar{x}_3 \bar{x}_4$ is essential. Consider next $x_1 x_2 \bar{x}_3$ and assume first that it will be included in the cover. Then the remaining three minterms, m_{10}, m_{11}, and m_{15}, will require two more prime implicants to be included in the cover. A possible implementation is

$$f = \bar{x}_3 \bar{x}_4 + x_1 x_2 \bar{x}_3 + x_1 x_3 x_4 + x_1 \bar{x}_2 x_3$$

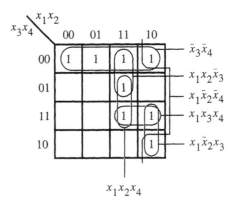

Figure 4.11   The function $f(x_1, \dots, x_4) = \sum m(0, 4, 8, 10, 11, 12, 13, 15)$.

The second possibility is that $x_1x_2\bar{x}_3$ is not included in the cover. Then $x_1x_2x_4$ becomes essential because there is no other way of covering m_{13}. Because $x_1x_2x_4$ also covers m_{15}, only m_{10} and m_{11} remain to be covered, which can be achieved with $x_1\bar{x}_2x_3$. Therefore, the alternative implementation is

$$f = \bar{x}_3\bar{x}_4 + x_1x_2x_4 + x_1\bar{x}_2x_3$$

Clearly, this implementation is a better choice.

Sometimes there may not be any essential prime implicants at all. An example is given in Figure 4.12. Choosing any of the prime implicants and first including it, then excluding it from the cover leads to two alternatives of equal cost. One includes the prime implicants indicated in black, which yields

$$f = \bar{x}_1\bar{x}_3\bar{x}_4 + x_2\bar{x}_3x_4 + x_1x_3x_4 + \bar{x}_2x_3\bar{x}_4$$

The other includes the prime implicants indicated in blue, which yields

$$f = \bar{x}_1\bar{x}_2\bar{x}_4 + \bar{x}_1x_2\bar{x}_3 + x_1x_2x_4 + x_1\bar{x}_2x_3$$

This procedure can be used to find minimum-cost implementations of both small and large logic functions. For our small examples it was convenient to use Karnaugh maps to determine the prime implicants of a function and then choose the final cover. Other techniques based on the same principles are much more suitable for use in CAD tools; we will introduce one such technique in sections 4.9 and 4.10.

The previous examples have been based on the sum-of-products form. We will next illustrate that the same concepts apply for the product-of-sums form.

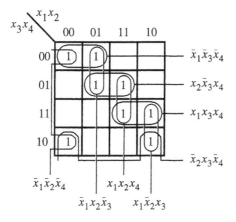

Figure 4.12   The function $f(x_1, \ldots, x_4) = \sum m(0, 2, 4, 5, 10, 11, 13, 15)$.

4.3 MINIMIZATION OF PRODUCT-OF-SUMS FORMS

Now that we know how to find the minimum-cost sum-of-products (SOP) implementations of functions, we can use the same techniques and the principle of duality to obtain minimum-cost product-of-sums (POS) implementations. In this case it is the maxterms for which $f = 0$ that have to be combined into sum terms that are as large as possible. Again, a sum term is considered larger if it covers more maxterms, and the larger the term, the less costly it is to implement.

Figure 4.13 depicts the same function as Figure 4.9 depicts. There are three maxterms that must be covered: M_4, M_5, and M_6. They can be covered by two sum terms shown in the figure, leading to the following implementation:

$$f = (\bar{x}_1 + x_2)(\bar{x}_1 + x_3)$$

A circuit corresponding to this expression has two OR gates and one AND gate, with two inputs for each gate. Its cost is greater than the cost of the equivalent SOP implementation derived in Figure 4.9, which requires only one OR gate and one AND gate.

The function from Figure 4.10 is reproduced in Figure 4.14. The maxterms for which $f = 0$ can be covered as shown, leading to the expression

$$f = (x_2 + x_3)(x_3 + x_4)(\bar{x}_1 + \bar{x}_2 + \bar{x}_3 + \bar{x}_4)$$

This expression represents a circuit with three OR gates and one AND gate. Two of the OR gates have two inputs, and the third has four inputs; the AND gate has three inputs. Assuming that both the complemented and uncomplemented versions of the input variables x_1 to x_4 are available at no extra cost, the cost of this circuit is 15. This compares favorably with the SOP implementation derived from Figure 4.10, which requires five gates and 13 inputs at a total cost of 18.

In general, as we already know from section 2.6.1, the SOP and POS implementations of a given function may or may not entail the same cost. The reader is encouraged to find the POS implementations for the functions in Figures 4.11 and 4.12 and compare the costs with the SOP forms.

We have shown how to obtain minimum-cost POS implementations by finding the largest sum terms that cover all maxterms for which $f = 0$. Another way of obtaining

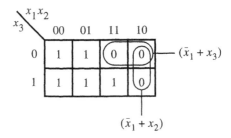

Figure 4.13   POS minimization of $f(x_1, x_2, x_3) = \Pi M(4, 5, 6)$.

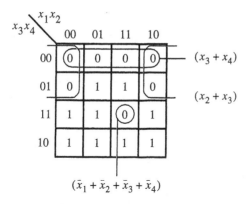

Figure 4.14   POS minimization of $f(x_1, \ldots, x_4) =$ $\Pi M(0, 1, 4, 8, 9, 12, 15)$.

the same result is by finding a minimum-cost SOP implementation of the complement of f. Then we can apply DeMorgan's theorem to this expression to obtain the simplest POS realization because $f = \bar{\bar{f}}$. For example, the simplest SOP implementation of $\bar{f}$ in Figure 4.13 is

$$\bar{f} = x_1 \bar{x}_2 + x_1 \bar{x}_3$$

Complementing this expression using DeMorgan's theorem yields

$$
\begin{aligned}
f = \bar{\bar{f}} &= \overline{x_1 \bar{x}_2 + x_1 \bar{x}_3} \\
&= \overline{x_1 \bar{x}_2} \cdot \overline{x_1 \bar{x}_3} \\
&= (\bar{x}_1 + x_2)(\bar{x}_1 + x_3)
\end{aligned}
$$

which is the same result as obtained above.

Using this approach for the function in Figure 4.14 gives

$$\bar{f} = \bar{x}_2 \bar{x}_3 + \bar{x}_3 \bar{x}_4 + x_1 x_2 x_3 x_4$$

Complementing this expression produces

$$
\begin{aligned}
f = \bar{\bar{f}} &= \overline{\bar{x}_2 \bar{x}_3 + \bar{x}_3 \bar{x}_4 + x_1 x_2 x_3 x_4} \\
&= \overline{\bar{x}_2 \bar{x}_3} \cdot \overline{\bar{x}_3 \bar{x}_4} \cdot \overline{x_1 x_2 x_3 x_4} \\
&= (x_2 + x_3)(x_3 + x_4)(\bar{x}_1 + \bar{x}_2 + \bar{x}_3 + \bar{x}_4)
\end{aligned}
$$

which matches the previously derived implementation.

4.4 INCOMPLETELY SPECIFIED FUNCTIONS

In digital systems it often happens that certain input conditions can never occur. For example, suppose that x_1 and x_2 control two interlocked switches such that both switches cannot be closed at the same time. Thus the only three possible states of the switches are that both switches are open or that one switch is open and the other switch is closed. Namely, the input valuations $(x_1, x_2) = 00, 01,$ and 10 are possible, but 11 is guaranteed not to occur. Then we say that $(x_1, x_2) = 11$ is a *don't-care condition*, meaning that a circuit with x_1 and x_2 as inputs can be designed by ignoring this condition. A function that has don't-care condition(s) is said to be *incompletely specified*.

Don't-care conditions, or *don't cares* for short, can be used to advantage in the design of logic circuits. Since these input valuations will never occur, the designer may assume that the function value for these valuations is either 1 or 0, whichever is more useful in trying to find a minimum-cost implementation. Figure 4.15 illustrates this idea. The required function has a value of 1 for minterms m_2, m_4, m_5, m_6, and m_{10}. Assuming the above-

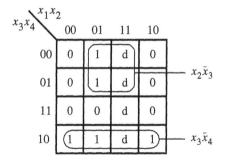

(a) SOP implementation

(b) POS implementation

Figure 4.15   Two implementations of the function $f(x_1, \ldots, x_4) = \sum m(2, 4, 5, 6, 10) + D(12, 13, 14, 15)$.

mentioned interlocked switches, the x_1 and x_2 inputs will never be equal to 1 at the same time; hence the minterms m_{12}, m_{13}, m_{14}, and m_{15} can all be used as don't cares. The don't cares are denoted by the letter d in the map. Using the shorthand notation, the function f is specified as

$$f(x_1, \ldots, x_4) = \sum m(2, 4, 5, 6, 10) + D(12, 13, 14, 15)$$

where D is the set of don't cares.

Part (a) of the figure indicates the best sum-of-products implementation. To form the largest possible groups of 1s, thus generating the lowest-cost prime implicants, it is necessary to assume that the don't cares D_{12}, D_{13}, and D_{14} (corresponding to minterms m_{12}, m_{13}, and m_{14}) have the value of 1 while D_{15} has the value of 0. Then there are only two prime implicants, which provide a complete cover of f. The resulting implementation is

$$f = x_2\bar{x}_3 + x_3\bar{x}_4$$

Part (b) shows how the best product-of-sums implementation can be obtained. The same values are assumed for the don't cares. The result is

$$f = (x_2 + x_3)(\bar{x}_3 + \bar{x}_4)$$

The freedom in choosing the value of don't cares leads to greatly simplified realizations. If we were to naively exclude the don't cares from the synthesis of the function, by assuming that they always have a value of 0, the resulting SOP expression would be

$$f = \bar{x}_1 x_2 \bar{x}_3 + \bar{x}_1 x_3 \bar{x}_4 + \bar{x}_2 x_3 \bar{x}_4$$

and the POS expression would be

$$f = (x_2 + x_3)(\bar{x}_3 + \bar{x}_4)(\bar{x}_1 + \bar{x}_2)$$

Both of these expressions have higher costs than the expressions obtained with a more appropriate assignment of values to don't cares.

Although don't-care values can be assigned arbitrarily, an arbitrary assignment may not lead to a minimum-cost implementation of a given function. If there are k don't cares, then there are 2^k possible ways of assigning 0 or 1 values to them. In the Karnaugh map we can usually see how best to do this assignment to find the simplest implementation.

Using interlocked switches to illustrate how don't-care conditions can occur in a real system may seem to be somewhat contrived. However, in Chapters 6, 8, and 9 we will encounter many examples of don't cares that occur in the course of practical design of digital circuits.

4.5 MULTIPLE-OUTPUT CIRCUITS

In all previous examples we have considered single functions and their circuit implementations. In practical digital systems it is necessary to implement a number of functions as part of some large logic circuit. Circuits that implement these functions can often be combined into a less-expensive single circuit with multiple outputs by sharing some of the gates needed in the implementation of individual functions.

Example 4.1   An example of gate sharing is given in Figure 4.16. Two functions, f_1 and f_2, of the same variables are to be implemented. The minimum-cost implementations for these functions are obtained as shown in parts (a) and (b) of the figure. This results in the expressions

$$f_1 = x_1\bar{x}_3 + \bar{x}_1x_3 + x_2\bar{x}_3x_4$$

$$f_2 = x_1\bar{x}_3 + \bar{x}_1x_3 + x_2x_3x_4$$

The cost of f_1 is four gates and 10 inputs, for a total of 14. The cost of f_2 is the same. Thus the total cost is 28 if both functions are implemented by separate circuits. A less-expensive

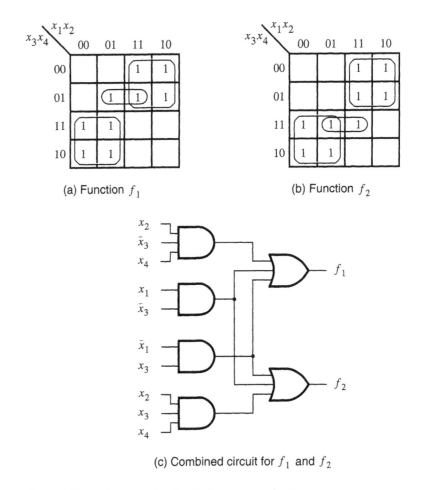

(a) Function f_1 (b) Function f_2

(c) Combined circuit for f_1 and f_2

Figure 4.16   An example of multiple-output synthesis.

realization is possible if the two circuits are combined into a single circuit with two outputs. Because the first two product terms are identical in both expressions, the AND gates that implement them need not be duplicated. The combined circuit is shown in Figure 4.16c. Its cost is six gates and 16 inputs, for a total of 22.

In this example we reduced the overall cost by finding minimum-cost realizations of f_1 and f_2 and then sharing the gates that implement the common product terms. This strategy does not necessarily always work the best, as the next example shows.

Figure 4.17 shows two functions to be implemented by a single circuit. Minimum-cost realizations of the individual functions f_3 and f_4 are obtained from parts (a) and (b) of the figure. **Example 4.2**

$$f_3 = \bar{x}_1 x_4 + x_2 x_4 + \bar{x}_1 x_2 x_3$$
$$f_4 = x_1 x_4 + \bar{x}_2 x_4 + \bar{x}_1 x_2 x_3 \bar{x}_4$$

None of the AND gates can be shared, which means that the cost of the combined circuit would be six AND gates, two OR gates, and 21 inputs, for a total of 29.

But several alternative realizations are possible. Instead of deriving the expressions for f_3 and f_4 using only prime implicants, we can look for other implicants that may be shared advantageously in the combined realization of the functions. Figure 4.17c shows the best choice of implicants, which yields the realization

$$f_3 = x_1 x_2 x_4 + \bar{x}_1 x_2 x_3 \bar{x}_4 + \bar{x}_1 x_4$$
$$f_4 = x_1 x_2 x_4 + \bar{x}_1 x_2 x_3 \bar{x}_4 + \bar{x}_2 x_4$$

The first two implicants are identical in both expressions. The resulting circuit is given in Figure 4.17d. It has the cost of six gates and 17 inputs, for a total of 23.

In Example 4.1 we sought the best SOP implementation for the functions f_1 and f_2 in Figure 4.16. We will now consider the POS implementation of the same functions. The minimum-cost POS expressions for f_1 and f_2 are **Example 4.3**

$$f_1 = (\bar{x}_1 + \bar{x}_3)(x_1 + x_2 + x_3)(x_1 + x_3 + x_4)$$
$$f_2 = (x_1 + x_3)(\bar{x}_1 + x_2 + \bar{x}_3)(\bar{x}_1 + \bar{x}_3 + x_4)$$

There are no common sum terms in these expressions that could be shared in the implementation. Moreover, from the Karnaugh maps in Figure 4.16, it is apparent that there is no sum term (covering the cells where $f_1 = f_2 = 0$) that can be profitably used in realizing both f_1 and f_2. Thus the best choice is to implement each function separately, according to the preceding expressions. Each function requires three OR gates, one AND gate, and 11 inputs. Therefore, the total cost of the circuit that implements both functions is 30. This realization is costlier than the SOP realization derived in Example 4.1.

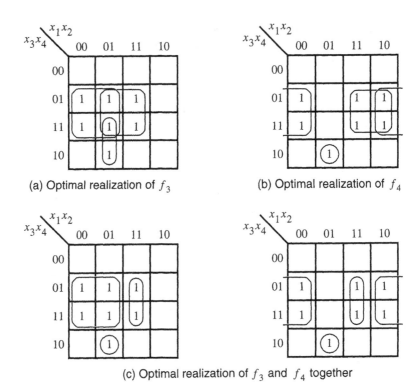

(a) Optimal realization of f_3

(b) Optimal realization of f_4

(c) Optimal realization of f_3 and f_4 together

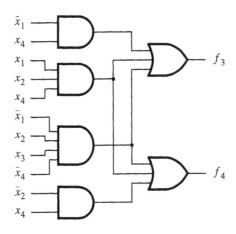

(d) Combined circuit for f_3 and f_4

Figure 4.17   Another example of multiple-output synthesis.

Consider now the POS realization of the functions f_3 and f_4 in Figure 4.17. The minimum-cost POS expressions for f_3 and f_4 are

Example 4.4

$$f_3 = (x_3 + x_4)(x_2 + x_4)(\overline{x}_1 + x_4)(\overline{x}_1 + x_2)$$
$$f_4 = (x_3 + x_4)(x_2 + x_4)(\overline{x}_1 + x_4)(x_1 + \overline{x}_2 + \overline{x}_4)$$

The first three sum terms are the same in both f_3 and f_4; they can be shared in a combined circuit. These terms require three OR gates and six inputs. In addition, one 2-input OR gate and one 4-input AND gate are needed for f_3, and one 3-input OR gate and one 4-input AND gate are needed for f_4. Thus the combined circuit comprises five OR gates, two AND gates, and 19 inputs, for a total cost of 26. This cost is slightly higher than the cost of the circuit derived in Example 4.2.

These examples show that the complexities of the best SOP or POS implementations of given functions may be quite different. For the functions in Figures 4.16 and 4.17, the SOP form gives better results. But if we are interested in implementing the complements of the four functions in these figures, then the POS form would be less costly.

Sophisticated CAD tools used to synthesize logic functions will automatically perform the types of optimizations illustrated in the preceding examples.

4.6 NAND AND NOR LOGIC NETWORKS

In Chapter 3 we saw that it is possible to design electronic circuits that realize basic logic functions other than AND, OR, and NOT, which have been the focus of our discussion to this point. From Figures 3.6 to 3.9 and Figures 3.13 to 3.15, it is obvious that NAND and NOR gates are simpler to implement than AND and OR gates. Then we should ask whether these gates can be used directly in the synthesis of logic circuits, rather than just being a part of the individual AND and OR gates. In section 2.5 we introduced DeMorgan's theorem. Its logic gate interpretation is shown in Figure 4.18. Identity 15a from section 2.5 is interpreted in part (a) of the figure. It specifies that a NAND of variables x_1 and x_2 is equivalent to first complementing each of the variables and then ORing them. Notice on the far-right side that we have indicated the NOT gates simply as small circles, which denote inversion of the logic value at that point. The other half of DeMorgan's theorem, identity 15b, appears in part (b) of the figure. It states that the NOR function is equivalent to first inverting the input variables and then ANDing them.

In previous sections we explained how any logic function can be implemented either in sum-of-products or product-of-sums form, which leads to logic networks that have either an AND-OR or an OR-AND structure, respectively. We will now show that such networks can be implemented using only NAND gates or only NOR gates.

Consider the network in Figure 4.19 as a representative of general AND-OR networks. This network can be transformed into a network of NAND gates as shown in the figure. First, each connection between the AND gate and an OR gate is replaced by a connection

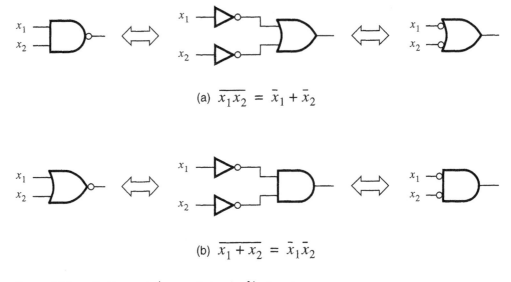

(a) $\overline{x_1 x_2} = \bar{x}_1 + \bar{x}_2$

(b) $\overline{x_1 + x_2} = \bar{x}_1 \bar{x}_2$

Figure 4.18   DeMorgan's theorem in terms of logic gates.

that includes two inversions of the signal: one inversion at the output of the AND gate and the other at the input of the OR gate. Such double inversion has no effect on the behavior of the network, as stated formally in theorem 9 in section 2.5. According to Figure 4.18a, the OR gate with inversions at its inputs is equivalent to a NAND gate. Thus we can redraw the network using only NAND gates, as shown in Figure 4.19. This example shows that

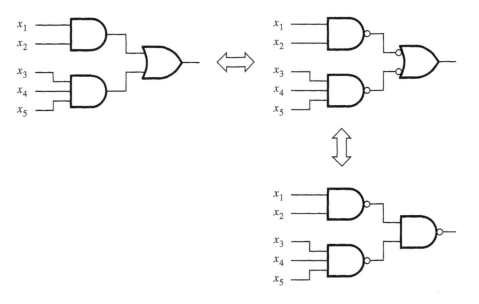

Figure 4.19   Using NAND gates to implement a sum-of-products.

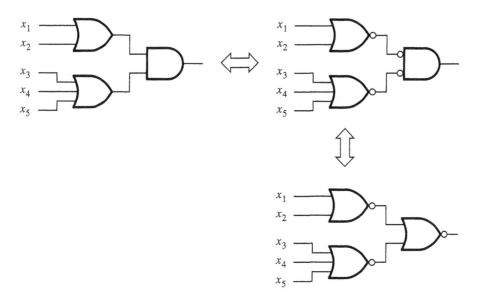

Figure 4.20   Using NOR gates to implement a product-of-sums.

any AND-OR network can be implemented as a NAND-NAND network having the same topology.

Figure 4.20 gives a similar construction for a product-of-sums network, which can be transformed into a circuit with only NOR gates. The procedure is exactly the same as the one described for Figure 4.19 except that now the identity in Figure 4.18b is applied. The conclusion is that any OR-AND network can be implemented as a NOR-NOR network having the same topology.

4.13 CONCLUDING REMARKS

This chapter has attempted to provide the reader with an understanding of various aspects of synthesis for logic functions and how synthesis is automated using modern CAD tools. Now that the reader is comfortable with the fundamental concepts, we can examine digital circuits of a more sophisticated nature. The next chapter describes circuits that perform arithmetic operations, which are a key part of computers.

PROBLEMS

4.1   Find the minimum-cost SOP and POS forms for the function $f(x_1, x_2, x_3) = \sum m(1, 2, 3, 5)$.

4.2   Repeat problem 4.1 for the function $f(x_1, x_2, x_3) = \sum m(1, 4, 7) + D(2, 5)$.

4.3   Repeat problem 4.1 for the function $f(x_1, \ldots, x_4) = \Pi M(0, 1, 2, 4, 5, 7, 8, 9, 10, 12, 14, 15)$.

4.4   Repeat problem 4.1 for the function $f(x_1, \ldots, x_4) = \sum m(0, 2, 8, 9, 10, 15) + D(1, 3, 6, 7)$.

4.5   Repeat problem 4.1 for the function $f(x_1, \ldots, x_5) = \Pi M(1, 4, 6, 7, 9, 12, 15, 17, 20, 21, 22, 23, 28, 31)$.

4.6   Repeat problem 4.1 for the function $f(x_1, \ldots, x_5) = \sum m(0, 1, 3, 4, 6, 8, 9, 11, 13, 14, 16, 19, 20, 21, 22, 24, 25) + D(5, 7, 12, 15, 17, 23)$.

4.7   Repeat problem 4.1 for the function $f(x_1, \ldots, x_5) = \sum m(1, 4, 6, 7, 9, 10, 12, 15, 17, 19, 20, 23, 25, 26, 27, 28, 30, 31) + D(8, 16, 21, 22)$.

4.8   Find 5 three-variable functions for which the product-of-sums form has lower cost than the sum-of-products form.

4.9   A four-variable logic function that is equal to 1 if any three or all four of its variables are equal to 1 is called a *majority* function. Design a minimum-cost circuit that implements this majority function.

4.10   Derive a minimum-cost realization of the four-variable function that is equal to 1 if exactly two or exactly three of its variables are equal to 1; otherwise it is equal to 0.

4.11   Prove or show a counter-example for the statement: If a function f has a unique minimum-cost SOP expression, then it also has a unique minimum-cost POS expression.

4.12   A circuit with two outputs has to implement the following functions

$$f(x_1, \ldots, x_4) = \sum m(0, 2, 4, 6, 7, 9) + D(10, 11)$$

$$g(x_1, \ldots, x_4) = \sum m(2, 4, 9, 10, 15) + D(0, 13, 14)$$

Design the minimum-cost circuit and compare its cost with combined costs of two circuits that implement f and g separately. Assume that the input variables are available in both uncomplemented and complemented forms.

4.13   Repeat problem 4.12 for the following functions

$$f(x_1, \ldots, x_5) = \sum m(1, 4, 5, 11, 27, 28) + D(10, 12, 14, 15, 20, 31)$$

$$g(x_1, \ldots, x_5) = \sum m(0, 1, 2, 4, 5, 8, 14, 15, 16, 18, 20, 24, 26, 28, 31)$$
$$+ D(10, 11, 12, 27)$$

4.14   Implement the logic circuit in Figure 4.26 using NAND gates only.

4.15   Implement the logic circuit in Figure 4.26 using NOR gates only.

4.16   Implement the logic circuit in Figure 4.28 using NAND gates only.

4.17   Implement the logic circuit in Figure 4.28 using NOR gates only.

4.18   Consider the function $f = x_3x_5 + \bar{x}_1x_2x_4 + x_1\bar{x}_2\bar{x}_4 + x_1x_3\bar{x}_4 + \bar{x}_1x_3x_4 + \bar{x}_1x_2x_5 + x_1\bar{x}_2x_5$. Derive a minimum-cost circuit that implements this function using NOT, AND, and OR gates.

4.19   Derive a minimum-cost circuit that implements the function $f(x_1, \ldots, x_4) = \sum m(4, 7, 8, 11) + D(12, 15)$.

4.20   Find the simplest realization of the function $f(x_1, \ldots, x_4) = \sum m(0, 3, 4, 7, 9, 10, 13, 14)$, assuming that the logic gates have a maximum fan-in of two.

4.21   Find the minimum-cost circuit for the function $f(x_1, \ldots, x_4) = \sum m(0, 4, 8, 13, 14, 15)$. Assume that the input variables are available in uncomplemented form only. (Hint: use functional decomposition.)

4.22   Use functional decomposition to find the best implementation of the function $f(x_1, \ldots, x_5) = \sum m(1, 2, 7, 9, 10, 18, 19, 25, 31) + D(0, 15, 20, 26)$. How does your implementation compare with the lowest-cost SOP implementation? Give the costs.

4.23   Show that the following distributive-like rules are valid

$$(A \cdot B)\#C = (A\#C) \cdot (B\#C)$$

$$(A + B)\#C = (A\#C) + (B\#C)$$

4.24   Use the cubical representation and the method discussed in section 4.10 to find a minimum-cost SOP realization of the function $f(x_1, \ldots, x_4) = \sum m(0, 2, 4, 5, 7, 8, 9, 15)$.

4.25   Repeat problem 4.24 for the function $f(x_1, \ldots, x_5) = \bar{x}_1\bar{x}_3\bar{x}_5 + x_1x_2\bar{x}_3 + x_2x_3\bar{x}_4x_5 + x_1\bar{x}_2\bar{x}_3x_4 + x_1x_2x_3x_4\bar{x}_5 + \bar{x}_1x_2x_4\bar{x}_5 + \bar{x}_1\bar{x}_3x_4x_5$.

4.26   Use the cubical representation and the method discussed in section 4.10 to find a minimum-cost SOP realization of the function $f(x_1, \ldots, x_4)$ defined by the ON-set ON = {00x0, 100x, x010, 1111} and the don't-care set DC = {00x1, 011x}.

4.27   In section 4.10.1 we showed how the ∗-product operation can be used to find the prime implicants of a given function f. Another possibility is to find the prime implicants by expanding the implicants in the initial cover of the function. An implicant is *expanded* by removing one literal to create a larger implicant (in terms of the number of vertices covered). A larger implicant is valid only if it does not include any vertices for which $f = 0$. The largest valid implicants obtained in the process of expansion are the prime

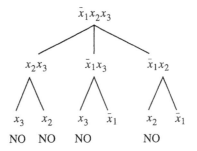

Figure P4.1   Expansion of implicant $\bar{x}_1 x_2 x_3$.

implicants. Figure P4.1 illustrates the expansion of the implicant $\bar{x}_1 x_2 x_3$ of the function in Figure 4.9, which is also used in Example 4.14. Note from Figure 4.9 that

$$\bar{f} = x_1 \bar{x}_2 \bar{x}_3 + x_1 \bar{x}_2 x_3 + x_1 x_2 \bar{x}_3$$

In Figure P4.1 the word NO is used to indicate that the expanded term is not valid, because it includes one or more vertices from $\bar{f}$. From the graph it is clear that the largest valid implicants that arise from this expansion are $x_2 x_3$ and $\bar{x}_1$; they are prime implicants of f.

Expand the other four implicants given in the initial cover in Example 4.14 to find all prime implicants of f. What is the relative complexity of this procedure compared to the ∗-product technique?

Note: A technique based on such expansion of implicants is used to find the prime implicants in the Espresso CAD program [19].

4.28   Repeat problem 4.27 for the function in Example 4.15. Expand the implicants given in the initial cover C^0.

4.29   Consider the logic expressions

$$f = x_1\bar{x}_2\bar{x}_5 + \bar{x}_1\bar{x}_2\bar{x}_4\bar{x}_5 + x_1 x_2 x_4 x_5 + \bar{x}_1\bar{x}_2 x_3\bar{x}_4 + x_1\bar{x}_2 x_3 x_5 + \bar{x}_2\bar{x}_3 x_4\bar{x}_5 + x_1 x_2 x_3 x_4\bar{x}_5$$

$$g = \bar{x}_2 x_3\bar{x}_4 + \bar{x}_2\bar{x}_3\bar{x}_4\bar{x}_5 + x_1 x_3 x_4\bar{x}_5 + x_1\bar{x}_2 x_4\bar{x}_5 + x_1 x_3 x_4 x_5 + \bar{x}_1\bar{x}_2\bar{x}_3\bar{x}_5 + x_1 x_2\bar{x}_3 x_4 x_5$$

Prove or disprove that $f = g$.

4.30   Consider the circuit in Figure P4.2, which implements functions f and g. What is the cost of this circuit, assuming that the input variables are available in both true and complemented forms? Redesign the circuit to implement the same functions, but at as low a cost as possible. What is the cost of your circuit?

4.31   Repeat problem 4.30 for the circuit in Figure P4.3. Use only NAND gates in your circuit.

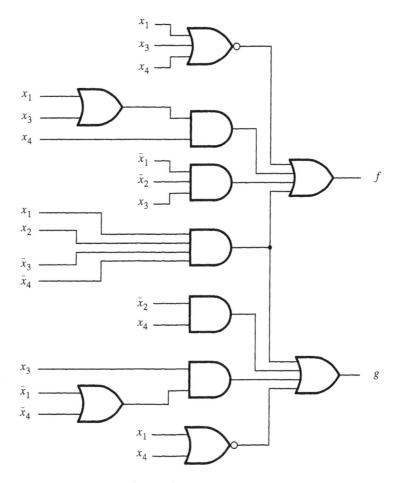

Figure P4.2   Circuit for problem 4.30.

REFERENCES

1. M. Karnaugh, "A Map Method for Synthesis of Combinatorial Logic Circuits," *Transactions of AIEE, Communications and Electronics* 72, part 1, November 1953, pp. 593–599.

2. R. L. Ashenhurst, "The Decomposition of Switching Functions," Proc. of the Symposium on the Theory of Switching, 1957, *Vol. 29 of Annals of Computation Laboratory* (Harvard University: Cambridge, MA, 1959), pp. 74–116.

3. F. J. Hill and G. R. Peterson, *Computer Aided Logical Design with Emphasis on VLSI*, 4th ed. (Wiley: New York, 1993).

4. T. Sasao, *Logic Synthesis and Optimization*, (Kluwer: Boston, Ma., 1993).

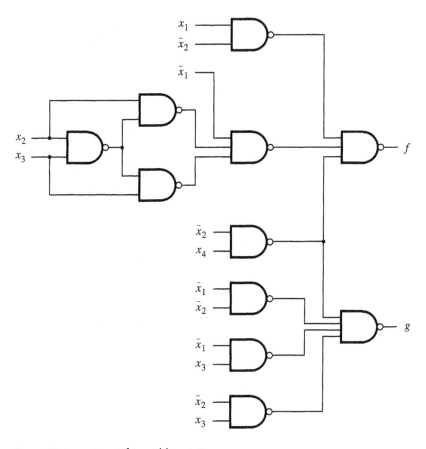

Figure P4.3   Circuit for problem 4.31.

5. S. Devadas, A. Gosh, and K. Keutzer, *Logic Synthesis* (McGraw-Hill: New York, 1994).

6. W. V. Quine, "The Problem of Simplifying Truth Functions," *Amer. Math. Monthly* 59 (1952), pp. 521–31.

7. E. J. McCluskey Jr., "Minimization of Boolean Functions," *Bell System Tech. Journal*, November 1956, pp. 521–31.

8. E. J. McCluskey, *Logic Design Principles* (Prentice-Hall: Englewood Cliffs, NJ, 1986).

9. J. F. Wakerly, *Digital Design Principles and Practices* (Prentice-Hall: Englewood Cliffs, NJ, 1990).

10. J. P. Hayes, *Introduction to Logic Design* (Addison-Wesley: Reading, MA, 1993).

11. C. H. Roth Jr., *Fundamentals of Logic Design*, 4th ed. (West: St. Paul, MN., 1993).

12. R. H. Katz, *Contemporary Logic Design* (Benjamin/Cummings: Redwood City, CA, 1994).

13. V. P. Nelson, H. T. Nagle, B. D. Carroll, and J. D. Irwin, *Digital Logic Circuit Analysis and Design* (Prentice-Hall: Englewood Cliffs, NJ, 1995).

14. J. P. Daniels, *Digital Design from Zero to One* (Wiley: New York, 1996).

15. P. K. Lala, *Practical Digital Logic Design and Testing* (Prentice-Hall: Englewood Cliffs, NJ, 1996).

16. A. Dewey, *Analysis and Design of Digital Systems with VHDL* (PWS Publishing Co.: Boston, MA, 1997).

17. M. M. Mano and C. R. Kime, *Logic and Computer Design Fundamentals* (Prentice-Hall: Upper Saddle River, NJ, 1997).

18. D. D. Gajski, *Principles of Digital Design* (Prentice-Hall: Upper Saddle River, NJ, 1997).

19. R. K. Brayton, G. D. Hachtel, C. T. McMullen, and A. L. Sangiovanni-Vincentelli, *Logic Minimization Algorithms for VLSI Synthesis* (Kluwer: Boston, MA, 1984).

20. R. K. Brayton, R. Rudell, A. Sangiovanni-Vincentelli, and A. R. Wang, "MIS: A Multiple-Level Logic Synthesis Optimization System," *IEEE Transactions on Computer-Aided Design*, CAD-6, November 1987, pp. 1062–81.

21. E. M. Sentovic, K. J. Singh, L. Lavagno, C. Moon, R. Murgai, A. Saldanha, H. Savoj, P. R. Stephan, R. K. Brayton, and A. Sangiovanni-Vincentelli, "SIS: A System for Sequential Circuit Synthesis," Technical Report UCB/ERL M92/41, Electronics Research Laboratory, Department of Electrical Engineering and Computer Science, University of California, Berkeley, 1992.

22. G. De Micheli, *Synthesis and Optimization of Digital Circuits* (McGraw-Hill: New York, 1994).

23. N. Sherwani, *Algorithms for VLSI Physical Design Automation* (Kluwer: Boston, MA, 1995).

24. B. Preas and M. Lorenzetti, *Physical Design Automation of VLSI Systems* (Benjamin/Cummings: Redwood City, CA, 1988).

5

NUMBER REPRESENTATION AND ARITHMETIC CIRCUITS

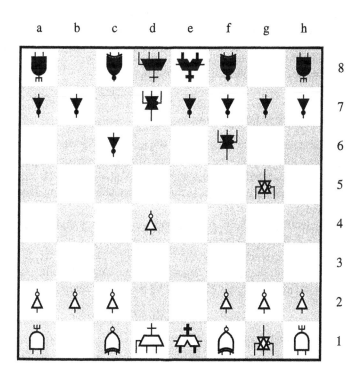

5. Ne4–g5, Ng8–f6

In this chapter we will discuss logic circuits that perform arithmetic operations. We will explain how numbers can be added, subtracted, and multiplied. We will also show how to write VHDL code to describe the arithmetic circuits. These circuits provide an excellent platform for illustrating the power and versatility of VHDL in specifying complex logic-circuit assemblies. The concepts involved in the design of the arithmetic circuits are easily applied to a wide variety of other circuits.

Before tackling the design of arithmetic circuits, it is necessary to discuss how numbers are represented in digital systems. In the previous chapters we dealt with logic variables in a general way, using variables to represent either the states of switches or some general conditions. Now we will use the variables to represent numbers. Several variables are needed to specify a number, with each variable corresponding to one digit of the number.

5.1 POSITIONAL NUMBER REPRESENTATION

When dealing with numbers and arithmetic operations, it is convenient to use standard symbols. Thus to represent addition we use the plus (+) symbol, and for subtraction we use the minus (−) symbol. In previous chapters we used the + symbol to represent the logical OR operation and − to denote the deletion of an element from a set. Even though we will now use the same symbols for two different purposes, the meaning of each symbol will usually be clear from the context of the discussion. In cases where there may be some ambiguity, the meaning will be stated explicitly.

5.1.1 UNSIGNED INTEGERS

The simplest numbers to consider are the integers. We will begin by considering positive integers and then expand the discussion to include negative integers. Numbers that are positive only are called *unsigned*, and numbers that can also be negative are called *signed*. Representation of numbers that include a radix point (real numbers) is discussed later in the chapter.

In the familiar decimal system, a number consists of digits that have 10 possible values, from 0 to 9, and each digit represents a multiple of a power of 10. For example, the number 8547 represents $8 \times 10^3 + 5 \times 10^2 + 4 \times 10^1 + 7 \times 10^0$. We do not normally write the powers of 10 with the number, because they are implied by the positions of the digits. In general, a decimal integer is expressed by an *n*-tuple comprising *n* decimal digits

$$D = d_{n-1}d_{n-2} \ldots d_1 d_0$$

which represents the value

$$V(D) = d_{n-1} \times 10^{n-1} + d_{n-2} \times 10^{n-2} + \ldots + d_1 \times 10^1 + d_0 \times 10^0$$

This is referred to as the *positional number representation*.

Because the digits have 10 possible values and each digit is weighted as a power of 10, we say that decimal numbers are *base*-10, or *radix*-10 numbers. Decimal numbers are familiar, convenient, and easy to understand. However, in digital circuits it is not practical to use digits that can assume 10 values. In digital systems we use the binary, or *base*-2, system in which digits can be 0 or 1. Each binary digit is called a *bit*. In the binary number system, the same positional number representation is used so that

$$B = b_{n-1}b_{n-2}\ldots b_1 b_0$$

represents an integer that has the value

$$V(B) = b_{n-1} \times 2^{n-1} + b_{n-2} \times 2^{n-2} + \ldots + b_1 \times 2^1 + b_0 \times 2^0 \qquad \textbf{[5.1]}$$

$$= \sum_{i=0}^{n-1} b_i \times 2^i$$

For example, the binary number 1101 represents the value

$$V = 1 \times 2^3 + 1 \times 2^2 + 0 \times 2^1 + 1 \times 2^0$$

Because a particular digit pattern has different meanings for different radices, we will indicate the radix as a subscript when there is potential for confusion. Thus to specify that 1101 is a base-2 number, we will write $(1101)_2$. Evaluating the preceding expression for V gives $V = 8 + 4 + 1 = 13$. Hence

$$(1101)_2 = (13)_{10}$$

Note that the range of integers that can be represented by a binary number depends on the number of bits used. For example, with four bits the largest number is $(1111)_2 = (15)_{10}$. An example of a larger number is $(10110111)_2 = (183)_{10}$. In general, using n bits allows representation of integers in the range 0 to $2^n - 1$.

In a binary number the right-most bit is usually referred to as the *least-significant bit (LSB)*. The left-most bit of an unsigned integer, which has the highest power of 2 associated with it, is called the *most-significant bit (MSB)*. In digital systems it is often convenient to consider several bits together as a group. A group of four bits is called a *nibble*, and a group of eight bits is called a *byte*.

5.1.2 CONVERSION BETWEEN DECIMAL AND BINARY SYSTEMS

A binary number is converted into a decimal number simply by applying Equation 5.1 and evaluating it using decimal arithmetic. Converting a decimal number into a binary number is not quite as straightforward. The conversion can be performed by successively dividing the decimal number by 2 as follows. Suppose that a decimal number $D = d_{k-1}\ldots d_1 d_0$, with a value V, is to be converted into a binary number $B = b_{n-1}\ldots b_2 b_1 b_0$. Thus

$$V = b_{n-1} \times 2^{n-1} + \ldots + b_2 \times 2^2 + b_1 \times 2^1 + b_0$$

If we divide V by 2, the result is

$$\frac{V}{2} = b_{n-1} \times 2^{n-2} + \ldots + b_2 \times 2^1 + b_1 + \frac{b_0}{2}$$

The quotient of this integer division is $b_{n-1} \times 2^{n-2} + \ldots + b_2 \times 2 + b_1$, and the remainder is b_0. If the remainder is 0, then $b_0 = 0$; if it is 1, then $b_0 = 1$. Observe that the quotient is just another binary number, which comprises $n - 1$ bits, rather than n bits. Dividing this number by 2 yields the remainder b_1. The new quotient is

$$b_{n-1} \times 2^{n-3} + \ldots + b_2$$

Continuing the process of dividing the new quotient by 2, and determining one bit in each step, will produce all bits of the binary number. The process continues until the quotient becomes 0. Figure 5.1 illustrates the conversion process, using the example $(857)_{10} = (1101011001)_2$. Note that the least-significant bit (LSB) is generated first and the most-significant bit (MSB) is generated last.

5.1.3 OCTAL AND HEXADECIMAL REPRESENTATIONS

The positional number representation can be used for any radix. If the radix is r, then the number

$$K = k_{n-1}k_{n-2} \ldots k_1 k_0$$

has the value

$$V(K) = \sum_{i=0}^{n-1} k_i \times r^i$$

Our interest is limited to those radices that are most practical. We will use decimal numbers because they are used by people, and we will use binary numbers because they are used by computers. In addition, two other radices are useful—8 and 16. Numbers represented with radix 8 are called *octal* numbers, while radix-16 numbers are called *hexadecimal* numbers. In octal representation the digit values range from 0 to 7. In hexadecimal representation

Convert $(857)_{10}$

				Remainder	
$857 \div 2$	=	428		1	LSB
$428 \div 2$	=	214		0	
$214 \div 2$	=	107		0	
$107 \div 2$	=	53		1	
$53 \div 2$	=	26		1	
$26 \div 2$	=	13		0	
$13 \div 2$	=	6		1	
$6 \div 2$	=	3		0	
$3 \div 2$	=	1		1	
$1 \div 2$	=	0		1	MSB

Result is $(1101011001)_2$

Figure 5.1   Conversion from decimal to binary.

(often abbreviated as *hex*), each digit can have one of 16 values. The first 10 are denoted the same as in the decimal system, namely, 0 to 9. Digits that correspond to the decimal values 10, 11, 12, 13, 14, and 15 are denoted by the letters, A, B, C, D, E, and F. Table 5.1 gives the first 18 integers in these number systems.

Table 5.1   Numbers in different systems.

Decimal	Binary	Octal	Hexadecimal
00	00000	00	00
01	00001	01	01
02	00010	02	02
03	00011	03	03
04	00100	04	04
05	00101	05	05
06	00110	06	06
07	00111	07	07
08	01000	10	08
09	01001	11	09
10	01010	12	0A
11	01011	13	0B
12	01100	14	0C
13	01101	15	0D
14	01110	16	0E
15	01111	17	0F
16	10000	20	10
17	10001	21	11
18	10010	22	12

In computers the dominant number system is binary. The reason for using the octal and hexadecimal systems is that they serve as a useful shorthand notation for binary numbers. One octal digit represents three bits. Thus a binary number is converted into an octal number by taking groups of three bits, starting from the least-significant bit, and replacing them with the corresponding octal digit. For example, 101011010111 is converted as

$$\underbrace{1\,0\,1}_{5}\quad \underbrace{0\,1\,1}_{3}\quad \underbrace{0\,1\,0}_{2}\quad \underbrace{1\,1\,1}_{7}$$

which means that $(101011010111)_2 = (5327)_8$. If the number of bits is not a multiple of three, then we add 0s to the left of the most-significant bit. For example, $(10111011)_2 = (273)_8$ because

$$\underbrace{0\,1\,0}_{2}\quad \underbrace{1\,1\,1}_{7}\quad \underbrace{0\,1\,1}_{3}$$

Conversion from octal to binary is just as straightforward; each octal digit is simply replaced by three bits that denote the same value.

Similarly, a hexadecimal digit is represented using four bits. For example, a 16-bit number is represented using four hex digits, as in

$$(1010111100100101)_2 = (AF25)_{16}$$

because

$$\underbrace{1\,0\,1\,0}_{A} \qquad \underbrace{1\,1\,1\,1}_{F} \qquad \underbrace{0\,0\,1\,0}_{2} \qquad \underbrace{0\,1\,0\,1}_{5}$$

Zeros are added to the left of the most-significant bit if the number of bits is not a multiple of four. For example, $(1101101000)_2 = (368)_{16}$ because

$$\underbrace{0\,0\,1\,1}_{3} \qquad \underbrace{0\,1\,1\,0}_{6} \qquad \underbrace{1\,0\,0\,0}_{8}$$

Conversion from hexadecimal to binary involves straightforward substitution of each hex digit by four bits that denote the same value.

Binary numbers used in modern computers often have 32 or 64 bits. Written as binary n-tuples (sometimes called bit vectors), such numbers are awkward for people to deal with. It is much simpler to deal with them in the form of 8- or 16-digit hex numbers. Because the arithmetic operations in a digital system usually involve binary numbers, we will focus on circuits that use such numbers. We will sometimes use the hexadecimal representation as a convenient shorthand description.

We have introduced the simplest numbers—unsigned integers. It is necessary to be able to deal with several other types of numbers. We will discuss the representation of signed numbers, fixed-point numbers, and floating-point numbers later in this chapter. But first we will examine some simple circuits that operate on numbers to give the reader a feeling for digital circuits that perform arithmetic operations and to provide motivation for further discussion.

5.2 ADDITION OF UNSIGNED NUMBERS

Binary addition is performed in the same way as decimal addition except that the values of individual digits can be only 0 or 1. The addition of 2 one-bit numbers entails four possible combinations, as indicated in Figure 5.2a. Two bits are needed to represent the result of the addition. The right-most bit is called the *sum*, *s*. The left-most bit, which is produced as a carry-out when both bits being added are equal to 1, is called the *carry*, *c*. The addition operation is defined in the form of a truth table in part (*b*) of the figure. The sum bit *s* is the XOR function, which was introduced in section 3.9.1. The carry *c* is the AND function of inputs *x* and *y*. A circuit realization of these functions is shown in Figure 5.2c. This circuit, which implements the addition of only two bits, is called a *half-adder*.

A more interesting case is when larger numbers that have multiple bits are involved. Then it is still necessary to add each pair of bits, but for each bit position i, the addition operation may include a *carry-in* from bit position $i - 1$.

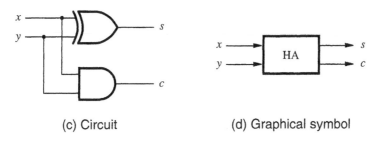

$$
\begin{array}{cccc}
x & 0 & 0 & 1 & 1 \\
+y & +0 & +1 & +0 & +1 \\
\hline
c\ s & 0\ 0 & 0\ 1 & 0\ 1 & 1\ 0
\end{array}
$$

Carry ⤒ ⤒ Sum

(a) The four possible cases

		Carry	Sum
x	y	c	s
0	0	0	0
0	1	0	1
1	0	0	1
1	1	1	0

(b) Truth table

(c) Circuit   (d) Graphical symbol

Figure 5.2   Half-adder.

Figure 5.3 gives an example of the addition operation. The operands are $X = (01111)_2 = (15)_{10}$ and $Y = (01010)_2 = (10)_{10}$. Note that five bits are used to represent X and Y. Using five bits, it is possible to represent integers in the range from 0 to 31; hence the sum $S = X + Y = (25)_{10}$ can also be denoted as a five-bit integer. Note also the labeling of individual bits, such that $X = x_4x_3x_2x_1x_0$ and $Y = y_4y_3y_2y_1y_0$. The figure shows the carries generated during the addition process. For example, a carry of 0 is generated when x_0 and y_0 are added, a carry of 1 is produced when x_1 and y_1 are added, and so on.

In Chapters 2 and 4 we designed logic circuits by first specifying their behavior in the form of a truth table. This approach is impractical in designing an adder circuit that can add the five-bit numbers in Figure 5.3. The required truth table would have 10 input variables, 5 for each number X and Y. It would have $2^{10} = 1024$ rows! A better approach is to consider the addition of each pair of bits, x_i and y_i, separately.

$$X = x_4x_3x_2x_1x_0 \qquad 0\ 1\ 1\ 1\ 1 \qquad (15)_{10}$$

$$+\ Y = y_4y_3y_2y_1y_0 \qquad 0\ 1\ 0\ 1\ 0 \qquad (10)_{10}$$

$$1\ 1\ 1\ 0 \quad \longleftarrow \quad \text{Generated carries}$$

$$S = s_4s_3s_2s_1s_0 \qquad 1\ 1\ 0\ 0\ 1 \qquad (25)_{10}$$

Figure 5.3   An example of addition.

For bit position 0, there is no carry-in, and hence the addition is the same as for Figure 5.2. For each other bit position i, the addition involves bits x_i and y_i, and a carry-in c_i. The sum and carry-out functions of variables x_i, y_i, and c_i are specified in the truth table in Figure 5.4a. The sum bit, s_i, is the modulo-2 sum of x_i, y_i, and c_i. The *carry-out*, c_{i+1}, is equal to 1 if the sum of x_i, y_i, and c_i is equal to either 2 or 3. Karnaugh maps for these functions are shown in part (b) of the figure. For the carry-out function the optimal sum-of-products realization is

$$c_{i+1} = x_iy_i + x_ic_i + y_ic_i$$

For the s_i function a sum-of-products realization is

$$s_i = \bar{x}_iy_i\bar{c}_i + x_i\bar{y}_i\bar{c}_i + \bar{x}_i\bar{y}_ic_i + x_iy_ic_i$$

A more attractive way of implementing this function is by using the XOR gates, as explained below.

Use of XOR Gates

The XOR function of two variables is defined as $x_1 \oplus x_2 = \bar{x}_1x_2 + x_1\bar{x}_2$. The preceding expression for the sum bit can be manipulated into a form that uses only XOR operations as follows

$$s_i = (\bar{x}_iy_i + x_i\bar{y}_i)\bar{c}_i + (\bar{x}_i\bar{y}_i + x_iy_i)c_i$$

$$= (x_i \oplus y_i)\bar{c}_i + \overline{(x_i \oplus y_i)}c_i$$

$$= (x_i \oplus y_i) \oplus c_i$$

The XOR operation is associative; hence we can write

$$s_i = x_i \oplus y_i \oplus c_i$$

Therefore, a single three-input XOR gate can be used to realize s_i.

The XOR gate generates as an output a modulo-2 sum of its inputs. The output is equal to 1 if an odd number of inputs have the value 1, and it is equal to 0 otherwise. For this reason the XOR is sometimes referred to as the *odd* function. Observe that the XOR has no minterms that can be combined into a larger product term, as evident from the checkerboard pattern for function s_i in the map in Figure 5.4b. The logic circuit implementing the truth table in Figure 5.4a is given in Figure 5.4c. This circuit is known as a *full-adder*.

c_i	x_i	y_i	c_{i+1}	s_i
0	0	0	0	0
0	0	1	0	1
0	1	0	0	1
0	1	1	1	0
1	0	0	0	1
1	0	1	1	0
1	1	0	1	0
1	1	1	1	1

(a) Truth table

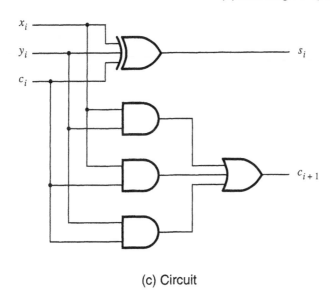

x_iy_i

c_i	00	01	11	10
0		1		1
1	1		1	

$$s_i = x_i \oplus y_i \oplus c_i$$

x_iy_i

c_i	00	01	11	10
0			1	
1		1	1	1

$$c_{i+1} = x_iy_i + x_ic_i + y_ic_i$$

(b) Karnaugh maps

(c) Circuit

Figure 5.4   Full-adder.

Another interesting feature of XOR gates is that a two-input XOR gate can be thought of as using one input as a control signal that determines whether the true or complemented value of the other input will be passed through the gate as the output value. This is clear from the definition of XOR, where $x_i \oplus y_i = \bar{x}y + x\bar{y}$. Consider x to be the control input. Then if $x = 0$, the output will be equal to the value of y. But if $x = 1$, the output will be equal to the complement of y. In the derivation above, we used algebraic manipulation to derive $s_i = (x_i \oplus y_i) \oplus c_i$. We could have obtained the same expression immediately by making the following observation. In the top half of the truth table in Figure 5.4a, c_i is equal to 0, and the sum function s_i is the XOR of x_i and y_i. In the bottom half of the table, c_i is equal to 1, while s_i is the complemented version of its top half. This observation leads directly to our expression using 2 two-input XOR operations. We will encounter an important example of using XOR gates to pass true or complemented signals under the control of another signal in section 5.3.3.

In the preceding discussion we encountered the complement of the XOR operation, which we denoted as $\overline{x \oplus y}$. This operation is used so commonly that it is given the distinct name *XNOR*. A special symbol, $\odot$, is often used to denote the XNOR operation, namely

$$x \odot y = \overline{x \oplus y}$$

The XNOR is sometimes also referred to as the *coincidence* operation because it produces the output of 1 when its inputs coincide in value; that is, they are both 0 or both 1.

5.2.1 DECOMPOSED FULL-ADDER

In view of the names used for the circuits, one can expect that a full-adder can be constructed using half-adders. This can be accomplished by creating a multilevel circuit of the type discussed in section 4.7.2. The circuit is given in Figure 5.5. It uses two half-adders to form a full-adder. The reader should verify the functional correctness of this circuit.

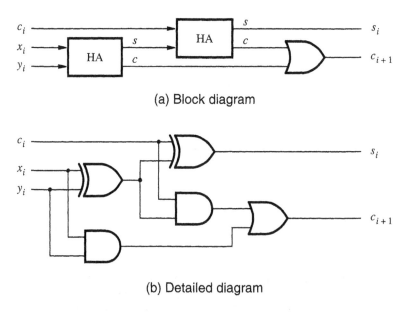

(a) Block diagram

(b) Detailed diagram

Figure 5.5   A decomposed implementation of the full-adder circuit.

5.2.2 RIPPLE-CARRY ADDER

To perform addition by hand, we start from the least-significant digit and add pairs of digits, progressing to the most-significant digit. If a carry is produced in position i, then this carry is added to the operands in position $i + 1$. The same arrangement can be used in a logic circuit that performs addition. For each bit position we can use a full-adder circuit, connected as shown in Figure 5.6. Note that to be consistent with the customary way of writing numbers, the least-significant bit position is on the right. Carries that are produced by the full-adders propagate to the left.

When the operands X and Y are applied as inputs to the adder, it takes some time before the output sum, S, is valid. Each full-adder introduces a certain delay before its s_i and c_{i+1} outputs are valid. Let this delay be denoted as Δt. Thus the carry-out from the first stage, c_1, arrives at the second stage Δt after the application of the x_0 and y_0 inputs. The carry-out from the second stage, c_2, arrives at the third stage with a $2\Delta t$ delay, and so on. The signal c_{n-1} is valid after a delay of $(n - 1)\Delta t$, which means that the complete sum is available after a delay of $n\Delta t$. Because of the way the carry signals "ripple" through the full-adder stages, the circuit in Figure 5.6 is called a *ripple-carry adder*.

The delay incurred to produce the final sum and carry-out in a ripple-carry adder depends on the size of the numbers. When 32- or 64-bit numbers are used, this delay may become unacceptably high. Because the circuit in each full-adder leaves little room for a drastic reduction in the delay, it may be necessary to seek different structures for implementation of n-bit adders. We will discuss a technique for building high-speed adders in section 5.4.

So far we have dealt with unsigned integers only. The addition of such numbers does not require a carry-in for stage 0. In Figure 5.6 we included c_0 in the diagram so that the ripple-carry adder can also be used for subtraction of numbers, as we will see in section 5.3.

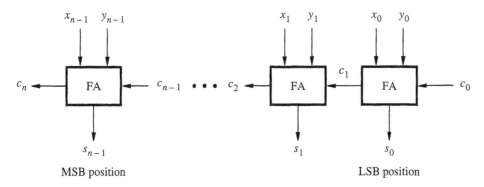

Figure 5.6 An n-bit ripple-carry adder.

5.2.3 DESIGN EXAMPLE

Suppose that we need a circuit that multiplies an eight-bit unsigned number by 3. Let $A = a_7a_6 \ldots a_1a_0$ denote the number and $P = p_9p_8 \ldots p_1p_0$ denote the product $P = 3A$. Note that 10 bits are needed to represent the product.

A simple approach to design the required circuit is to use two ripple-carry adders to add three copies of the number A, as illustrated in Figure 5.7a. The symbol that denotes each adder is a commonly used graphical symbol for adders. The letters x_i, y_i, s_i, and c_i indicate the meaning of the inputs and outputs according to Figure 5.6. The first adder produces $A + A = 2A$. Its result is represented as eight sum bits and the carry from the most-significant bit. The second adder produces $2A + A = 3A$. It has to be a nine-bit adder to be able to handle the nine bits of $2A$, which are generated by the first adder. Because the y_i inputs have to be driven only by the eight bits of A, the ninth input y_8 is connected to a constant 0.

This approach is straightforward, but not very efficient. Because $3A = 2A + A$, we can observe that $2A$ can be generated by shifting the bits of A one bit-position to the left, which gives the bit pattern $a_7a_6a_5a_4a_3a_2a_1a_00$. According to equation 5.1, this pattern is equal to $2A$. Then a single ripple-carry adder suffices for implementing $3A$, as shown in Figure 5.7b. This is essentially the same circuit as the second adder in part (a) of the figure. Note that the input x_0 is connected to a constant 0. Note also that in the second adder in part (a) the value of x_0 is always 0, even though it is driven by the least-significant bit, s_0, of the sum of the first adder. Because $x_0 = y_0 = a_0$ in the first adder, the sum bit s_0 will be 0, whether a_0 is 0 or 1.

5.3 SIGNED NUMBERS

In the decimal system the sign of a number is indicated by a $+$ or $-$ symbol to the left of the most-significant digit. In the binary system the *sign* of a number is denoted by the left-most bit. For a positive number the left-most bit is equal to 0, and for a negative number it is equal to 1. Therefore, in signed numbers the left-most bit represents the sign, and the remaining $n - 1$ bits represent the magnitude, as illustrated in Figure 5.8. It is important to note the difference in the location of the most-significant bit (MSB). In unsigned numbers all bits represent the magnitude of a number; hence all n bits are *significant* in defining the magnitude. Therefore, the MSB is the left-most bit, b_{n-1}. In signed numbers there are $n - 1$ significant bits, and the MSB is in bit position b_{n-2}.

5.3.1 NEGATIVE NUMBERS

Positive numbers are represented using the positional number representation as explained in the previous section. Negative numbers can be represented in three different ways: sign-and-magnitude, 1's complement, and 2's complement.

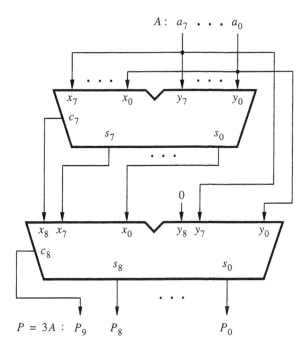

(a) Naive approach

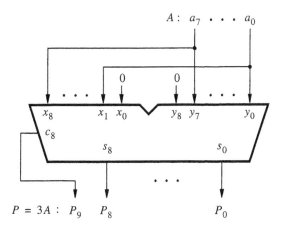

(b) Efficient design

Figure 5.7   Circuit that multiplies an eight-bit unsigned number by 3.

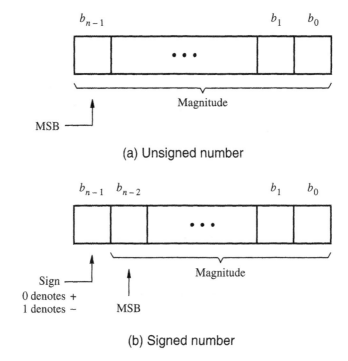

Figure 5.8   Formats for representation of integers.

Sign-and-Magnitude Representation

In the familiar decimal representation, the magnitude of both positive and negative numbers is expressed in the same way. The sign symbol distinguishes a number as being positive or negative. This scheme is called the *sign-and-magnitude* number representation. The same scheme can be used with binary numbers in which case the sign bit is 0 or 1 for positive or negative numbers, respectively. For example, if we use four-bit numbers, then $+5 = 0101$ and $-5 = 1101$. Because of its similarity to decimal sign-and-magnitude numbers, this representation is easy to understand. However, as we will see shortly, this representation is not well suited for use in computers. More suitable representations are based on complementary systems, explained below.

1's Complement Representation

In a complementary number system, the negative numbers are defined according to a subtraction operation involving positive numbers. We will consider two schemes for binary numbers: the 1's complement and the 2's complement. In the *1's complement* scheme, an n-bit negative number, K, is obtained by subtracting its equivalent positive number, P, from $2^n - 1$; that is, $K = (2^n - 1) - P$. For example, if $n = 4$, then $K = (2^4 - 1) - P = (15)_{10} - P = (1111)_2 - P$. If we convert $+5$ to a negative, we get $-5 = 1111 - 0101 = 1010$. Similarly, $+3 = 0011$ and $-3 = 1111 - 0011 = 1100$. Clearly, the 1's complement can be obtained simply by complementing each bit of the number, including the sign bit. While 1's complement numbers are easy to derive, they have some drawbacks when used in arithmetic operations, as we will see in the next section.

2's Complement Representation

In the 2's complement scheme, a negative number, K, is obtained by subtracting its equivalent positive number, P, from 2^n; namely, $K = 2^n - P$. Using our four-bit example, $-5 = 10000 - 0101 = 1011$, and $-3 = 10000 - 0011 = 1101$. Finding 2's complements in this manner requires performing a subtraction operation that involves borrows. However, we can observe that if K_1 is the 1's complement of P and K_2 is the 2's complement of P, then

$$K_1 = (2^n - 1) - P$$
$$K_2 = 2^n - P$$

It follows that $K_2 = K_1 + 1$. Thus a simpler way of finding a 2's complement of a number is to add 1 to its 1's complement because finding a 1's complement is trivial. This is how 2's complement numbers are obtained in logic circuits that perform arithmetic operations.

The reader will need to develop an ability to find 2's complement numbers quickly. There is a simple rule that can be used for this purpose.

Rule for Finding 2's Complements   Given a signed number, $B = b_{n-1}b_{n-2}\ldots b_1 b_0$, its 2's complement, $K = k_{n-1}k_{n-2}\ldots k_1 k_0$, can be found by examining the bits of B from right to left and taking the following action: copy all bits of B that are 0 and the first bit that is 1; then simply complement the rest of the bits.

For example, if $B = 0110$, then we copy $k_0 = b_0 = 0$ and $k_1 = b_1 = 1$, and complement the rest so that $k_2 = \bar{b}_2 = 0$ and $k_3 = \bar{b}_3 = 1$. Hence $K = 1010$. As another example, if $B = 10110100$, then $K = 01001100$. We leave the proof of this rule as an exercise for the reader.

Table 5.2 illustrates the interpretation of all 16 four-bit patterns in the three signed-number representations that we have considered. Note that for both sign-and-magnitude representation and for 1's complement representation there are two patterns that represent the value zero. For 2's complement there is only one such pattern. Also, observe that the range of numbers that can be represented with four bits in 2's complement form is -8 to $+7$, while in the other two representations it is -7 to $+7$.

Using 2's-complement representation, an n-bit number $B = b_{n-1}b_{n-2}\ldots b_1 b_0$ represents the value

$$V(B) = (-b_{n-1} \times 2^{n-1}) + b_{n-2} \times 2^{n-2} + \ldots + b_1 \times 2^1 + b_0 \times 2^0 \qquad \textbf{[5.2]}$$

Thus the largest negative number, $100\ldots00$, has the value -2^{n-1}. The largest positive number, $011\ldots11$, has the value $2^{n-1} - 1$.

Table 5.2   Interpretation of four-bit signed integers.

$b_3b_2b_1b_0$	Sign and magnitude	1's complement	2's complement
0111	+7	+7	+7
0110	+6	+6	+6
0101	+5	+5	+5
0100	+4	+4	+4
0011	+3	+3	+3
0010	+2	+2	+2
0001	+1	+1	+1
0000	+0	+0	+0
1000	−0	−7	−8
1001	−1	−6	−7
1010	−2	−5	−6
1011	−3	−4	−5
1100	−4	−3	−4
1101	−5	−2	−3
1110	−6	−1	−2
1111	−7	−0	−1

5.3.2 ADDITION AND SUBTRACTION

To assess the suitability of different number representations, it is necessary to investigate their use in arithmetic operations—particularly in addition and subtraction. We can illustrate the good and bad aspects of each representation by considering very small numbers. We will use four-bit numbers, consisting of a sign bit and three significant bits. Thus the numbers have to be small enough so that the magnitude of their sum can be expressed in three bits, which means that the sum cannot exceed the value 7.

Addition of positive numbers is the same for all three number representations. It is actually the same as the addition of unsigned numbers discussed in section 5.2. But there are significant differences when negative numbers are involved. The difficulties that arise become apparent if we consider operands with different combinations of signs.

Sign-and-Magnitude Addition

If both operands have the same sign, then the addition of sign-and-magnitude numbers is simple. The magnitudes are added, and the resulting sum is given the sign of the operands. However, if the operands have opposite signs, the task becomes more complicated. Then it is necessary to subtract the smaller number from the larger one. This means that logic circuits that compare and subtract numbers are also needed. We will see shortly that it is possible to perform subtraction without the need for this circuitry. For this reason, the sign-and-magnitude representation is not used in computers.

1's Complement Addition

An obvious advantage of the 1's complement representation is that a negative number is generated simply by complementing all bits of the corresponding positive number. Figure 5.9 shows what happens when two numbers are added. There are four cases to consider in terms of different combinations of signs. As seen in the top half of the figure, the computation of $5 + 2 = 7$ and $(-5) + 2 = (-3)$ is straightforward; a simple addition of the operands gives the correct result. Such is not the case with the other two possibilities. Computing $5 + (-2) = 3$ produces the bit vector 10010. Because we are dealing with four-bit numbers, there is a carry-out from the sign-bit position. Also, the four bits of the result represent the number 2 rather than 3, which is a wrong result. Interestingly, if we take the carry-out from the sign-bit position and add it to the result in the least-significant bit position, the new result is the correct sum of 3. This correction is indicated in blue in the figure. A similar situation arises when adding $(-5) + (-2) = (-7)$. After the initial addition the result is wrong because the four bits of the sum are 0111, which represents $+7$ rather than -7. But again, there is a carry-out from the sign-bit position, which can be used to correct the result by adding it in the LSB position, as shown in Figure 5.9.

The conclusion from these examples is that the addition of 1's complement numbers may or may not be simple. In some cases a correction is needed, which amounts to an extra addition that must be performed. Consequently, the time needed to add two 1's complement numbers may be twice as long as the time needed to add two unsigned numbers.

2's Complement Addition

Consider the same combinations of numbers as used in the 1's complement example. Figure 5.10 indicates how the addition is performed using 2's complement numbers. Adding $5 + 2 = 7$ and $(-5) + 2 = (-3)$ is straightforward. The computation $5 + (-2) = 3$ generates the correct four bits of the result, namely 0011. There is a carry-out from the sign-bit position, which we can simply ignore. The fourth case is $(-5) + (-2) = (-7)$. Again, the four bits of the result, 1001, give the correct sum (-7). In this case also, the carry-out from the sign-bit position can be ignored.

(+ 5)	0 1 0 1	(−5)	1 0 1 0
+ (+ 2)	+ 0 0 1 0	+ (+ 2)	+ 0 0 1 0
(+ 7)	0 1 1 1	(−3)	1 1 0 0

(+ 5)	0 1 0 1	(−5)	1 0 1 0
+ (−2)	+ 1 1 0 1	+ (−2)	+ 1 1 0 1
(+ 3)	1 0 0 1 0 ⟶ 1	(−7)	1 0 1 1 1 ⟶ 1
	0 0 1 1		1 0 0 0

Figure 5.9   Examples of 1's complement addition.

(+ 5)	0 1 0 1	(−5)	1 0 1 1
+ (+ 2)	+ 0 0 1 0	+ (+ 2)	+ 0 0 1 0
(+ 7)	0 1 1 1	(−3)	1 1 0 1

(+ 5)	0 1 0 1	(−5)	1 0 1 1
+ (−2)	+ 1 1 1 0	+ (−2)	+ 1 1 1 0
(+ 3)	1 0 0 1 1	(−7)	1 1 0 0 1

ignore   ignore

Figure 5.10   Examples of 2's complement addition.

As illustrated by these examples, the addition of 2's complement numbers is very simple. When the numbers are added, the result is always correct. If there is a carry-out from the sign-bit position, it is simply ignored. Therefore, the addition process is the same, regardless of the signs of the operands. It can be performed by an adder circuit, such as the one shown in Figure 5.6. Hence the 2's complement notation is highly suitable for the implementation of addition operations. We will now consider its use in subtraction operations.

2's Complement Subtraction

The easiest way of performing subtraction is to negate the subtrahend and add it to the minuend. This is done by finding the 2's complement of the subtrahend and then performing the addition. Figure 5.11 illustrates the process. The operation $5 - (+2) = 3$ involves finding the 2's complement of +2, which is 1110. When this number is added to 0101, the result is $0011 = (+3)$ and a carry-out from the sign-bit position occurs, which is ignored. A similar situation arises for $(−5) − (+2) = (−7)$. In the remaining two cases there is no carry-out, and the result is correct.

As a graphical aid to visualize the addition and subtraction examples in Figures 5.10 and 5.11, we can place all possible four-bit patterns on a modulo-16 circle given in Figure 5.12. If these bit patterns represented unsigned integers, they would be numbers 0 to 15. If they represent 2's-complement integers, then the numbers range from −8 to +7, as shown. The addition operation is done by stepping in the clockwise direction by the magnitude of the number to be added. For example, $−5 + 2$ is determined by starting at 1011 (= −5) and moving clockwise two steps, giving the result 1101 (= −3). Subtraction is performed by stepping in the counterclockwise direction. For example, $−5 − (+2)$ is determined by starting at 1011 and moving counterclockwise two steps, which gives 1001 (= −7).

The key conclusion of this section is that the subtraction operation can be realized as the addition operation, using a 2's complement of the subtrahend, regardless of the signs of

```
(+ 5)        0 1 0 1              0 1 0 1
- (+ 2)     - 0 0 1 0    ⇒      + 1 1 1 0
─────       ─────────            ─────────
(+ 3)                           1 0 0 1 1
                                   ↑
                                   │
                                ignore


(- 5)        1 0 1 1              1 0 1 1
- (+ 2)     - 0 0 1 0    ⇒      + 1 1 1 0
─────       ─────────            ─────────
(- 7)                           1 1 0 0 1
                                   ↑
                                   │
                                ignore


(+ 5)        0 1 0 1              0 1 0 1
- (- 2)     - 1 1 1 0    ⇒      + 0 0 1 0
─────       ─────────            ─────────
(+ 7)                             0 1 1 1


(- 5)        1 0 1 1              1 0 1 1
- (- 2)     - 1 1 1 0    ⇒      + 0 0 1 0
─────       ─────────            ─────────
(- 3)                             1 1 0 1
```

Figure 5.11   Examples of 2's complement subtraction.

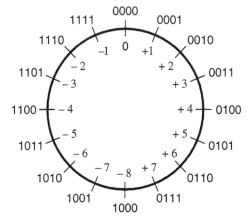

Figure 5.12   Graphical interpretation of four-bit 2's complement numbers.

the two operands. Therefore, it should be possible to use the same adder circuit to perform both addition and subtraction.

5.3.3 ADDER AND SUBTRACTOR UNIT

The only difference between performing addition and subtraction is that for subtraction it is necessary to use the 2's complement of one operand. Let X and Y be the two operands, such that Y serves as the subtrahend in subtraction. From section 5.3.1 we know that a 2's complement can be obtained by adding 1 to the 1's complement of Y. Adding 1 in the least-significant bit position can be accomplished simply by setting the carry-in bit c_0 to 1. A 1's complement of a number is obtained by complementing each of its bits. This could be done with NOT gates, but we need a more flexible circuit where we can use the true value of Y for addition and its complement for subtraction.

In section 5.2 we explained that two-input XOR gates can be used to choose between true and complemented versions of an input value, under the control of the other input. This idea can be applied in the design of the adder/subtractor unit as follows. Assume that there exists a control signal that chooses whether addition or subtraction is to be performed. Let this signal be called $\overline{\text{Add}}$/Sub. Also, let its value be 0 for addition and 1 for subtraction. To indicate this fact, we placed a bar over Add. This is a commonly used convention, where a bar over a name means that the action specified by the name is to be taken if the control signal has the value 0. Now let each bit of Y be connected to one input of an XOR gate, with the other input connected to $\overline{\text{Add}}$/Sub. The outputs of the XOR gates represent Y if $\overline{\text{Add}}$/Sub = 0, and they represent the 1's complement of Y if $\overline{\text{Add}}$/Sub = 1. This leads to the circuit in Figure 5.13. The main part of the circuit is an n-bit adder, which can be implemented using the ripple-carry structure of Figure 5.6. Note that the control signal $\overline{\text{Add}}$/Sub is also

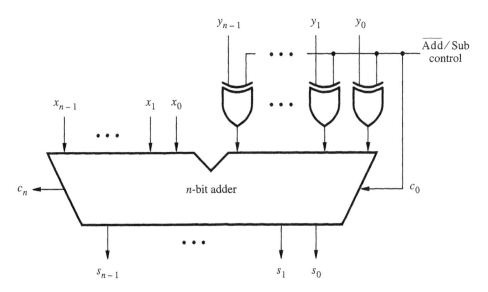

Figure 5.13   Adder/subtractor unit.

connected to the carry-in c_0. This makes $c_0 = 1$ when subtraction is to be performed, thus adding the 1 that is needed to form the 2's complement of Y. When the addition operation is performed, we will have $c_i = 0$.

The combined adder/subtractor unit is a good example of an important concept in the design of logic circuits. It is useful to design circuits to be as flexible as possible and to exploit common portions of circuits for as many tasks as possible. This approach minimizes the number of gates needed to implement such circuits, and it reduces the wiring complexity substantially.

5.3.4 RADIX-COMPLEMENT SCHEMES

The idea of performing a subtraction operation by addition of a complement of the subtrahend is not restricted to binary numbers. We can gain some insight into the workings of the 2's complement scheme by considering its counterpart in the decimal number system. Consider the subtraction of two-digit decimal numbers. Computing a result such as $74 - 33 = 41$ is simple because each digit of the subtrahend is smaller than the corresponding digit of the minuend; therefore, no borrow is needed in the computation. But computing $74 - 36 = 38$ is not as simple because a borrow is needed in subtracting the least-significant digit. If a borrow occurs, the computation becomes more complicated.

Suppose that we restructure the required computation as follows

$$74 - 36 = 74 + 100 - 100 - 36$$
$$= 74 + (100 - 36) - 100$$

Now two subtractions are needed. Subtracting 36 from 100 still involves borrows. But noting that $100 = 99 + 1$, these borrows can be avoided by writing

$$74 - 36 = 74 + (99 + 1 - 36) - 100$$
$$= 74 + (99 - 36) + 1 - 100$$

The subtraction in parentheses does not require borrows; it is performed by subtracting each digit of the subtrahend from 9. We can see a direct correlation between this expression and the one used for 2's complement, as reflected in the circuit in Figure 5.13. The operation $(99 - 36)$ is analogous to complementing the subtrahend Y to find its 1's complement, which is the same as subtracting each bit from 1. Using decimal numbers, we find the *9's complement* of the subtrahend by subtracting each digit from 9. In Figure 5.13 we add the carry-in of 1 to form the 2's complement of Y. In our decimal example we perform $(99 - 36) + 1 = 64$. Here 64 is the 10's complement of 36. For an n-digit decimal number, N, its *10's complement*, K_{10}, is defined as $K_{10} = 10^n - N$, while its 9's complement, K_9, is $K_9 = (10^n - 1) - N$.

Thus the required subtraction $(74 - 36)$ can be performed by addition of the 10's complement of the subtrahend, as in

$$74 - 36 = 74 + 64 - 100$$
$$= 138 - 100$$
$$= 38$$

The subtraction $138 - 100$ is trivial because it means that the leading digit in 138 is simply deleted. This is analogous to ignoring the carry-out from the circuit in Figure 5.13, as discussed for the subtraction examples in Figure 5.11.

Example 5.1   Suppose that A and B are n-digit decimal numbers. Using the above 10's-complement approach, B can be subtracted from A as follows:

$$A - B = A + (10^n - B) - 10^n$$

If $A \geq B$, then the operation $A + (10^n - B)$ produces a carry-out of 1. This carry is equivalent to 10^n; hence it can be simply ignored.

But if $A < B$, then the operation $A + (10^n - B)$ produces a carry-out of 0. Let the result obtained be M, so that

$$A - B = M - 10^n$$

We can rewrite this as

$$10^n - (B - A) = M$$

The left side of this equation is the 10's complement of $(B - A)$. The 10's complement of a positive number represents a negative number that has the same magnitude. Hence M correctly represents the negative value obtained from the computation $A - B$ when $A < B$. This concept is illustrated in the examples that follow.

Example 5.2   When dealing with binary signed numbers we use 0 in the left-most bit position to denote a positive number and 1 to denote a negative number. If we wanted to build hardware that operates on signed decimal numbers, we could use a similar approach. Let 0 in the left-most digit position denote a positive number and let 9 denote a negative number. Note that 9 is the 9's complement of 0 in the decimal system, just as 1 is the 1's complement of 0 in the binary system.

Thus, using three-digit signed numbers, $A = 045$ and $B = 027$ are positive numbers with magnitudes 45 and 27, respectively. The number B can be subtracted from A as follows

$$\begin{aligned}
A - B &= 045 - 027 \\
&= 045 + 1000 - 1000 - 027 \\
&= 045 + (999 - 027) + 1 - 1000 \\
&= 045 + 972 + 1 - 1000 \\
&= 1018 - 1000 \\
&= 018
\end{aligned}$$

This gives the correct answer of $+18$.

Next consider the case where the minuend has lower value than the subtrahend. This is illustrated by the computation

$$B - A = 027 - 045$$
$$= 027 + 1000 - 1000 - 045$$
$$= 027 + (999 - 045) + 1 - 1000$$
$$= 027 + 954 + 1 - 1000$$
$$= 982 - 1000$$

From this expression it appears that we still need to perform the subtraction $982 - 1000$. But as seen in Example 5.1, this can be rewritten as

$$982 = 1000 + B - A$$
$$= 1000 - (A - B)$$

Therefore, 982 is the negative number that results when forming the 10's complement of $(A - B)$. From the previous computation we know that $(A - B) = 018$, which denotes $+18$. Thus the signed number 982 is the 10's complement representation of -18, which is the required result.

Let $C = 955$ and $D = 973$; hence the values of C and D are -45 and -27, respectively. **Example 5.3**
The number D can be subtracted from C as follows

$$C - D = 955 - 973$$
$$= 955 + 1000 - 1000 - 973$$
$$= 955 + (999 - 973) + 1 - 1000$$
$$= 955 + 026 + 1 - 1000$$
$$= 982 - 1000$$

The number 982 is the 10's complement representation of -18, which is the correct result.
   Consider now the case $D - A$, where $D = 973$ and $A = 045$:

$$D - A = 973 - 045$$
$$= 973 + 1000 - 1000 - 045$$
$$= 973 + (999 - 045) + 1 - 1000$$
$$= 973 + 954 + 1 - 1000$$
$$= 1928 - 1000$$
$$= 928$$

The result 928 is the 10's complement representation of -72.
   These examples illustrate that signed numbers can be subtracted without using a subtraction operation that involves borrows. The only subtraction needed is in forming the 9's complement of the subtrahend, in which case each digit is simply subtracted from 9.

Thus a circuit that forms the 9's complement, combined with a normal adder circuit, will suffice for both addition and subtraction of decimal signed numbers. A key point is that the hardware needs to deal only with n digits if n-digit numbers are used. Any carry that may be generated from the left-most digit position is simply ignored.

The concept of subtracting a number by adding its radix-complement is general. If the radix is r, then the r's complement, K_r, of an n-digit number, N, is determined as $K_r = r^n - N$. The $(r-1)$'s complement, K_{r-1}, is defined as $K_{r-1} = (r^n - 1) - N$; it is computed simply by subtracting each digit of N from the value $(r-1)$. The $(r-1)$'s complement is referred to as the *diminished-radix complement*. Circuits for forming the $(r-1)$'s complements are simpler than those for general subtraction that involves borrows. The circuits are particularly simple in the binary case, where the 1's complement requires just inverting each bit.

Example 5.4   In Figure 5.11 we illustrated the subtraction operation on binary numbers given in 2's-complement representation. Consider the computation $(+5) - (+2) = (+3)$, using the approach discussed above. Each number is represented by a four-bit pattern. The value 2^4 is represented as 10000. Then

$$0101 - 0010 = 0101 + (10000 - 0010) - 10000$$
$$= 0101 + (1111 - 0010) + 1 - 10000$$
$$= 0101 + 1101 + 1 - 10000$$
$$= 10011 - 10000$$
$$= 0011$$

Because $5 > 2$, there is a carry from the fourth bit position. It represents the value 2^4, denoted by the pattern 10000.

Example 5.5   Consider now the computation $(+2) - (+5) = (-3)$, which gives

$$0010 - 0101 = 0010 + (10000 - 0101) - 10000$$
$$= 0010 + (1111 - 0101) + 1 - 10000$$
$$= 0010 + 1010 + 1 - 10000$$
$$= 1101 - 10000$$

Because $2 < 5$, there is no carry from the fourth bit position. The answer, 1101, is the 2's-complement representation of -3. Note that

$$1101 = 10000 + 0010 - 0101$$
$$= 10000 - (0101 - 0010)$$
$$= 10000 - 0011$$

indicating that 1101 is the 2's complement of 0011 (+3).

Finally, consider the case where the subtrahend is a negative number. The computation **Example 5.6**
$(+5) - (-2) = (+7)$ is done as follows

$$0101 - 1110 = 0101 + (10000 - 1110) - 10000$$
$$= 0101 + (1111 - 1110) + 1 - 10000$$
$$= 0101 + 0001 + 1 - 10000$$
$$= 0111 - 10000$$

While $5 > (-2)$, the pattern 1110 is greater than the pattern 0101 when the patterns are treated as unsigned numbers. Therefore, there is no carry from the fourth bit position. The answer 0111 is the 2's complement representation of +7. Note that

$$0111 = 10000 + 0101 - 1110$$
$$= 10000 - (1110 - 0101)$$
$$= 10000 - 1001$$

and 1001 represents -7.

5.3.5 ARITHMETIC OVERFLOW

The result of addition or subtraction is supposed to fit within the significant bits used to represent the numbers. If n bits are used to represent signed numbers, then the result must be in the range -2^{n-1} to $2^{n-1} - 1$. If the result does not fit in this range, then we say that *arithmetic overflow* has occurred. To ensure the correct operation of an arithmetic circuit, it is important to be able to detect the occurrence of overflow.

Figure 5.14 presents the four cases where 2's-complement numbers with magnitudes of 7 and 2 are added. Because we are using four-bit numbers, there are three significant bits, b_{2-0}. When the numbers have opposite signs, there is no overflow. But if both numbers have the same sign, the magnitude of the result is 9, which cannot be represented with just three significant bits; therefore, overflow occurs. The key to determining whether overflow

$$
\begin{array}{rr}
(+7) & 0\,1\,1\,1 \\
+\,(+2) & +\,0\,0\,1\,0 \\
\hline
(+9) & 1\,0\,0\,1 \\
& c_4 = 0 \\
& c_3 = 1
\end{array}
\qquad
\begin{array}{rr}
(-7) & 1\,0\,0\,1 \\
+\,(+2) & +\,0\,0\,1\,0 \\
\hline
(-5) & 1\,0\,1\,1 \\
& c_4 = 0 \\
& c_3 = 0
\end{array}
$$

$$
\begin{array}{rr}
(+7) & 0\,1\,1\,1 \\
+\,(-2) & +\,1\,1\,1\,0 \\
\hline
(+5) & 1\,0\,1\,0\,1 \\
& c_4 = 1 \\
& c_3 = 1
\end{array}
\qquad
\begin{array}{rr}
(-7) & 1\,0\,0\,1 \\
+\,(-2) & +\,1\,1\,1\,0 \\
\hline
(-9) & 1\,0\,1\,1\,1 \\
& c_4 = 1 \\
& c_3 = 0
\end{array}
$$

Figure 5.14 Examples for determination of overflow.

occurs is the carry-out from the MSB position, called c_3 in the figure, and from the sign-bit position, called c_4. The figure indicates that overflow occurs when these carry-outs have different values, and a correct sum is produced when they have the same value. Indeed, this is true in general for both addition and subtraction of 2's-complement numbers. As a quick check of this statement, consider the examples in Figure 5.10 where the numbers are small enough so that overflow does not occur in any case. In the top two examples in the figure, there is a carry-out of 0 from both sign and MSB positions. In the bottom two examples, there is a carry-out of 1 from both positions. Therefore, for the examples in Figures 5.10 and 5.14, the occurrence of overflow is detected by

$$\text{Overflow} = c_3\bar{c}_4 + \bar{c}_3c_4$$
$$= c_3 \oplus c_4$$

For n-bit numbers we have

$$\text{Overflow} = c_{n-1} \oplus c_n$$

Thus the circuit in Figure 5.13 can be modified to include overflow checking with the addition of one XOR gate.

5.3.6 PERFORMANCE ISSUES

When buying a digital system, such as a computer, the buyer pays particular attention to the performance that the system is expected to provide and to the cost of acquiring the system. Superior performance usually comes at a higher cost. However, a large increase in performance can often be achieved at a modest increase in cost. A commonly used indicator of the value of a system is its *price/performance ratio*.

The addition and subtraction of numbers are fundamental operations that are performed frequently in the course of a computation. The speed with which these operations are performed has a strong impact on the overall performance of a computer. In light of this, let us take a closer look at the speed of the adder/subtractor unit in Figure 5.13. We are interested in the largest delay from the time the operands X and Y are presented as inputs, until the time all bits of the sum S and the final carry-out, c_n, are valid. Most of this delay is caused by the n-bit adder circuit. Assume that the adder is implemented using the ripple-carry structure in Figure 5.6 and that each full-adder stage is the circuit in Figure 5.4c. The delay for the carry-out signal in this circuit, Δt, is equal to two gate delays. From section 5.2.2 we know that the final result of the addition will be valid after a delay of $n\Delta t$, which is equal to $2n$ gate delays. In addition to the delay in the ripple-carry path, there is also a delay in the XOR gates that feed either the true or complemented value of Y to the adder inputs. If this delay is equal to one gate delay, then the total delay of the circuit in Figure 5.13 is $2n+1$ gate delays. For a large n, say $n = 32$ or $n = 64$, the delay would lead to unacceptably poor performance. Therefore, it is important to find faster circuits to perform addition.

The speed of any circuit is limited by the longest delay along the paths through the circuit. In the case of the circuit in Figure 5.13, the longest delay is along the path from the y_i input, through the XOR gate and through the carry circuit of each adder stage. The longest delay is often referred to as the *critical-path delay*, and the path that causes this delay is called the *critical path*.

5.4 FAST ADDERS

The performance of a large digital system is dependent on the speed of circuits that form its various functional units. Obviously, better performance can be achieved using faster circuits. This can be accomplished by using superior (usually newer) technology in which the delays in basic gates are reduced. But it can also be accomplished by changing the overall structure of a functional unit, which may lead to even more impressive improvement. In this section we will discuss an alternative for implementation of an *n*-bit adder, which substantially reduces the time needed to add numbers.

5.4.1 CARRY-LOOKAHEAD ADDER

To reduce the delay caused by the effect of carry propagation through the ripple-carry adder, we can attempt to evaluate quickly for each stage whether the carry-in from the previous stage will have a value 0 or 1. If a correct evaluation can be made in a relatively short time, then the performance of the complete adder will be improved.

From Figure 5.4*b* the carry-out function for stage *i* can be realized as

$$c_{i+1} = x_i y_i + x_i c_i + y_i c_i$$

If we factor this expression as

$$c_{i+1} = x_i y_i + (x_i + y_i)c_i$$

then it can be written as

$$c_{i+1} = g_i + p_i c_i \qquad \text{[5.3]}$$

where

$$g_i = x_i y_i$$
$$p_i = x_i + y_i$$

The function g_i is equal to 1 when both inputs x_i and y_i are equal to 1, regardless of the value of the incoming carry to this stage, c_i. Since in this case stage *i* is guaranteed to generate a carry-out, g is called the *generate* function. The function p_i is equal to 1 when at least one of the inputs x_i and y_i is equal to 1. In this case a carry-out is produced if $c_i = 1$. The effect is that the carry-in of 1 is propagated through stage *i*; hence p_i is called the *propagate* function.

Expanding the expression 5.3 in terms of stage $i - 1$ gives

$$c_{i+1} = g_i + p_i(g_{i-1} + p_{i-1}c_{i-1})$$
$$= g_i + p_i g_{i-1} + p_i p_{i-1} c_{i-1}$$

The same expansion for other stages, ending with stage 0, gives

$$c_{i+1} = g_i + p_i g_{i-1} + p_i p_{i-1} g_{i-2} + \dots + p_i p_{i-1} \cdots p_2 p_1 g_0 + p_i p_{i-1} \cdots p_1 p_0 c_0 \quad \textbf{[5.4]}$$

This expression represents a two-level AND-OR circuit in which c_{i+1} is evaluated very quickly. An adder based on this expression is called a *carry-lookahead adder*.

To appreciate the physical meaning of expression 5.4, it is instructive to consider its effect on the construction of a fast adder in comparison with the details of the ripple-carry adder. We will do so by examining the detailed structure of the two stages that add the least-significant bits, namely, stages 0 and 1. Figure 5.15 shows the first two stages of a ripple-carry adder in which the carry-out functions are implemented as indicated in expression 5.3. Each stage is essentially the circuit from Figure 5.4c except that an extra OR gate is used (which produces the p_i signal), instead of an AND gate because we factored the sum-of-products expression for c_{i+1}.

The slow speed of the ripple-carry adder is caused by the long path along which a carry signal must propagate. In Figure 5.15 the critical path is from inputs x_0 and y_0 to the output c_2. It passes through five gates, as highlighted in blue. The path in other stages of an n-bit adder is the same as in stage 1. Therefore, the total delay along the critical path is $2n + 1$.

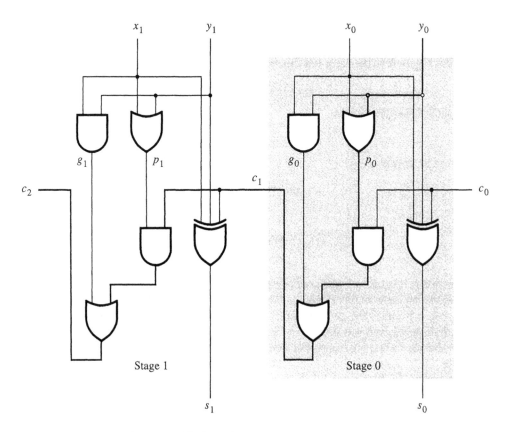

Figure 5.15   A ripple-carry adder based on expression 5.3.

Figure 5.16 gives the first two stages of the carry-lookahead adder, using expression 5.4 to implement the carry-out functions. Thus

$$c_1 = g_0 + p_0 c_0$$
$$c_2 = g_1 + p_1 g_0 + p_1 p_0 c_0$$

The critical path for producing the c_2 signal is highlighted in blue. In this circuit, c_2 is produced just as quickly as c_1, after a total of three gate delays. Extending the circuit to n bits, the final carry-out signal c_n would also be produced after only three gate delays because expression 5.4 is just a large two-level (AND-OR) circuit.

The total delay in the n-bit carry-lookahead adder is four gate delays. The values of all g_i and p_i signals are determined after one gate delay. It takes two more gate delays to evaluate all carry signals. Finally, it takes one more gate delay (XOR) to generate all sum bits. The key to the good performance of the adder is quick evaluation of carry signals.

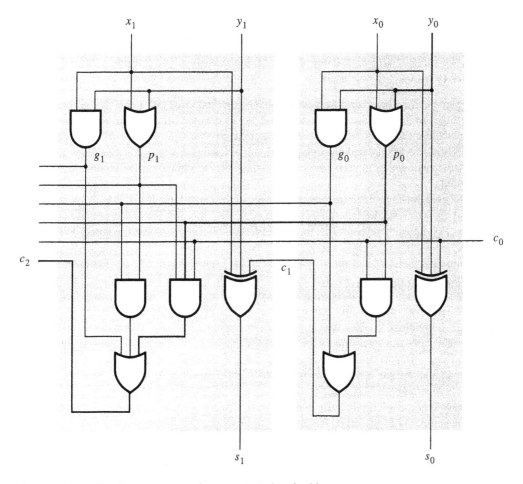

Figure 5.16 The first two stages of a carry-lookahead adder.

The expression 5.4 can be evaluated quickly by an AND-OR circuit. However, the number of inputs to some of the gates needed to realize this expression is large for high values of i. We know from Chapters 3 and 4 that the technology used to implement the gates limits the fan-in to a rather small number of inputs. Thus the reality of fan-in constraints must be taken into account. To illustrate this problem, consider the expressions for the first eight carries:

$$c_1 = g_0 + p_0 c_0$$
$$c_2 = g_1 + p_1 g_0 + p_1 p_0 c_0$$
$$\vdots$$
$$c_8 = g_7 + p_7 g_6 + p_7 p_6 g_5 + p_7 p_6 p_5 g_4 + p_7 p_6 p_5 p_4 g_3 + p_7 p_6 p_5 p_4 p_3 g_2$$
$$+ p_7 p_6 p_5 p_4 p_3 p_2 g_1 + p_7 p_6 p_5 p_4 p_3 p_2 p_1 g_0 + p_7 p_6 p_5 p_4 p_3 p_2 p_1 p_0 c_0$$

Suppose that the maximum fan-in of the gates is four inputs. Then it is impossible to implement all of these expressions with a two-level AND-OR circuit. The biggest problem is c_8, where one of the AND gates requires nine inputs; moreover, the OR gate also requires nine inputs. To meet the fan-in constraint, we can rewrite the expression for c_8 as

$$c_8 = (g_7 + p_7 g_6 + p_7 p_6 g_5 + p_7 p_6 p_5 g_4) + [(p_7 p_6 p_5 p_4)(g_3 + p_3 g_2 + p_3 p_2 g_1 + p_3 p_2 p_1 g_0)]$$
$$+ (p_7 p_6 p_5 p_4)(p_3 p_2 p_1 p_0) c_0$$

To implement this expression we need 11 AND gates and three OR gates. The propagation delay in generating c_8 consists of one gate delay to develop all g_i and p_i, two gate delays to produce the sum-of-products terms in parentheses, one gate delay to form the product term in square brackets, and one delay for the final ORing of terms. Hence c_8 is valid after five gate delays, rather than the three gates delays that would be needed without the fan-in constraint.

Because fan-in limitations reduce the speed of the carry-lookahead adder, some devices that are characterized by low fan-in include dedicated circuitry for implementation of fast adders. Examples of such devices include FPGAs whose logic blocks are based on lookup tables.

The complexity of an n-bit carry-lookahead adder increases rapidly as n becomes larger. To reduce the complexity, we can use a *hierarchical* approach in designing large adders. Suppose that we want to design a 32-bit adder. We can divide this adder into 4 eight-bit blocks, such that bits b_{7-0} are block 0, bits b_{15-8} are block 1, bits b_{23-16} are block 2, and bits b_{31-24} are block 3. Then we can implement each block as an eight-bit carry-lookahead adder. The carry-out signals from the four blocks are c_8, c_{16}, c_{24}, and c_{32}. Now we have two possibilities. We can connect the four blocks as four stages in a ripple-carry adder. Thus while carry-lookahead is used within each block, the carries ripple between the blocks. This circuit is illustrated in Figure 5.17.

Instead of using a ripple-carry approach between blocks, a faster circuit can be designed in which a second-level carry-lookahead is performed to produce quickly the carry signals between blocks. The structure of this "hierarchical carry-lookahead adder" is shown in Figure 5.18. Each block in the top row includes an eight-bit carry-lookahead adder, based on generate signals, g_i, and propagate signals, p_i, for each stage in the block, as discussed

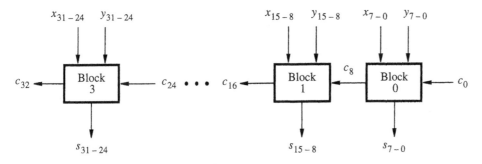

Figure 5.17   A hierarchical carry-lookahead adder with ripple-carry between blocks.

before. However, instead of producing a carry-out signal from the most-significant bit of the block, each block produces generate and propagate signals for the entire block. Let G_j and P_j denote these signals for each block j. Now G_j and P_j can be used as inputs to a second-level carry-lookahead circuit, at the bottom of Figure 5.18, which evaluates all carries between blocks. We can derive the block generate and propagate signals for block

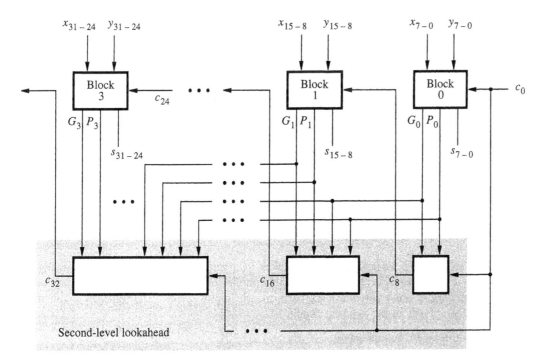

Figure 5.18   A hierarchical carry-lookahead adder.

0 by examining the expression shown above for c_8

$$c_8 = g_7 + p_7 g_6 + p_7 p_6 g_5 + p_7 p_6 p_5 g_4 + p_7 p_6 p_5 p_4 g_3 + p_7 p_6 p_5 p_4 p_3 g_2$$
$$+ p_7 p_6 p_5 p_4 p_3 p_2 g_1 + p_7 p_6 p_5 p_4 p_3 p_2 p_1 g_0 + p_7 p_6 p_5 p_4 p_3 p_2 p_1 p_0 c_0$$

The last term in this expression specifies that if all eight propagate functions are 1, then the carry-in c_0 is propagated through the entire block. Hence

$$P_0 = p_7 p_6 p_5 p_4 p_3 p_2 p_1 p_0$$

The rest of the terms in the expression for c_8 represent all other cases when the block produces a carry-out. Thus

$$G_0 = g_7 + p_7 g_6 + p_7 p_6 g_5 + \ldots + p_7 p_6 p_5 p_4 p_3 p_2 p_1 g_0$$

The expression for c_8 in the hierarchical adder is given by

$$c_8 = G_0 + P_0 c_0$$

For block 1 the expressions for G_1 and P_1 have the same form as for G_0 and P_0 except that each subscript i is replaced by $i + 8$. The expressions for G_2, P_2, G_3, and P_3 are derived in the same way. The expression for the carry-out of block 1, c_{16}, is

$$c_{16} = G_1 + P_1 c_8$$
$$= G_1 + P_1 G_0 + P_1 P_0 c_0$$

Similarly, the expressions for G_2, P_2, G_3, and P_3 are

$$c_{24} = G_2 + P_2 G_1 + P_2 P_1 G_0 + P_2 P_1 P_0 c_0$$
$$c_{32} = G_3 + P_3 G_2 + P_3 P_2 G_1 + P_3 P_2 P_1 G_0 + P_3 P_2 P_1 P_0 c_0$$

Using this scheme, it takes two more gate delays to produce the carry signals c_8, c_{16}, and c_{24} than the time needed to generate the G_j and P_j functions. Therefore, assuming a fan-in constraint of four inputs, the time needed to add two 32-bit numbers involves five gate delays to develop G_j and P_j (as we determined in the previous derivation of the c_8 signal), three gate delays for the second-level lookahead (because two gates in the expression for c_{32} require five inputs and hence must be factored), and one gate delay (XOR) to produce the final sum bits. The total time is nine gate delays. Actually, the final sum is generated after eight delays because c_{32} is not used to determine the sum bits. However, c_{32} is used to determine whether overflow occurs, since $overflow = c_{31} \oplus c_{32}$. Therefore, the complete addition operation, including the determination of the overflow condition, takes nine gate delays.

In section 5.3.5 we determined that it takes $2n+1$ gate delays to add two numbers using a ripple-carry adder. For 32-bit numbers this implies 65 gate delays. It is clear that the carry-lookahead adder offers a large performance improvement. The trade-off is much greater complexity of the required circuit.

Technology Considerations

Before we leave the topic of the carry-lookahead adder, we should consider an alternative implementation of the structure in Figure 5.16. The same functionality can be achieved by using the circuit in Figure 5.19. In this case stage 0 is implemented using the circuit of

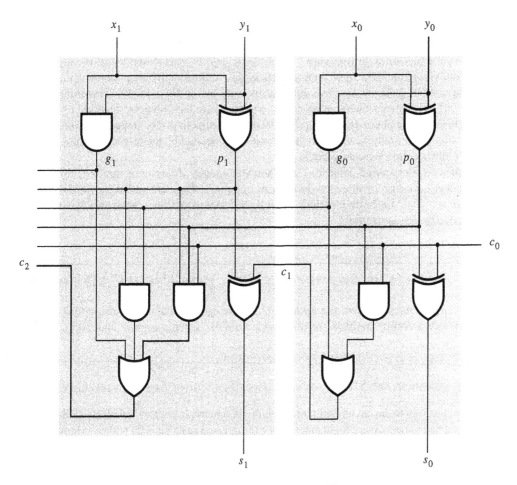

Figure 5.19   An alternative design for a carry-lookahead adder.

Figure 5.5 in which 2 two-input XOR gates are used to generate the sum bit, rather than having 1 three-input XOR gate. The output of the first XOR gate can also serve as the propagate signal p_0. Thus the corresponding OR gate in Figure 5.16 is not needed. Stage 1 is constructed using the same approach.

The circuits in Figures 5.16 and 5.19 require the same number of gates. But is one of them better in some way? The answer must be sought by considering the specific aspects of the technology that is used to implement the circuits. If a CPLD or an FPGA is used, such as those in Figures 3.33 and 3.39, then it does not matter which circuit is chosen. A three-input XOR function can be realized by one macrocell in the CPLD, using the sum-of-products expression .

$$s_i = x_i \bar{y}_i \bar{c}_i + \bar{x}_i y_i \bar{c}_i + \bar{x}_i \bar{y}_i c_i + x_i y_i c_i$$

because the macrocell allows for implementation of four product terms.

In the FPGA any three-input function can be implemented in a single logic cell; hence it is easy to realize a three-input XOR. However, suppose that we want to build a carry-lookahead adder on a custom chip. If the XOR gate is constructed using the approach discussed in section 3.9.1, then a three-input XOR would actually be implemented using 2 two-input XOR gates, as we have done for the sum bits in Figure 5.19. Therefore, if the first XOR gate realizes the function $x_i \oplus y_i$, which is also the propagate function p_i, then it is obvious that the alternative in Figure 5.19 is more attractive. The important point of this discussion is that optimization of logic circuits may depend on the target technology. The CAD tools take this fact into account.

The carry-lookahead adder is a well-known concept. There exist standard chips that implement a portion of the carry-lookahead circuitry. They are called *carry-lookahead generators*. CAD tools often include predesigned subcircuits for adders, which designers can use to design larger units.

5.6 MULTIPLICATION

Before we discuss the general issue of multiplication, we should note that a binary number, B, can be multiplied by 2 simply by adding a zero to the right of its least-significant bit. This effectively moves all bits of B to the left, and we say that B is *shifted* left by one bit position. Thus if $B = b_{n-1}b_{n-2}\ldots b_1 b_0$, then $2 \times B = b_{n-1}b_{n-2}\ldots b_1 b_0 0$. (We have already used this fact in section 5.2.3.) Similarly, a number is multiplied by 2^k by shifting it left by k bit positions. This is true for both unsigned and signed numbers.

We should also consider what happens if a binary number is shifted right by k bit positions. According to the positional number representation, this action divides the number by 2^k. For unsigned numbers the shifting amounts to adding k zeros to the left of the most-significant bit. For example, if B is an unsigned number, then $B \div 2 = 0 b_{n-1}b_{n-2}\ldots b_2 b_1$. Note that bit b_0 is lost when shifting to the right. For signed numbers it is necessary to preserve the sign. This is done by shifting the bits to the right and filling from the left with the value of the sign bit. Hence if B is a signed number, then $B \div 2 = b_{n-1}b_{n-1}b_{n-2}\ldots b_2 b_1$. For instance, if $B = 011000 = (24)_{10}$, then $B \div 2 = 001100 = (12)_{10}$ and $B \div 4 = 000110 = (6)_{10}$. Similarly, if $B = 101000 = -(24)_{10}$, then $B \div 2 = 110100 = -(12)_{10}$ and $B \div 4 = 111010 = -(6)_{10}$. The reader should also observe that the smaller the positive number, the more 0s there are to the left of the first 1, while for a negative number there are more 1s to the left of the first 0.

Now we can turn our attention to the general task of multiplication. Two binary numbers can be multiplied using the same method as we use for decimal numbers. We will focus our discussion on multiplication of unsigned numbers. Figure 5.32a shows how multiplication is performed manually, using four-bit numbers. Each multiplier bit is examined from right to left. If a bit is equal to 1, an appropriately shifted version of the multiplicand is added to form a *partial product*. If the multiplier bit is equal to 0, then nothing is added. The sum of all shifted versions of the multiplicand is the desired product. Note that the product occupies eight bits.

The same scheme can be used to design a multiplier circuit. We will stay with four-bit numbers to keep the discussion simple. Let the multiplicand, multiplier, and product be denoted as $M = m_3 m_2 m_1 m_0$, $Q = q_3 q_2 q_1 q_0$, and $P = p_7 p_6 p_5 p_4 p_3 p_2 p_1 p_0$, respectively. One simple way of implementing the multiplication scheme is to use a sequential approach, where an eight-bit adder is used to compute partial products. As a first step, the bit q_0 is examined. If $q_0 = 1$, then M is added to the initial partial product, which is initialized to 0. If $q_0 = 0$, then 0 is added to the partial product. Next q_1 is examined. If $q_1 = 1$, then the value $2 \times M$ is added to the partial product. The value $2 \times M$ is created simply by shifting M one bit position to the left. Similarly, $4 \times M$ is added to the partial product if $q_2 = 1$, and $8 \times M$ is added if $q_3 = 1$. We will show in Chapter 10 how such a circuit may be implemented.

This sequential approach leads to a relatively slow circuit, primarily because a single eight-bit adder is used to perform all additions needed to generate the partial products and the final product. A much faster circuit can be obtained if multiple adders are used to compute the partial products.

5.6.1   ARRAY MULTIPLIER FOR UNSIGNED NUMBERS

Figure 5.32b indicates how multiplication may be performed by using multiple adders. In each step a four-bit adder is used to compute the new partial product. Note that as the computation progresses, the least-significant bits are not affected by subsequent additions; hence they can be passed directly to the final product, as indicated by blue arrows. Of course, these bits are a part of the partial products as well.

A fast multiplier circuit can be designed using an array structure that is similar to the organization in Figure 5.32b. Consider a 4 × 4 example, where the multiplicand and

$$
\begin{array}{llr}
\text{Multiplicand M} & (14) & 1\,1\,1\,0 \\
\text{Multiplier Q} & (11) & \times\ 1\,0\,1\,1 \\
\hline
& & 1\,1\,1\,0 \\
& & 1\,1\,1\,0 \\
& & 0\,0\,0\,0 \\
& & 1\,1\,1\,0 \\
\hline
\text{Product P} & (154) & 1\,0\,0\,1\,1\,0\,1\,0
\end{array}
$$

(a) Multiplication by hand

$$
\begin{array}{llr}
\text{Multiplicand M} & (11) & 1\,1\,1\,0 \\
\text{Multiplier Q} & (14) & \times\ 1\,0\,1\,1 \\
\hline
\text{Partial product 0} & & 1\,1\,1\,0 \\
& & +\ 1\,1\,1\,0 \\
\hline
\text{Partial product 1} & & 1\,0\,1\,0\,1 \\
& & +\ 0\,0\,0\,0 \\
\hline
\text{Partial product 2} & & 0\,1\,0\,1\,0 \\
& & +\ 1\,1\,1\,0 \\
\hline
\text{Product P} & (154) & 1\,0\,0\,1\,1\,0\,1\,0
\end{array}
$$

(b) Multiplication for implementation in hardware

Figure 5.32   Multiplication of unsigned numbers.

multiplier are $M = m_3m_2m_1m_0$ and $Q = q_3q_2q_1q_0$, respectively. The partial product 0, $PP0 = pp0_3\ pp0_2\ pp0_1\ pp0_0$, can be generated using the AND of q_0 with each bit of M. Thus

$$PP0 = m_3q_0\ \ m_2q_0\ \ m_1q_0\ \ m_0q_0$$

Partial product 1, $PP1$, is generated using the AND of q_1 with M and adding it to $PP0$ as follows

$PP0$:		0	$pp0_3$	$pp0_2$	$pp0_1$	$pp0_0$
$+$	m_3q_1	m_2q_1	m_1q_1	m_0q_0	0
$PP1$:		$pp1_4$	$pp1_3$	$pp1_2$	$pp1_1$	$pp1_0$

Similarly, partial product 2, $PP2$, is generated using the AND of q_2 with M and adding to $PP1$, and so on.

A circuit that implements the preceding operations is arranged in an array, as shown in Figure 5.33a. There are two types of blocks in the array. Part (b) of the figure shows the details of the blocks in the top row, and part (c) shows the block used in the second and third rows. Observe that the shifted versions of the multiplicand are provided by routing the m_k signals diagonally from one block to another. The full-adder included in each block implements a ripple-carry adder to generate each partial product. It is possible to design even faster multipliers by using other types of adders [1].

5.6.2 MULTIPLICATION OF SIGNED NUMBERS

Multiplication of unsigned numbers illustrates the main issues involved in the design of multiplier circuits. Multiplication of signed numbers is somewhat more complex.

If the multiplier operand is positive, it is possible to use essentially the same scheme as for unsigned numbers. For each bit of the multiplier operand that is equal to 1, a properly shifted version of the multiplicand must be added to the partial product. The multiplicand can be either positive or negative.

Since shifted versions of the multiplicand are added to the partial products, it is important to ensure that the numbers involved are represented correctly. For example, if the two right-most bits of the multiplier are both equal to 1, then the first addition must produce the partial product $PP1 = M + 2M$, where M is the multiplicand. If $M = m_{n-1}m_{n-2}\ldots m_1m_0$, then $PP1 = m_{n-1}m_{n-2}\ldots m_1m_0 + m_{n-1}m_{n-2}\ldots m_1m_00$. The adder that performs this addition comprises circuitry that adds two operands of equal length. Since shifting the multiplicand to the left, to generate $2M$, results in one of the operands having $n + 1$ bits, the required addition has to be performed using the second operand, M, represented also as an $(n+1)$-bit number. An n-bit signed number is represented as an $(n+1)$-bit number by replicating the sign bit as the new left-most bit. Thus $M = m_{n-1}m_{n-2}\ldots m_1m_0$ is represented using $(n + 1)$ bits as $M = m_{n-1}m_{n-1}m_{n-2}\ldots m_1m_0$. The value of a positive number does not change if 0s are appended as the most-significant bits; the value of a negative number does not change if 1s are appended as the most-significant bits. Such replication of the sign bit is called *sign extension*.

When a shifted version of the multiplicand is added to a partial product, overflow has to be avoided. Hence the new partial product must be larger by one extra bit. Figure

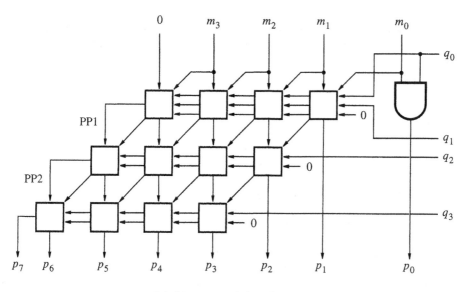

(a) Structure of the circuit

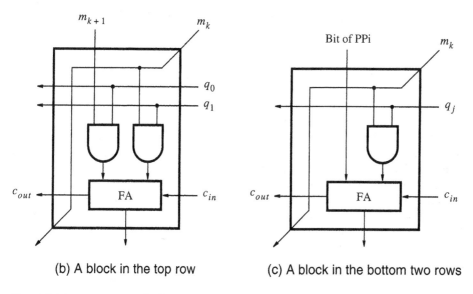

(b) A block in the top row

(c) A block in the bottom two rows

Figure 5.33 A 4×4 multiplier circuit.

5.34a illustrates the process of multiplying two positive numbers. The sign-extended bits are shown in blue. Part (b) of the figure involves a negative multiplicand. Note that the resulting product has $2n$ bits in both cases.

For a negative multiplier operand, it is possible to convert both the multiplier and the multiplicand into their 2's complements because this will not change the value of the result. Then the scheme for a positive multiplier can be used.

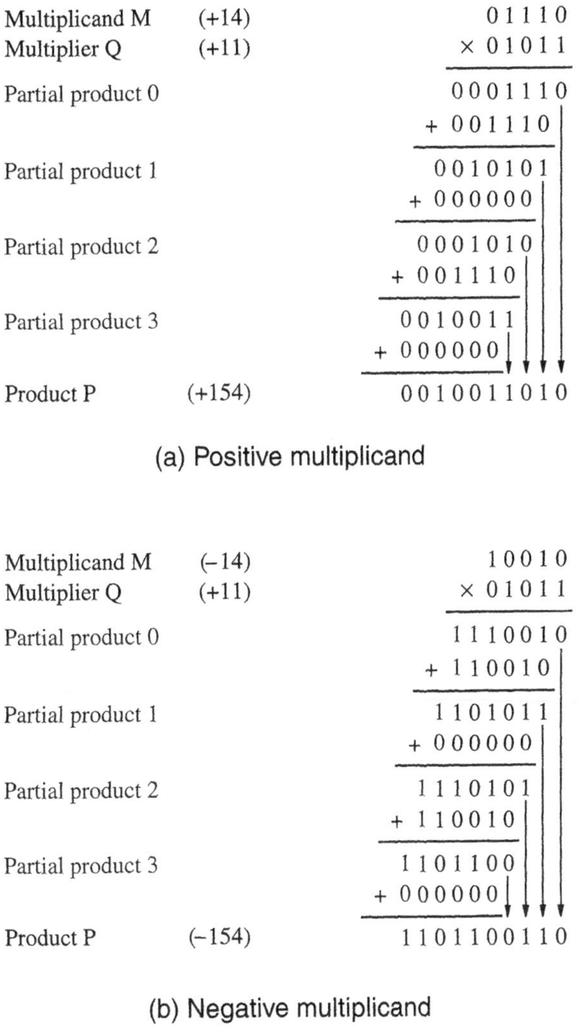

| Multiplicand M | (+14) | 0 1 1 1 0 |
| Multiplier Q | (+11) | × 0 1 0 1 1 |

Partial product 0
```
         0 0 0 1 1 1 0
       + 0 0 1 1 1 0
```

Partial product 1
```
         0 0 1 0 1 0 1
       + 0 0 0 0 0 0
```

Partial product 2
```
         0 0 0 1 0 1 0
       + 0 0 1 1 1 0
```

Partial product 3
```
         0 0 1 0 0 1 1
       + 0 0 0 0 0 0
```

| Product P | (+154) | 0 0 1 0 0 1 1 0 1 0 |

(a) Positive multiplicand

| Multiplicand M | (−14) | 1 0 0 1 0 |
| Multiplier Q | (+11) | × 0 1 0 1 1 |

Partial product 0
```
         1 1 1 0 0 1 0
       + 1 1 0 0 1 0
```

Partial product 1
```
         1 1 0 1 0 1 1
       + 0 0 0 0 0 0
```

Partial product 2
```
         1 1 1 0 1 0 1
       + 1 1 0 0 1 0
```

Partial product 3
```
         1 1 0 1 1 0 0
       + 0 0 0 0 0 0
```

| Product P | (−154) | 1 1 0 1 1 0 0 1 1 0 |

(b) Negative multiplicand

Figure 5.34   Multiplication of signed numbers.

We have presented a relatively simple scheme for multiplication of signed numbers. There exist other techniques that are more efficient but also more complex. We will not pursue these techniques, but an interested reader may consult reference [1].

We have discussed circuits that perform addition, subtraction, and multiplication. Another arithmetic operation that is needed in computer systems is division. Circuits that perform division are more complex; we will present an example in Chapter 10. Various techniques for performing division are usually discussed in books on the subject of computer organization, and can be found in references [1, 2].

5.7 OTHER NUMBER REPRESENTATIONS

In the previous sections we dealt with binary integers represented in the positional number representation. Other types of numbers are also used in digital systems. In this section we will discuss briefly three other types: fixed-point, floating-point, and binary-coded decimal numbers.

5.7.1 FIXED-POINT NUMBERS

A *fixed-point* number consists of integer and fraction parts. It can be written in the positional number representation as

$$B = b_{n-1}b_{n-2} \cdots b_1 b_0 . b_{-1}b_{-2} \cdots b_{-k}$$

The value of the number is

$$V(B) = \sum_{i=-k}^{n-1} b_i \times 2^i$$

The position of the radix point is assumed to be fixed; hence the name fixed-point number. If the radix point is not shown, then it is assumed to be to the right of the least-significant digit, which means that the number is an integer.

Logic circuits that deal with fixed-point numbers are essentially the same as those used for integers. We will not discuss them separately.

5.7.2 FLOATING-POINT NUMBERS

Fixed-point numbers have a range that is limited by the significant digits used to represent the number. For example, if we use eight digits and a sign to represent decimal integers, then the range of values that can be represented is 0 to ± 99999999. If eight digits are used to represent a fraction, then the representable range is 0.00000001 to ± 0.99999999. In scientific applications it is often necessary to deal with numbers that are very large or very small. Instead of using the fixed-point representation, which would require many significant digits, it is better to use the floating-point representation in which numbers are represented by a *mantissa* comprising the significant digits and an *exponent* of the radix R. The format is

$$Mantissa \times R^{Exponent}$$

The numbers are often *normalized*, such that the radix point is placed to the right of the first nonzero digit, as in 5.234×10^{43} or 6.31×10^{-28}.

Binary floating-point representation has been standardized by the Institute of Electrical and Electronic Engineers (IEEE) [3]. Two sizes of formats are specified in this standard— a *single-precision* 32-bit format and a *double-precision* 64-bit format. Both formats are illustrated in Figure 5.35.

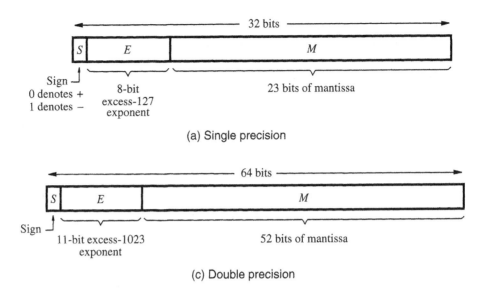

Figure 5.35   IEEE standard floating-point formats.

Single-Precision Floating-Point Format

Figure 5.35*a* depicts the single-precision format. The left-most bit is the sign bit—0 for positive and 1 for negative numbers. There is an 8-bit exponent field, E, and a 23-bit mantissa field, M. The exponent is with respect to the radix 2. Because it is necessary to be able to represent both very large and very small numbers, the exponent can be either positive or negative. Instead of simply using an 8-bit signed number as the exponent, which would allow exponent values in the range -128 to 127, the IEEE standard specifies the exponent in the *excess-127* format. In this format the value 127 is added to the value of the actual exponent so that

$$Exponent = E - 127$$

In this way E becomes a positive integer. This format is convenient for adding and subtracting floating-point numbers because the first step in these operations involves comparing the exponents to determine whether the mantissas must be appropriately shifted to add/subtract the significant bits. The range of E is 0 to 255. The extreme values of $E = 0$ and $E = 255$ are taken to denote the exact zero and infinity, respectively. Therefore, the normal range of the exponent is -126 to 127, which is represented by the values of E from 1 to 254.

The mantissa is represented using 23 bits. The IEEE standard calls for a normalized mantissa, which means that the most-significant bit is always equal to 1. Thus it is not necessary to include this bit explicitly in the mantissa field. Therefore, if M is the bit vector in the mantissa field, the actual value of the mantissa is $1.M$, which gives a 24-bit mantissa. Consequently, the floating-point format in Figure 5.35*a* represents the number

$$Value = \pm 1.M \times 2^{E-127}$$

The size of the mantissa field allows the representation of numbers that have the precision of about seven decimal digits. The exponent field range of 2^{-126} to 2^{127} corresponds to about $10^{\pm 38}$.

Double-Precision Floating-Point Format

Figure 5.35b shows the double-precision format, which uses 64 bits. Both the exponent and mantissa fields are larger. This format allows greater range and precision of numbers. The exponent field has 11 bits, and it specifies the exponent in the *excess-1023* format, where

$$Exponent = E - 1023$$

The range of E is 0 to 2047, but again the values $E = 0$ and $E = 2047$ are used to indicate the exact 0 and infinity, respectively. Thus the normal range of the exponent is -1022 to 1023, which is represented by the values of E from 1 to 2046.

The mantissa field has 52 bits. Since the mantissa is assumed to be normalized, its actual value is again 1.M. Therefore, the value of a floating-point number is

$$Value = \pm 1.M \times 2^{E-1023}$$

This format allows representation of numbers that have the precision of about 16 decimal digits and the range of approximately $10^{\pm 308}$.

Arithmetic operations using floating-point operands are significantly more complex than signed integer operations. Because this is a rather specialized domain, we will not elaborate on the design of logic circuits that can perform such operations. For a more complete discussion of floating-point operations, the reader may consult references [1, 2].

5.7.3 BINARY-CODED-DECIMAL REPRESENTATION

In digital systems it is possible to represent decimal numbers simply by encoding each digit in binary form. This is called the *binary-coded-decimal (BCD)* representation. Because there are 10 digits to encode, it is necessary to use four bits per digit. Each digit is encoded by the binary pattern that represents its unsigned value, as shown in Table 5.3. Note that only 10 of the 16 available patterns are used in BCD, which means that the remaining 6 patterns should not occur in logic circuits that operate on BCD operands; these patterns are usually treated as don't-care conditions in the design process. BCD representation was used in some early computers as well as in many handheld calculators. Its main virtue is that it provides a format that is convenient when numerical information is to be displayed on a simple digit-oriented display. Its drawbacks are complexity of circuits that perform arithmetic operations and the fact that six of the possible code patterns are wasted.

Even though the importance of BCD representation has diminished, it is still encountered. To give the reader an indication of the complexity of the required circuits, we will consider BCD addition in some detail.

BCD Addition

The addition of two BCD digits is complicated by the fact that the sum may exceed 9, in which case a correction will have to be made. Let $X = x_3x_2x_1x_0$ and $Y = y_3y_2y_1y_0$

Table 5.3	Binary-coded decimal digits.
Decimal digit	**BCD code**
0	0000
1	0001
2	0010
3	0011
4	0100
5	0101
6	0110
7	0111
8	1000
9	1001

represent the two BCD digits and let $S = s_3 s_2 s_1 s_0$ be the desired sum digit, $S = X + Y$. Obviously, if $X + Y \leq 9$, then the addition is the same as the addition of 2 four-bit unsigned binary numbers. But, if $X + Y > 9$, then the result requires two BCD digits. Moreover, the four-bit sum obtained from the four-bit adder may be incorrect.

There are two cases where some correction has to be made: when the sum is greater than 9 but no carry-out is generated using four bits, and when the sum is greater than 15 so that a carry-out is generated using four bits. Figure 5.36 illustrates these cases. In the first

$$
\begin{array}{rrr}
X & 0\,1\,1\,1 & 7 \\
+\ Y & +\ 0\,1\,0\,1 & +\ 5 \\
\hline
Z & 1\,1\,0\,0 & 12 \\
& +\ 0\,1\,1\,0 & \\
\hline
\text{carry} \longrightarrow & 1\,0\,0\,1\,0 & \\
& \underbrace{}_{S\,=\,2} &
\end{array}
$$

$$
\begin{array}{rrr}
X & 1\,0\,0\,0 & 8 \\
+\ Y & +\ 1\,0\,0\,1 & +\ 9 \\
\hline
Z & 1\,0\,0\,0\,1 & 17 \\
& +\ 0\,1\,1\,0 & \\
\hline
\text{carry} \longrightarrow & 1\,0\,1\,1\,1 & \\
& \underbrace{}_{S\,=\,7} &
\end{array}
$$

Figure 5.36 Addition of BCD digits.

case the four-bit addition yields $7 + 5 = 12 = Z$. To obtain a correct BCD result, we must generate $S = 2$ and a carry-out of 1. The necessary correction is apparent from the fact that the four-bit addition is a modulo-16 scheme, whereas decimal addition is a modulo-10 scheme. Therefore, a correct decimal digit can be generated by adding 6 to the result of four-bit addition whenever this result exceeds 9. Thus we can arrange the computation as follows

$$Z = X + Y$$

If $Z \leq 9$, then $S = Z$ and carry-out $= 0$

if $Z > 9$, then $X = Z + 6$ and carry-out $= 1$

The second example in Figure 5.36 shows what happens when $X + Y > 15$. In this case the four least-significant bits of Z represent the digit 1, which is wrong. But a carry is generated, which corresponds to the value 16, that must be taken into account. Again adding 6 to the intermediate sum Z provides the necessary correction.

Figure 5.37 gives a block diagram of a one-digit BCD adder that is based on this scheme. The block that detects whether $Z > 9$ produces an output signal, Adjust, which controls the multiplexer that provides the correction when needed. A second four-bit adder generates the corrected sum bits. If Adjust $= 0$, then $S = Z + 0$; if Adjust $= 1$, then $S = Z + 6$ and carry-out $= 1$.

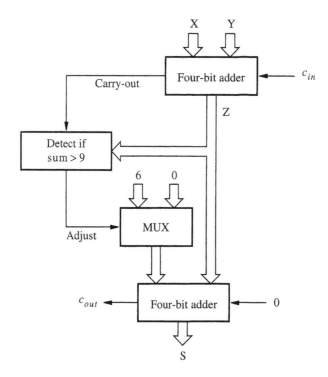

Figure 5.37   Block diagram for a one-digit BCD adder.

An implementation of this block diagram, using VHDL code, is shown in Figure 5.38. Inputs X and Y are defined as four-bit numbers. The sum output, S, is defined as a five-bit number, which allows for the carry-out to appear in bit S_4, while the sum is produced in bits S_{3-0}. The intermediate sum Z is also defined as a five-bit number. Recall from the discussion in section 5.5.4 that VHDL requires at least one of the operands of an arithmetic operation to have the same number of bits as in the result. This requirement explains why we have concatenated a 0 to input X in the expression $Z <= ('0' \& X) + Y$.

The statement

$$Adjust <= '1' \text{ WHEN } Z > 9 \text{ ELSE } '0' ;$$

uses a type of VHDL signal assignment statement that we have not seen before. It is called a *selected signal assignment* and is used to assign one of multiple values to a signal, based on some criterion. In this case the criterion is the condition $Z > 9$. If this condition is satisfied, the statement assigns 1 to Adjust; otherwise, it assigns 0 to Adjust. Other examples of the selected signal assignment are given in Chapter 6.

We should also note that we have included the *Adjust* signal in the VHDL code only to be consistent with Figure 5.37. We could just as easily have eliminated the *Adjust* signal and written the expression as

$$S <= Z \text{ WHEN } Z < 10 \text{ ELSE } Z + 6 ;$$

To verify the functional correctness of the code, we performed a functional simulation. An example of the obtained results is given in Figure 5.39.

If we wish to derive a circuit to implement the block diagram in Figure 5.37 by hand, instead of by using VHDL, then the following approach can be used. To define the *Adjust* function, we can observe that the intermediate sum will exceed 9 if the carry-out from the four-bit adder is equal to 1, or if $z_3 = 1$ and either z_2 or z_1 (or both) are equal to 1. Hence

```
LIBRARY ieee ;
USE ieee.std_logic_1164.all ;
USE ieee.std_logic_unsigned.all ;

ENTITY BCD IS
    PORT ( X, Y  : IN    STD_LOGIC_VECTOR(3 DOWNTO 0) ;
               S    : OUT  STD_LOGIC_VECTOR(4 DOWNTO 0) ) ;
END BCD ;

ARCHITECTURE Behavior OF BCD IS
    SIGNAL Z : STD_LOGIC_VECTOR(4 DOWNTO 0) ;
    SIGNAL Adjust : STD_LOGIC ;
BEGIN
    Z <= ('0' & X) + Y ;
    Adjust <= '1' WHEN Z > 9 ELSE '0' ;
    S <= Z WHEN (Adjust = '0') ELSE Z + 6 ;
END Behavior ;
```

Figure 5.38   VHDL code for a one-digit BCD adder.

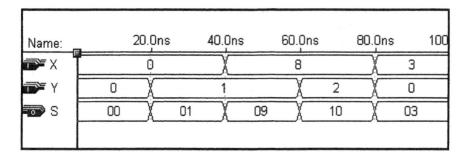

Figure 5.39   Functional simulation of the VHDL code in Figure 5.38.

the logic expression for this function is

$$\text{Adjust} = \text{Carry-out} + z_3(z_2 + z_1)$$

Instead of implementing another complete four-bit adder to perform the correction, we can use a simpler circuit because the addition of constant 6 does not require the full capability of a four-bit adder. Note that the least-significant bit of the sum, s_0, is not affected at all; hence $s_0 = z_0$. A two-bit adder may be used to develop bits s_2 and s_1. Bit s_3 is the same as z_3 if the carry-out from the two-bit adder is 0, and it is equal to $\bar{z}_3$ if this carry-out is equal to 1. A complete circuit that implements this scheme is shown in Figure 5.40. Using the one-digit BCD adder as a basic block, it is possible to build larger BCD adders in the same way as a binary full-adder is used to build larger ripple-carry binary adders.

Subtraction of BCD numbers can be handled with the radix-complement approach. Just as we use 2's complement representation to deal with negative binary numbers, we can use 10's complement representation to deal with decimal numbers. We leave the development of such a scheme as an exercise for the reader (see problem 5.19).

5.8   ASCII CHARACTER CODE

The most popular code for representing information in digital systems is used for both letters and numbers, as well as for some control characters. It is known as the *ASCII code*, which stands for the American Standard Code for Information Interchange. The code specified by this standard is presented in Table 5.4.

The ASCII code uses seven-bit patterns to denote 128 different characters. Ten of the characters are decimal digits 0 to 9. Note that the high-order bits have the same pattern, $b_6b_5b_4 = 011$, for all 10 digits. Each digit is identified by the low-order four bits, b_{3-0}, using the binary patterns for these digits. Capital and lowercase letters are encoded in a way that makes sorting of textual information easy. The codes for A to Z are in ascending numerical sequence, which means that the task of sorting letters (or words) is accomplished by a simple arithmetic comparison of the codes that represent the letters.

Characters that are either letters of the alphabet or numbers are referred to as *alphanumeric* characters. In addition to these characters, the ASCII code includes punctuation marks such as ! and ?; commonly used symbols such as & and %; and a collection of control characters. The control characters are those needed in computer systems to handle

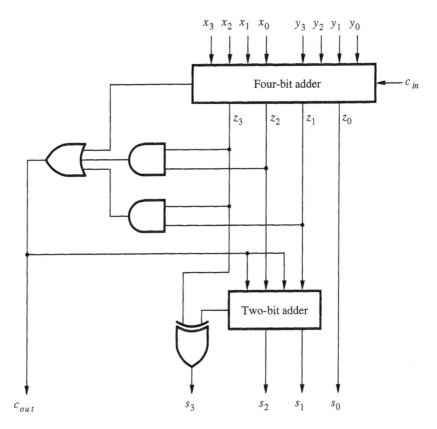

Figure 5.40   Circuit for a one-digit BCD adder.

and transfer data among various devices. For example, the carriage return character, which is abbreviated as CR in the table, indicates that the carriage, or cursor position, of an output device, say, printer or display, should return to the left-most column.

The ASCII code is used to encode information that is handled as text. It is not convenient for representation of numbers that are used as operands in arithmetic operations. For this purpose, it is best to convert ASCII-encoded numbers into a binary representation that we discussed before.

The ASCII standard uses seven bits to encode a character. In computer systems a more natural size is eight bits, or one byte. There are two common ways of fitting an ASCII-encoded character into a byte. One is to set the eighth bit, b_7, to 0. Another is to use this bit to indicate the parity of the other seven bits, which means showing whether the number of 1s in the seven-bit code is even or odd.

Parity

The concept of *parity* is widely used in digital systems for error-checking purposes. When digital information is transmitted from one point to another, perhaps by long wires, it is possible for some bits to become corrupted during the transmission process. For example,

Table 5.4   The seven-bit ASCII code.

Bit positions	Bit positions 654						
3210	000	001	010	011	100	101	110	111
0000	NUL	DLE	SPACE	0	@	P	`	p
0001	SOH	DC1	!	1	A	Q	a	q
0010	STX	DC2	"	2	B	R	b	r
0011	ETX	DC3	#	3	C	S	c	s
0100	EOT	DC4	$	4	D	T	d	t
0101	ENQ	NAK	%	5	E	U	e	u
0110	ACK	SYN	&	6	F	V	f	v
0111	BEL	ETB	'	7	G	W	g	w
1000	BS	CAN	(	8	H	X	h	x
1001	HT	EM	)	9	I	Y	i	y
1010	LF	SUB	*	:	J	Z	j	z
1011	VT	ESC	+	;	K	[	k	{
1100	FF	FS	,	<	L	\	l	|
1101	CR	GS	-	=	M	]	m	}
1110	SO	RS	.	>	N	^	n	~
1111	SI	US	/	?	O	—	o	DEL

NUL	Null/Idle	SI	Shift in
SOH	Start of header	DLE	Data link escape
STX	Start of text	DC1-DC4	Device control
ETX	End of text	NAK	Negative acknowledgement
EOT	End of transmitted	SYN	Synchronous idle
ENQ	Enquiry	ETB	End of transmitted block
ACQ	Acknowledgement	CAN	Cancel (error in data)
BEL	Audible signal	EM	End of medium
BS	Back space	SUB	Special sequence
HT	Horizontal tab	ESC	Escape
LF	Line feed	FS	File separator
VT	Vertical tab	GS	Group separator
FF	Form feed	RS	Record separator
CR	Carriage return	US	Unit separator
SO	Shift out	DEL	Delete/Idle

Bit positions of code format = | 6 | 5 | 4 | 3 | 2 | 1 | 0 |

the sender may transmit a bit whose value is equal to 1, but the receiver observes a bit whose value is 0. Suppose that a data item consists of n bits. A simple error-checking mechanism can be implemented by including an extra bit, p, which indicates the parity of the n-bit item. Two kinds of parity can be used. For *even parity* the p bit is given the value such that the total number of 1s in the $n + 1$ transmitted bits (comprising the n-bit data and the parity bit

p) is even. For *odd parity* the p bit is given the value that makes the total number of 1s odd. The sender generates the p bit based on the n-bit data item that is to be transmitted. The receiver checks whether the parity of the received item is correct.

Parity generating and checking circuits can be realized with XOR gates. For example, for a four-bit data item consisting of bits $x_3x_2x_1x_0$, the even parity bit can be generated as

$$p = x_3 \oplus x_2 \oplus x_1 \oplus x_0$$

At the receiving end the checking is done using

$$c = p \oplus x_3 \oplus x_2 \oplus x_1 \oplus x_0$$

If $c = 0$, then the received item shows the correct parity. If $c = 1$, then an error has occurred. Note that observing $c = 0$ is not a guarantee that the received item is correct. If two or any even number of bits have their values inverted during the transmission, the parity of the data item will not be changed; hence the error will not be detected. But if an odd number of bits are corrupted, then the error will be detected.

The attractiveness of parity checking lies in its simplicity. There exist other more sophisticated schemes that provide more reliable error-checking mechanisms [4]. We will discuss parity circuits again in section 9.3.

PROBLEMS

5.1   Determine the decimal values of the following unsigned numbers:
(a) $(0111011110)_2$
(b) $(1011100111)_2$
(c) $(3751)_8$
(d) $(A25F)_{16}$
(e) $(F0F0)_{16}$

5.2   Determine the decimal values of the following 1's complement numbers:
(a) 0111011110
(b) 1011100111
(c) 1111111110

5.3   Determine the decimal values of the following 2's complement numbers:
(a) 0111011110
(b) 1011100111
(c) 1111111110

5.4   Convert the decimal numbers 73, 1906, −95, and −1630 into signed 12-bit numbers in the following representations:
(a) Sign and magnitude
(b) 1's complement
(c) 2's complement

5.5   Perform the following operations involving eight-bit 2's complement numbers and indicate whether arithmetic overflow occurs. Check your answers by converting to decimal sign-and-magnitude representation.

$$\begin{array}{r} 00110110 \\ +01000101 \\ \hline 00110110 \\ -00101011 \end{array} \qquad \begin{array}{r} 01110101 \\ +11011110 \\ \hline 01110101 \\ -11010110 \end{array} \qquad \begin{array}{r} 11011111 \\ +10111000 \\ \hline 11010011 \\ -11101100 \end{array}$$

5.6 Prove that the XOR operation is associative, which means that $x_i \oplus (y_i \oplus z_i) = (x_i \oplus y_i) \oplus z_i$.

5.7 Show that the circuit in Figure 5.5 implements the full-adder specified in Figure 5.4a.

5.8 Prove the validity of the simple rule for finding the 2's complement of a number, which was presented in section 5.3. Recall that the rule states that scanning a number from right to left, all 0s and the first 1 are copied; then all remaining bits are complemented.

5.9 Prove the validity of the expression Overflow = $c_n \oplus c_{n-1}$ for addition of n-bit signed numbers.

5.10 In section 5.5.4 we stated that a carry-out signal, c_k, from bit position $k - 1$ of an adder circuit can be generated as $c_k = x_k \oplus y_k \oplus s_k$, where x_k and y_k are inputs and s_k is the sum bit. Verify the correctness of this statement.

5.11 Consider the circuit in Figure P5.1. Can this circuit be used as one stage in a carry-ripple adder? Discuss the pros and cons.

5.12 Determine the number of gates needed to implement an n-bit carry-lookahead adder, assuming no fan-in constraints. Use AND, OR, and XOR gates with any number of inputs.

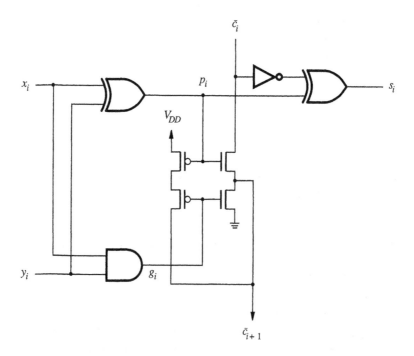

Figure P5.1   Circuit for problem 5.11.

5.13   Determine the number of gates needed to implement an eight-bit carry-lookahead adder assuming that the maximum fan-in for the gates is four.

5.14   In Figure 5.18 we presented the structure of a hierarchical carry-lookahead adder. Show the complete circuit for a four-bit version of this adder, built using 2 two-bit blocks.

5.15   What is the critical delay path in the multiplier in Figure 5.33? What is the delay along this path in terms of the number of gates?

5.16   (a) Write a VHDL entity to describe the circuit block in Figure 5.33*b*. Use MAX+plusII to synthesize a circuit from the code and verify its functional correctness.
(b) Write a VHDL entity to describe the circuit block in Figure 5.33*c*. Use MAX+plusII to synthesize a circuit from the code and verify its functional correctness.
(c) Write a VHDL entity to describe the 4×4 multiplier shown in Figure 5.33*a*. Your code should be hierarchical and should use the subcircuits designed in parts (*a*) and (*b*). Synthesize a circuit from the code and verify its functional correctness.

5.17   Consider the VHDL code in Figure P5.2. Given the relationship between the signals Input and Output, what is the functionality of the circuit described by the code? Comment on whether or not this code represents a good style to use for the functionality that it represents.

```
LIBRARY ieee ;
USE ieee.std_logic_1164.all ;

ENTITY problem IS
      PORT ( Input   : IN    STD_LOGIC_VECTOR(3 DOWNTO 0) ;
             Output  : OUT  STD_LOGIC_VECTOR(3 DOWNTO 0) ) ;
END problem ;

ARCHITECTURE LogicFunc OF problem IS
BEGIN
      WITH Input SELECT
          Output <= "0001" WHEN "0101",
                    "0010" WHEN "0110",
                    "0011" WHEN "0111",
                    "0010" WHEN "1001",
                    "0100" WHEN "1010",
                    "0110" WHEN "1011",
                    "0011" WHEN "1101",
                    "0110" WHEN "1110",
                    "1001" WHEN "1111",
                    "0000" WHEN OTHERS ;
END LogicFunc ;
```

Figure P5.2   The VHDL code for problem 5.17.

5.18 Design a circuit that generates the 9's complement of a BCD digit. Note that the 9's complement of d is $9 - d$.

5.19 Derive a scheme for performing subtraction using BCD operands. Show a block diagram for the subtractor circuit.
Hint: Subtraction can be performed easily if the operands are in the 10's complement (radix complement) representation. In this representation the sign digit is 0 for a positive number and 9 for a negative number.

5.20 Write complete VHDL code for the circuit that you derived in problem 5.19.

5.21 Suppose that we want to determine how many of the bits in a three-bit unsigned number are equal to 1. Design the simplest circuit that can accomplish this task.

5.22 Repeat problem 5.21 for a six-bit unsigned number.

5.23 Repeat problem 5.21 for an eight-bit unsigned number.

5.24 Show a graphical interpretation of three-digit decimal numbers, similar to Figure 5.12. The left-most digit is 0 for positive numbers and 9 for negative numbers. Verify the validity of your answer by trying a few examples of addition and subtraction.

5.25 In a ternary number system there are three digits: 0, 1, and 2. Figure P5.3 defines a ternary half-adder. Design a circuit that implements this half-adder using binary-encoded signals, such that two bits are used for each ternary digit. Let $A = a_1 a_0$, $B = b_1 b_0$, and $Sum = s_1 s_0$; note that $Carry$ is just a binary signal. Use the following encoding: $00 = (0)_3$, $01 = (1)_3$, and $10 = (2)_3$. Minimize the cost of the circuit.

A B	Carry	Sum
0 0	0	0
0 1	0	1
0 2	0	2
1 0	0	1
1 1	0	2
1 2	1	0
2 0	0	2
2 1	1	0
2 2	1	1

Figure P5.3   Ternary half-adder.

5.26   Design a ternary full-adder circuit, using the approach described in problem 5.25.

5.27   Consider the subtractions $26 - 27 = 99$ and $18 - 34 = 84$. Using the concepts presented in section 5.3.4, explain how these answers (99 and 84) can be interpreted as the correct signed results of these subtractions.

REFERENCES

1.   V. C. Hamacher, Z. G. Vranesic and S. G. Zaky, *Computer Organization*, 4th ed. (McGraw-Hill: New York, 1996).

2.   D. A. Patterson and J. L. Hennessy, *Computer Organization and Design—The Hardware/Software Interface*, 2nd ed. (Morgan Kaufmann: San Francisco, CA, 1998).

3.   Institute of Electrical and Electronic Engineers (IEEE), "A Proposed Standard for Floating-Point Arithmetic," *Computer* 14, no. 3 (March 1981), pp. 51–62.

4.   W. W. Peterson and E. J. Weldon Jr., *Error-Correcting Codes*, 2nd ed. (MIT Press: Boston, MA, 1972).

6

COMBINATIONAL-CIRCUIT BUILDING BLOCKS

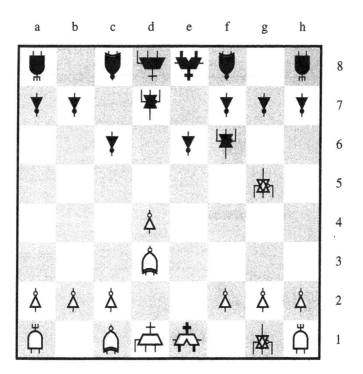

6. Bf1–d3, e7–e6

Previous chapters have introduced the basic techniques for design of logic circuits. In practice, a few types of logic circuits are often used as building blocks in larger designs. This chapter discusses a number of these blocks and gives examples of their use. The chapter also includes a major section on VHDL, which describes several key features of the language.

6.1 MULTIPLEXERS

Multiplexers were introduced briefly in Chapters 2 and 3. A multiplexer circuit has a number of data inputs, one or more select inputs, and one output. It passes the signal value on one of the data inputs to the output. The data input is selected by the values of the select inputs. Figure 6.1 shows a 2-to-1 multiplexer. Part (a) gives the symbol commonly used. The *select* input, s, chooses as the output of the multiplexer either input w_0 or w_1. The multiplexer's functionality can be described in the form of a truth table as shown in part (b) of the figure. Part (c) gives a sum-of-products implementation of the 2-to-1 multiplexer, and part (d) illustrates how it can be constructed with transmission gates.

Figure 6.2a depicts a larger multiplexer with four data inputs, $w_0, \ldots, w_3$, and two select inputs, s_1 and s_0. As shown in the truth table in part (b) of the figure, the two-bit number represented by $s_1 s_0$ selects one of the data inputs as the output of the multiplexer. A sum-of-products implementation of the 4-to-1 multiplexer appears in Figure 6.2c. It

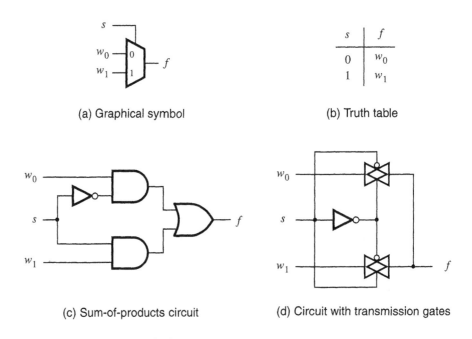

(a) Graphical symbol

(b) Truth table

(c) Sum-of-products circuit

(d) Circuit with transmission gates

Figure 6.1   A 2-to-1 multiplexer.

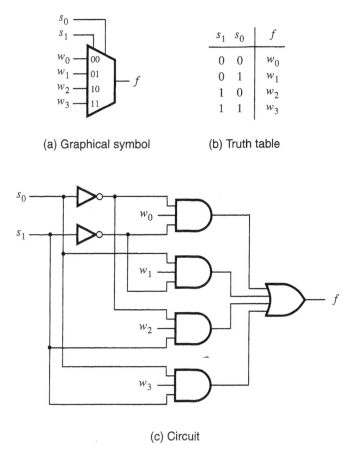

s_1	s_0	f
0	0	w_0
0	1	w_1
1	0	w_2
1	1	w_3

(a) Graphical symbol   (b) Truth table

(c) Circuit

Figure 6.2   A 4-to-1 multiplexer.

realizes the multiplexer function

$$f = \bar{s}_1\bar{s}_0 w_0 + \bar{s}_1 s_0 w_1 + s_1 \bar{s}_0 w_2 + s_1 s_0 w_3$$

It is possible to build larger multiplexers using the same approach. Usually, the number of data inputs, n, is an integer power of two. A multiplexer that has n data inputs, $w_0, \ldots, w_{n-1}$, requires $\lceil \log_2 n \rceil$ select inputs. Larger multiplexers can also be constructed from smaller multiplexers. For example, the 4-to-1 multiplexer can be built using three 2-to-1 multiplexers as illustrated in Figure 6.3. If the 4-to-1 multiplexer is implemented using transmission gates, then the structure in this figure is always used. Figure 6.4 shows how a 16-to-1 multiplexer is constructed with five 4-to-1 multiplexers.

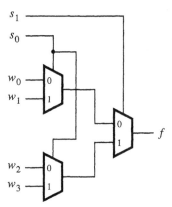

Figure 6.3   Using 2-to-1 multiplexers to build a 4-to-1 multiplexer.

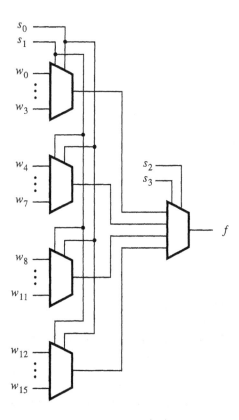

Figure 6.4   A 16-to-1 multiplexer.

Figure 6.5 shows a circuit that has two inputs, x_1 and x_2, and two outputs, y_1 and y_2. As indicated by the blue lines, the function of the circuit is to allow either of its inputs to be connected to either of its outputs, under the control of another input, s. A circuit that has n inputs and k outputs, whose sole function is to provide a capability to connect any input to any output, is usually referred to as an $n \times k$ crossbar switch. Crossbars of various sizes can be created, with different numbers of inputs and outputs. When there are two inputs and two outputs, it is called a 2×2 crossbar.

Example 6.1

Figure 6.5b shows how the 2×2 crossbar can be implemented using 2-to-1 multiplexers. The multiplexer select inputs are controlled by the signal s. If $s = 0$, the crossbar connects x_1 to y_1 and x_2 to y_2, while if $s = 1$, the crossbar connects x_1 to y_2 and x_2 to y_1. Crossbar switches are useful in many practical applications in which it is necessary to be able to connect one set of wires to another set of wires, where the connection pattern changes from time to time.

We introduced field-programmable gate array (FPGA) chips in section 3.6.5. Figure 3.39 depicts a small FPGA that is programmed to implement a particular circuit. The logic blocks in the FPGA have two inputs, and there are four tracks in each routing channel. Each of the programmable switches that connects a logic block input or output to an interconnection wire is shown as an X. A small part of Figure 3.39 is reproduced in Figure 6.6a. For clarity, the figure shows only a single logic block and the interconnection wires and switches associated with its input terminals.

Example 6.2

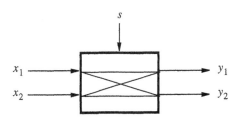

(a) A 2x2 crossbar switch

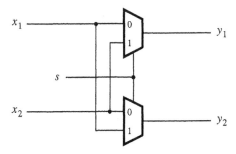

(b) Implementation using multiplexers

Figure 6.5   A practical application of multiplexers.

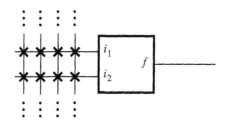

(a) Part of the FPGA in Figure 3.39

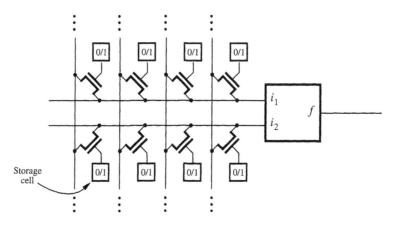

(b) Implementation using pass transistors

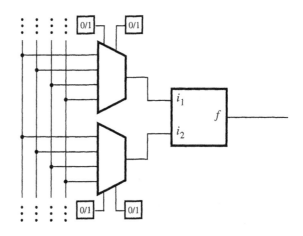

(c) Implementation using multiplexers

Figure 6.6   Implementing programmable switches in an FPGA.

One way in which the programmable switches can be implemented is illustrated in Figure 6.6b. Each X in part (a) of the figure is realized using an NMOS transistor controlled by a storage cell. This type of programmable switch was also shown in Figure 3.68. We described storage cells briefly in section 3.6.5 and will discuss them in more detail in section 10.1. Each cell stores a single logic value, either 0 or 1, and provides this value as the output of the cell. Each storage cell is built by using several transistors. Thus the eight cells shown in the figure use a significant amount of chip area.

The number of storage cells needed can be reduced by using multiplexers, as shown in Figure 6.6c. Each logic block input is fed by a 4-to-1 multiplexer, with the select inputs controlled by storage cells. This approach requires only four storage cells, instead of eight. In commercial FPGAs the multiplexer-based approach is usually adopted.

6.1.1 SYNTHESIS OF LOGIC FUNCTIONS USING MULTIPLEXERS

Multiplexers are useful in many practical applications, such as those described above. They can also be used in a more general way to synthesize logic functions. Consider the example in Figure 6.7a. The truth table defines the function $f = w_1 \oplus w_2$. This function can be implemented by a 4-to-1 multiplexer in which the values of f in each row of the truth table are connected as constants to the multiplexer data inputs. The multiplexer select inputs are driven by w_1 and w_2. Thus for each valuation of w_1w_2, the output f is equal to the function value in the corresponding row of the truth table.

The above implementation is straightforward, but it is not very efficient. A better implementation can be derived by manipulating the truth table as indicated in Figure 6.7b, which allows f to be implemented by a single 2-to-1 multiplexer. One of the input signals, w_1 in this example, is chosen as the select input of the 2-to-1 multiplexer. The truth table is redrawn to indicate the value of f for each value of w_1. When $w_1 = 0, f$ has the same value as input w_2, and when $w_1 = 1, f$ has the value of $\overline{w}_2$. The circuit that implements this truth table is given in Figure 6.7c. This procedure can be applied to synthesize a circuit that implements any logic function.

Figure 6.8a gives the truth table for the three-input majority function, and it shows how the truth table can be modified to implement the function using a 4-to-1 multiplexer. Any two of the three inputs may be chosen as the multiplexer select inputs. We have chosen w_1 and w_2 for this purpose, resulting in the circuit in Figure 6.8b.

Example 6.3

Figure 6.9a indicates how the function $f = w_1 \oplus w_2 \oplus w_3$ can be implemented using 2-to-1 multiplexers. When $w_1 = 0, f$ is equal to the XOR of w_2 and w_3, and when $w_1 = 1, f$ is the XNOR of w_2 and w_3. The left multiplexer in the circuit produces $w_2 \oplus w_3$, using the result from Figure 6.7, and the right multiplexer uses the value of w_1 to select either $w_2 \oplus w_3$ or its

Example 6.4

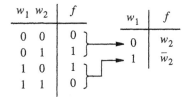

w_1	w_2	f
0	0	0
0	1	1
1	0	1
1	1	0

(a) Implementation using a 4-to-1 multiplexer

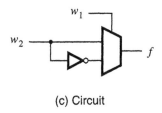

w_1	w_2	f
0	0	0
0	1	1
1	0	1
1	1	0

w_1	f
0	w_2
1	$\overline{w}_2$

(b) Modified truth table

(c) Circuit

Figure 6.7   Synthesis of a logic function using mutiplexers.

complement. Note that we could have derived this circuit directly by writing the function as $f = (w_2 \oplus w_3) \oplus w_1$.

Figure 6.10 gives an implementation of the three-input XOR function using a 4-to-1 multiplexer. Choosing w_1 and w_2 for the select inputs results in the circuit shown.

6.1.2 MULTIPLEXER SYNTHESIS USING SHANNON'S EXPANSION

Figures 6.8 through 6.10 illustrate how truth tables can be interpreted to implement logic functions using multiplexers. In each case the inputs to the multiplexers are the constants 0 and 1, or some variable or its complement. Besides using such simple inputs, it is possible to connect more complex circuits as inputs to a multiplexer, allowing functions to be synthesized using a combination of multiplexers and other logic gates. Suppose that we

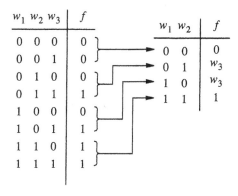

(a) Modified truth table

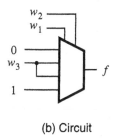

(b) Circuit

Figure 6.8 Implementation of the three-input majority function using a 4-to-1 multiplexer.

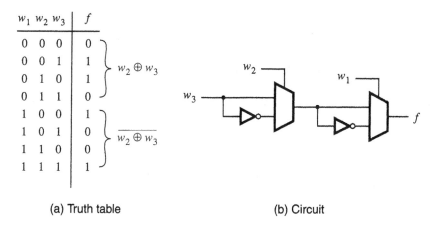

(a) Truth table   (b) Circuit

Figure 6.9 Three-input XOR implemented with 2-to-1 multiplexers.

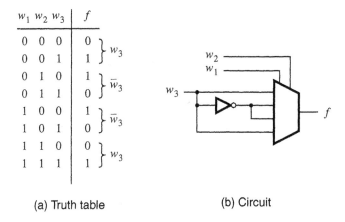

w_1 w_2 w_3	f	
0 0 0	0	} w_3
0 0 1	1	
0 1 0	1	} $\overline{w}_3$
0 1 1	0	
1 0 0	1	} $\overline{w}_3$
1 0 1	0	
1 1 0	0	} w_3
1 1 1	1	

(a) Truth table   (b) Circuit

Figure 6.10   Three-input XOR implemented with a 4-to-1 multiplexer.

want to implement the three-input majority function in Figure 6.8 using a 2-to-1 multiplexer in this way. Figure 6.11 shows an intuitive way of realizing this function. The truth table can be modified as shown on the right. If $w_1 = 0$, then $f = w_2 w_3$, and if $w_1 = 1$, then $f = w_2 + w_3$. Using w_1 as the select input for a 2-to-1 multiplexer leads to the circuit in Figure 6.11b.

This implementation can be derived using algebraic manipulation as follows. The function in Figure 6.11a is expressed in sum-of-products form as

$$f = \overline{w}_1 w_2 w_3 + w_1 \overline{w}_2 w_3 + w_1 w_2 \overline{w}_3 + w_1 w_2 w_3$$

It can be manipulated into

$$f = \overline{w}_1 (w_2 w_3) + w_1 (\overline{w}_2 w_3 + w_2 \overline{w}_3 + w_2 w_3)$$
$$= \overline{w}_1 (w_2 w_3) + w_1 (w_2 + w_3)$$

which corresponds to the circuit in Figure 6.11b.

Multiplexer implementations of logic functions require that a given function be decomposed in terms of the variables that are used as the select inputs. This can be accomplished by means of a theorem proposed by Claude Shannon [1].

Shannon's Expansion Theorem   Any Boolean function $f(w_1, \ldots, w_n)$ can be written in the form

$$f(w_1, w_2, \ldots, w_n) = \overline{w}_1 \cdot f(0, w_2, \ldots, w_n) + w_1 \cdot f(1, w_2, \ldots, w_n)$$

This expansion can be done in terms of any of the n variables. We will leave the proof of the theorem as an exercise for the reader (see problem 6.9).

To illustrate its use, we can apply the theorem to the three-input majority function, which can be written as

$$f(w_1, w_2, w_3) = w_1 w_2 + w_1 w_3 + w_2 w_3$$

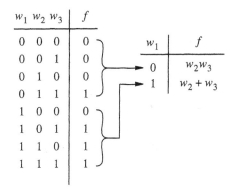

w_1 w_2 w_3	f
0 0 0	0
0 0 1	0
0 1 0	0
0 1 1	1
1 0 0	0
1 0 1	1
1 1 0	1
1 1 1	1

w_1	f
0	$w_2 w_3$
1	$w_2 + w_3$

(a) Truth table

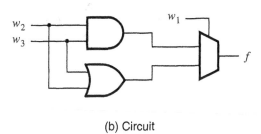

(b) Circuit

Figure 6.11 The three-input majority function implemented using a 2-to-1 multiplexer.

Expanding this function in terms of w_1 gives

$$f = \overline{w}_1(w_2 w_3) + w_1(w_2 + w_3)$$

which is the expression that we derived above.

For the three-input XOR function, we have

$$f = w_1 \oplus w_2 \oplus w_3$$
$$= \overline{w}_1 \cdot (w_2 \oplus w_3) + w_1 \cdot (\overline{w_2 \oplus w_3})$$

which gives the circuit in Figure 6.9b.

In Shannon's expansion the term $f(0, w_2, \ldots, w_n)$ is called the *cofactor* of f with respect to $\overline{w}_1$; it is denoted in shorthand notation as $f_{\overline{w}_1}$. Similarly, the term $f(1, w_2, \ldots, w_n)$ is called the cofactor of f with respect to w_1, written f_{w_1}. Hence we can write

$$f = \overline{w}_1 f_{\overline{w}_1} + w_1 f_{w_1}$$

In general, if the expansion is done with respect to variable w_i, then f_{w_i} denotes $f(w_1, \ldots, w_{i-1}, 1, w_{i+1}, \ldots, w_n)$ and

$$f(w_1, \ldots, w_n) = \overline{w_i} f_{\overline{w_i}} + w_i f_{w_i}$$

The complexity of the logic expression may vary, depending on which variable, w_i, is used, as illustrated in Example 6.5.

Example 6.5   For the function $f = \overline{w}_1 w_3 + w_2 \overline{w}_3$, decomposition using w_1 gives

$$f = \overline{w}_1 f_{\overline{w}_1} + w_1 f_{w_1}$$
$$= \overline{w}_1 (w_3 + w_2) + w_1 (w_2 \overline{w}_3)$$

Using w_2 instead of w_1 produces

$$f = \overline{w}_2 f_{\overline{w}_2} + w_2 f_{w_2}$$
$$= \overline{w}_2 (\overline{w}_1 w_3) + w_2 (\overline{w}_1 + \overline{w}_3)$$

Finally, using w_3 gives

$$f = \overline{w}_3 f_{\overline{w}_3} + w_3 f_{w_3}$$
$$= \overline{w}_3 (w_2) + w_3 (\overline{w}_1)$$

The results generated using w_1 and w_2 have the same cost, but the expression produced using w_3 has a lower cost. In practice, the CAD tools that perform decompositions of this type try a number of alternatives and choose the one that produces the best result.

Shannon's expansion can be done in terms of more than one variable. For example, expanding a function in terms of w_1 and w_2 gives

$$f(w_1, \ldots, w_n) = \overline{w}_1 \overline{w}_2 \cdot f(0, 0, w_3, \ldots, w_n) + \overline{w}_1 w_2 \cdot f(0, 1, w_3, \ldots, w_n) +$$
$$w_1 \overline{w}_2 \cdot f(1, 0, w_3, \ldots, w_n) + w_1 w_2 \cdot f(1, 1, w_3, \ldots, w_n)$$

This expansion gives a form that can be implemented using a 4-to-1 multiplexer. If Shannon's expansion is done in terms of all n variables, then the result is the canonical sum-of-products form, which was defined in section 2.6.1.

Example 6.6   Assume that we wish to implement the function

$$f = \overline{w}_1 \overline{w}_3 + w_1 w_2 + w_1 w_3$$

using a 2-to-1 multiplexer and any other necessary gates. Shannon's expansion using w_1 gives

$$f = \overline{w}_1 f_{\overline{w}_1} + w_1 f_{w_1}$$
$$= \overline{w}_1 (\overline{w}_3) + w_1 (w_2 + w_3)$$

The corresponding circuit is shown in Figure 6.12a. Assume now that we wish to use a 4-to-1 multiplexer instead. Further decomposition using w_2 gives

$$f = \overline{w}_1 \overline{w}_2 f_{\overline{w}_1 \overline{w}_2} + \overline{w}_1 w_2 f_{\overline{w}_1 w_2} + w_1 \overline{w}_2 f_{w_1 \overline{w}_2} + w_1 w_2 f_{w_1 w_2}$$
$$= \overline{w}_1 \overline{w}_2 (\overline{w}_3) + \overline{w}_1 w_2 (\overline{w}_3) + w_1 \overline{w}_2 (w_3) + w_1 w_2 (1)$$

The circuit is shown in Figure 6.12b.

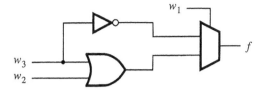

(a) Using a 2-to-1 multiplexer

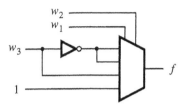

(b) Using a 4-to-1 multiplexer

Figure 6.12   The circuits synthesized in Example 6.6.

C onsider the three-input majority function

Example 6.7

$$f = w_1w_2 + w_1w_3 + w_2w_3$$

We wish to implement this function using only 2-to-1 multiplexers. Shannon's expansion using w_1 yields

$$f = \overline{w}_1(w_2w_3) + w_1(w_2 + w_3 + w_2w_3)$$
$$= \overline{w}_1(w_2w_3) + w_1(w_2 + w_3)$$

Let $g = w_2w_3$ and $h = w_2 + w_3$. Expansion of both g and h using w_2 gives

$$g = \overline{w}_2(0) + w_2(w_3)$$
$$h = \overline{w}_2(w_3) + w_2(1)$$

The corresponding circuit is shown in Figure 6.13. It is equivalent to the 4-to-1 multiplexer circuit derived using a truth table in Figure 6.8.

I n section 3.6.5 we said that most FPGAs use lookup tables for their logic blocks. Assume **Example 6.8** that an FPGA exists in which each logic block is a three-input lookup table (3-LUT). Because it stores a truth table, a 3-LUT can realize any logic function of three variables. Using Shannon's expansion, any four-variable function can be realized with at most three 3-LUTs. Consider the function

$$f = \overline{w}_2w_3 + \overline{w}_1w_2\overline{w}_3 + w_2\overline{w}_3w_4 + w_1\overline{w}_2\overline{w}_4$$

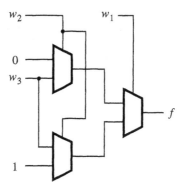

Figure 6.13   The circuit synthesized in Example 6.7.

Expansion in terms of w_1 produces

$$f = \overline{w}_1 f_{\overline{w}_1} + w_1 f_{w_1}$$
$$= \overline{w}_1(\overline{w}_2 w_3 + w_2 \overline{w}_3 + w_2 \overline{w}_3 w_4) + w_1(\overline{w}_2 w_3 + w_2 \overline{w}_3 w_4 + \overline{w}_2 \overline{w}_4)$$
$$= \overline{w}_1(\overline{w}_2 w_3 + w_2 \overline{w}_3) + w_1(\overline{w}_2 w_3 + w_2 \overline{w}_3 w_4 + \overline{w}_2 \overline{w}_4)$$

A circuit with three 3-LUTs that implements this expression is shown in Figure 6.14a. Decomposition of the function using w_2, instead of w_1, gives

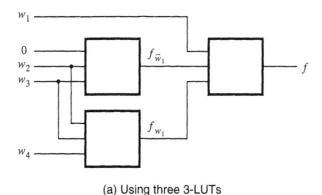

(a) Using three 3-LUTs

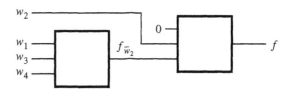

(b) Using two 3-LUTs

Figure 6.14   Circuits synthesized in Example 6.8.

$$f = \overline{w}_2 f_{\overline{w}_2} + w_2 f_{w_2}$$
$$= \overline{w}_2 (w_3 + w_1 \overline{w}_4) + w_2 (\overline{w}_1 \overline{w}_3 + \overline{w}_3 w_4)$$

Observe that $\overline{f}_{\overline{w}_2} = f_{w_2}$; hence only two 3-LUTs are needed, as illustrated in Figure 6.14b. The LUT on the right implements the two-variable function $\overline{w}_2 f_{\overline{w}_2} + w_2 \overline{f}_{\overline{w}_2}$.

Since it is possible to implement any logic function using multiplexers, general-purpose chips exist that contain multiplexers as their basic logic resources. Both Actel Corporation [2] and QuickLogic Corporation [3] offer FPGAs in which the logic block comprises an arrangement of multiplexers. Texas Instruments offers gate array chips that have multiplexer-based logic blocks [4].

6.2 DECODERS

Decoder circuits are used to decode encoded information. A binary decoder, depicted in Figure 6.15, is a logic circuit with n inputs and 2^n outputs. Only one output is asserted at a time, and each output corresponds to one valuation of the inputs. The decoder also has an enable input, En, that is used to disable the outputs; if $En = 0$, then none of the decoder outputs is asserted. If $En = 1$, the valuation of $w_{n-1} \ldots w_1 w_0$ determines which of the outputs is asserted. An n-bit binary code in which exactly one of the bits is set to 1 at a time is referred to as *one-hot encoded*, meaning that the single bit that is set to 1 is deemed to be "hot." The outputs of a binary decoder are one-hot encoded.

A 2-to-4 decoder is given in Figure 6.16. The two data inputs are w_1 and w_0. They represent a two-bit number that causes the decoder to assert one of the outputs $y_0, \ldots, y_3$. Although a decoder can be designed to have either active-high or active-low outputs, in Figure 6.16 active-high outputs are assumed. Setting the inputs $w_1 w_0$ to 00, 01, 10, or 11 causes the output y_0, y_1, y_2, or y_3 to be set to 1, respectively. A graphical symbol for the decoder is given in part (b) of the figure, and a logic circuit is shown in part (c).

Larger decoders can be built using the sum-of-products structure in Figure 6.16c, or else they can be constructed from smaller decoders. Figure 6.17 shows how a 3-to-8 decoder is built with two 2-to-4 decoders. The w_2 input drives the enable inputs of the two decoders. The top decoder is enabled if $w_2 = 0$, and the bottom decoder is enabled if $w_2 = 1$. This concept can be applied for decoders of any size. Figure 6.18 shows how five 2-to-4 decoders can be used to construct a 4-to-16 decoder. Because of its treelike structure, this type of circuit is often referred to as a *decoder tree*.

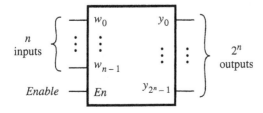

Figure 6.15   An n-to-2^n binary decoder.

En	w_1	w_0	y_0	y_1	y_2	y_3
1	0	0	1	0	0	0
1	0	1	0	1	0	0
1	1	0	0	0	1	0
1	1	1	0	0	0	1
0	x	x	0	0	0	0

(a) Truth table

(b) Graphical symbol

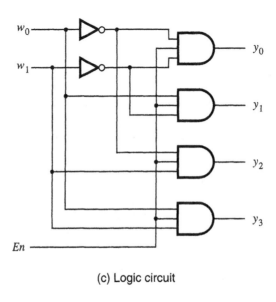

(c) Logic circuit

Figure 6.16   A 2-to-4 decoder.

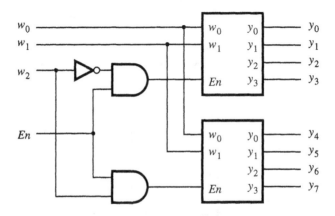

Figure 6.17   A 3-to-8 decoder using two 2-to-4 decoders.

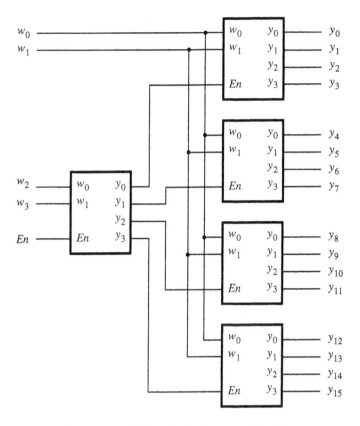

Figure 6.18   A 4-to-16 decoder built using a decoder tree.

Decoders are useful for many practical purposes. In Figure 6.2c we showed the sum-of-products implementation of the 4-to-1 multiplexer, which requires AND gates to distinguish the four different valuations of the select inputs s_1 and s_0. Since a decoder evaluates the values on its inputs, it can be used to build a multiplexer as illustrated in Figure 6.19. The enable input of the decoder is not needed in this case, and it is set to 1. The four outputs of the decoder represent the four valuations of the select inputs.   **Example 6.9**

In Figure 3.59 we showed how a 2-to-1 multiplexer can be constructed using two tri-state buffers. This concept can be applied to any size of multiplexer, with the addition of a decoder. An example is shown in Figure 6.20. The decoder enables one of the tri-state buffers for each valuation of the select lines, and that tri-state buffer drives the output, f, with the selected data input. We have now seen that multiplexers can be implemented in various ways. The choice of whether to employ the sum-of-products form, transmission gates, or tri-state buffers depends on the resources available in the chip being used.   **Example 6.10**

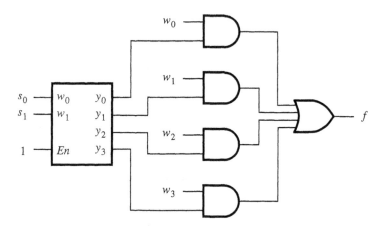

Figure 6.19   A 4-to-1 multiplexer built using a decoder.

For instance, most FPGAs that use lookup tables for their logic blocks do not contain tri-state buffers. Hence multiplexers must be implemented in the sum-of-products form using the lookup tables (see problem 6.15).

6.2.1 DEMULTIPLEXERS

We showed in section 6.1 that a multiplexer has one output, n data inputs, and $\lceil \log_2 n \rceil$ select inputs. The purpose of the multiplexer circuit is to *multiplex* the n data inputs onto the single data output under control of the select inputs. A circuit that performs the opposite function, namely, placing the value of a single data input onto multiple data outputs, is

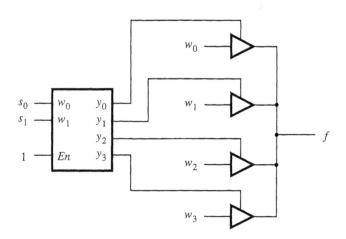

Figure 6.20   A 4-to-1 multiplexer built using a decoder and tri-state buffers.

called a *demultiplexer*. The demultiplexer can be implemented using a decoder circuit. For example, the 2-to-4 decoder in Figure 6.16 can be used as a 1-to-4 demultiplexer. In this case the *En* input serves as the data input for the demultiplexer, and the y_0 to y_3 outputs are the data outputs. The valuation of w_1w_0 determines which of the outputs is set to the value of *En*. To see how the circuit works, consider the truth table in Figure 6.16a. When $En = 0$, all the outputs are set to 0, including the one selected by the valuation of w_1w_0. When $En = 1$, the valuation of w_1w_0 sets the appropriate output to 1.

In general, an n-to-2^n decoder circuit can be used as a 1-to-n demultiplexer. However, in practice decoder circuits are used much more often as decoders rather than as demultiplexers. In many applications the decoder's *En* input is not actually needed; hence it can be omitted. In this case the decoder always asserts one of its data outputs, $y_0, \ldots, y_{2^n-1}$, according to the valuation of the data inputs, $w_{n-1} \ldots w_0$. Example 6.11 uses a decoder that does not have the *En* input.

One of the most important applications of decoders is in memory blocks, which are used to store information. Such memory blocks are included in digital systems, such as computers, where there is a need to store large amounts of information electronically. One type of memory block is called a *read-only memory* (ROM). A ROM consists of a collection of storage cells, where each cell permanently stores a single logic value, either 0 or 1. Figure 6.21 shows an example of a ROM block. The storage cells are arranged in 2^m rows with n

Example 6.11

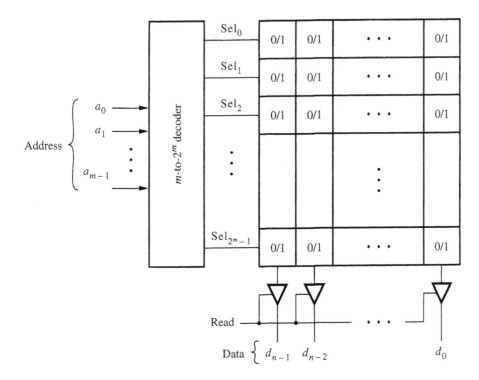

Figure 6.21 A $2^m \times n$ read-only memory (ROM) block.

cells per row. Thus each row stores n bits of information. The location of each row in the ROM is identified by its *address*. In the figure the row at the top of the ROM has address 0, and the row at the bottom has address $2^m - 1$. The information stored in the rows can be accessed by asserting the select lines, Sel_0 to Sel_{2^m-1}. As shown in the figure, a decoder with m inputs and 2^m outputs is used to generate the signals on the select lines. Since the inputs to the decoder choose the particular address (row) selected, they are called the *address* lines. The information stored in the row appears on the data outputs of the ROM, $d_{n-1}, \ldots, d_0$, which are called the *data* lines. Figure 6.21 shows that each data line has an associated tri-state buffer that is enabled by the ROM input named *Read*. To access, or *read*, data from the ROM, the address of the desired row is placed on the address lines and *Read* is set to 1.

Many different types of memory blocks exist. In a ROM the stored information can be read out of the storage cells, but it cannot be changed (see problem 6.33). Another type of ROM allows information to be both read out of the storage cells and stored, or *written*, into them. Reading its contents is the normal operation, whereas writing requires a special procedure. Such a memory block is called a programmable ROM (PROM). The storage cells in a PROM are usually implemented using EEPROM transistors. We discussed EEPROM transistors in section 3.10 to show how they are used in PLDs. Other types of memory blocks are discussed in section 10.1.

6.3   ENCODERS

An encoder performs the opposite function of a decoder. It encodes given information into a more compact form.

6.3.1   BINARY ENCODERS

A *binary encoder* encodes information from 2^n inputs into an n-bit code, as indicated in Figure 6.22. Exactly one of the input signals should have a value of 1, and the outputs present the binary number that identifies which input is equal to 1. The truth table for a 4-to-2 encoder is provided in Figure 6.23a. Observe that the output y_0 is 1 when either input w_1 or w_3 is 1, and output y_1 is 1 when input w_2 or w_3 is 1. Hence these outputs can be generated by the circuit in Figure 6.23b. Note that we assume that the inputs are one-hot

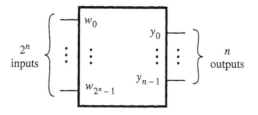

Figure 6.22   A 2^n-to-n binary encoder.

w_3	w_2	w_1	w_0	y_1	y_0
0	0	0	1	0	0
0	0	1	0	0	1
0	1	0	0	1	0
1	0	0	0	1	1

(a) Truth table

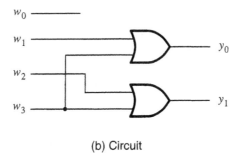

(b) Circuit

Figure 6.23   A 4-to-2 binary encoder.

encoded. All input patterns that have multiple inputs set to 1 are not shown in the truth table, and they are treated as don't-care conditions.

Encoders are used to reduce the number of bits needed to represent given information. A practical use of encoders is for transmitting information in a digital system. Encoding the information allows the transmission link to be built using fewer wires. Encoding is also useful if information is to be stored for later use because fewer bits need to be stored.

6.3.2 PRIORITY ENCODERS

Another useful class of encoders is based on the priority of input signals. In a *priority encoder* each input has a priority level associated with it. The encoder outputs indicate the active input that has the highest priority. When an input with a high priority is asserted, the other inputs with lower priority are ignored. The truth table for a 4-to-2 priority encoder is shown in Figure 6.24. It assumes that w_0 has the lowest priority and w_3 the highest. The outputs y_1 and y_0 represent the binary number that identifies the highest priority input set to 1. Since it is possible that none of the inputs is equal to 1, an output, z, is provided to indicate this condition. It is set to 1 when at least one of the inputs is equal to 1. It is set to 0 when all inputs are equal to 0. The outputs y_1 and y_0 are not meaningful in this case, and hence the first row of the truth table can be treated as a don't-care condition for y_1 and y_0.

The behavior of the priority encoder is most easily understood by first considering the last row in the truth table. It specifies that if input w_3 is 1, then the outputs are set to $y_1y_0 = 11$. Because w_3 has the highest priority level, the values of inputs w_2, w_1, and w_0

w_3	w_2	w_1	w_0	y_1	y_0	z
0	0	0	0	d	d	0
0	0	0	1	0	0	1
0	0	1	x	0	1	1
0	1	x	x	1	0	1
1	x	x	x	1	1	1

Figure 6.24   Truth table for a 4-to-2 priority encoder.

do not matter. To reflect the fact that their values are irrelevant, w_2, w_1, and w_0 are denoted by the symbol x in the truth table. The second-last row in the truth table stipulates that if $w_2 = 1$, then the outputs are set to $y_1 y_0 = 10$, but only if $w_3 = 0$. Similarly, input w_1 causes the outputs to be set to $y_1 y_0 = 01$ only if both w_3 and w_2 are 0. Input w_0 produces the outputs $y_1 y_0 = 00$ only if w_0 is the only input that is asserted.

A logic circuit that implements the truth table can be synthesized by using the techniques developed in Chapter 4. However, a more convenient way to derive the circuit is to define a set of intermediate signals, $i_0, \ldots, i_3$, based on the observations above. Each signal, i_k, is equal to 1 only if the input with the same index, w_k, represents the highest-priority input that is set to 1. The logic expressions for $i_0, \ldots, i_3$ are

$$i_0 = \overline{w}_3 \overline{w}_2 \overline{w}_1 w_0$$
$$i_1 = \overline{w}_3 \overline{w}_2 w_1$$
$$i_2 = \overline{w}_3 w_2$$
$$i_3 = w_3$$

Using the intermediate signals, the rest of the circuit for the priority encoder has the same structure as the binary encoder in Figure 6.23, namely

$$y_0 = i_1 + i_3$$
$$y_1 = i_2 + i_3$$

The output z is given by

$$z = i_1 + i_2 + i_3 + i_4$$

6.4 CODE CONVERTERS

The purpose of the decoder and encoder circuits is to convert from one type of input encoding to a different output encoding. For example, a 3-to-8 binary decoder converts from a binary number on the input to a one-hot encoding at the output. An 8-to-3 binary encoder performs the opposite conversion. There are many other possible types of code converters. One common example is a BCD-to-7-segment decoder, which converts one binary-coded decimal (BCD) digit into information suitable for driving a digit-oriented display. As illustrated in Figure 6.25a, the circuit converts the BCD digit into seven signals that are used to drive the segments in the display. Each segment is a small light-emitting diode (LED), which glows when driven by an electrical signal. The segments are labeled from a to g in the figure. The truth table for the BCD-to-7-segment decoder is given in Figure 6.25c. For each valuation of the inputs $w_3, \ldots, w_0$, the seven outputs are set to display the appropriate BCD digit. Note that the last 6 rows of a complete 16-row truth table are not shown. They represent don't-care conditions because they are not legal BCD codes and will never occur in a circuit that deals with BCD data. A circuit that implements the truth table can be derived using the synthesis techniques discussed in Chapter 4. Finally, we should note that although the word *decoder* is traditionally used for this circuit, a more appropriate term is *code converter*. The term *decoder* is more appropriate for circuits that produce one-hot encoded outputs.

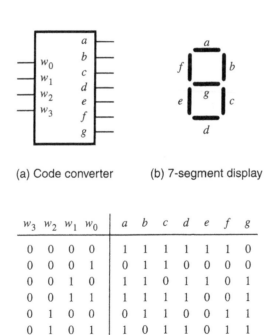

(a) Code converter   (b) 7-segment display

w_3	w_2	w_1	w_0	a	b	c	d	e	f	g
0	0	0	0	1	1	1	1	1	1	0
0	0	0	1	0	1	1	0	0	0	0
0	0	1	0	1	1	0	1	1	0	1
0	0	1	1	1	1	1	1	0	0	1
0	1	0	0	0	1	1	0	0	1	1
0	1	0	1	1	0	1	1	0	1	1
0	1	1	0	1	0	1	1	1	1	1
0	1	1	1	1	1	1	0	0	0	0
1	0	0	0	1	1	1	1	1	1	1
1	0	0	1	1	1	1	1	0	1	1

(c) Truth table

Figure 6.25   A BCD-to-7-segment display code converter.

6.5   ARITHMETIC COMPARISON CIRCUITS

Chapter 5 presented arithmetic circuits that perform addition, subtraction, and multiplication of binary numbers. Another useful type of arithmetic circuit compares the relative sizes of two binary numbers. Such a circuit is called a *comparator*. This section considers the design of a comparator that has two n-bit inputs, A and B, which represent unsigned binary numbers. The comparator produces three outputs, called $AeqB$, $AgtB$, and $AltB$. The $AeqB$ output is set to 1 if A and B are equal. The $AgtB$ output is 1 if A is greater than B, and the $AltB$ output is 1 if A is less than B.

The desired comparator can be designed by creating a truth table that specifies the three outputs as functions of A and B. However, even for moderate values of n, the truth table is large. A better approach is to derive the comparator circuit by considering the bits of A and B in pairs. We can illustrate this by a small example, where $n = 4$.

Let $A = a_3a_2a_1a_0$ and $B = b_3b_2b_1b_0$. Define a set of intermediate signals called i_3, i_2, i_1, and i_0. Each signal, i_k, is 1 if the bits of A and B with the same index are equal. That is, $i_k = \overline{a_k \oplus b_k}$. The comparator's $AeqB$ output is then given by

$$AeqB = i_3 i_2 i_1 i_0$$

An expression for the $AgtB$ output can be derived by considering the bits of A and B in the order from the most-significant bit to the least-significant bit. The first bit-position, k, at which a_k and b_k differ determines whether A is less than or greater than B. If $a_k = 0$ and $b_k = 1$, then $A < B$. But if $a_k = 1$ and $b_k = 0$, then $A > B$. The $AgtB$ output is defined by

$$AgtB = a_3\overline{b}_3 + i_3 a_2 \overline{b}_2 + i_3 i_2 a_1 \overline{b}_1 + i_3 i_2 i_1 a_0 \overline{b}_0$$

The i_k signals ensure that only the first digits, considered from the left to the right, of A and B that differ determine the value of $AgtB$.

The $AltB$ output can be derived by using the other two outputs as

$$AltB = \overline{AeqB + AltB}$$

A logic circuit that implements the four-bit comparator circuit is shown in Figure 6.26. This approach can be used to design a comparator for any value of n.

6.7   CONCLUDING REMARKS

This chapter has introduced a number of circuit building blocks. Examples using these blocks to construct larger circuits will be presented in Chapters 7 and 10. To describe the building block circuits efficiently, several VHDL constructs have been introduced. In many cases a given circuit can be described in various ways, using different constructs. A circuit that can be described using a selected signal assignment can also be described using a case statement. Circuits that fit well with conditional signal assignments are also well-suited to if-then-else statements. In general, there are no clear rules that dictate when one type of assignment statement should be preferred over another. With experience the user develops a sense for which types of statements work well in a particular design situation. Personal preference also influences how the code is written.

VHDL is not a programming language, and VHDL code should not be written as if it were a computer program. The concurrent and sequential assignment statements discussed in this chapter can be used to create large, complex circuits. A good way to design such circuits is to construct them using well-defined modules, in the manner that we illustrated

```
LIBRARY ieee ;
USE ieee.std_logic_1164.all ;
USE ieee.std_logic_unsigned.all ;

ENTITY alu IS
    PORT ( s    : IN    STD_LOGIC_VECTOR(2 DOWNTO 0) ;
           A, B : IN    STD_LOGIC_VECTOR(3 DOWNTO 0) ;
           F    : OUT  STD_LOGIC_VECTOR(3 DOWNTO 0) ) ;
END alu ;

ARCHITECTURE Behavior OF alu IS
BEGIN
    PROCESS ( s, A, B )
    BEGIN
        CASE s IS
            WHEN "000" =>
                F <= "0000" ;
            WHEN "001" =>
                F <= B − A ;
            WHEN "010" =>
                F <= A − B ;
            WHEN "011" =>
                F <= A + B ;
            WHEN "100" =>
                F <= A XOR B ;
            WHEN "101" =>
                F <= A OR B ;
            WHEN "110" =>
                F <= A AND B ;
            WHEN OTHERS =>
                F <= "1111" ;
        END CASE ;
    END PROCESS ;
END Behavior ;
```

Figure 6.48   Code that represents the functionality of the 74381 ALU chip.

for the multiplexers, decoders, encoders, and so on. Additional examples using the VHDL statements introduced in this chapter are given in Chapters 7 and 8. In Chapter 10 we provide a number of examples of using VHDL code to describe larger digital systems. For more information on VHDL, the reader can consult more specialized books [5–10].

In the next chapter we introduce logic circuits that include the ability to store logic signal values in memory elements.

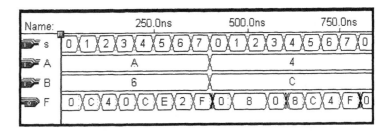

Figure 6.49   Timing simulation for the code in Figure 6.48.

PROBLEMS

6.1   Show how the function $f(w_1, w_2, w_3) = \sum m(0, 2, 3, 4, 5, 7)$ can be implemented using a 3-to-8 binary decoder and an OR gate.

6.2   Show how the function $f(w_1, w_2, w_3) = \sum m(1, 2, 3, 5, 6)$ can be implemented using a 3-to-8 binary decoder and an OR gate.

6.3   Consider the function $f = \overline{w}_1 \overline{w}_3 + w_2 \overline{w}_3 + \overline{w}_1 w_2$. Use the truth table to derive a circuit for f that uses a 2-to-1 multiplexer.

6.4   Repeat problem 6.3 for the function $f = \overline{w}_2 \overline{w}_3 + w_1 w_2$.

6.5   For the function $f(w_1, w_2, w_3) = \sum m(0, 2, 3, 6)$, use Shannon's expansion to derive an implementation using a 2-to-1 multiplexer and any other necessary gates.

6.6   Repeat problem 6.5 for the function $f(w_1, w_2, w_3) = \sum m(0, 4, 6, 7)$.

6.7   Consider the function $f = \overline{w}_2 + \overline{w}_1 \overline{w}_3 + w_1 w_3$. Show how repeated application of Shannon's expansion can be used to derive the minterms of f.

6.8   Repeat problem 6.7 for $f = w_2 + \overline{w}_1 \overline{w}_3$.

6.9   Prove Shannon's expansion theorem presented in section 6.1.2.

6.10   Section 6.1.2 shows Shannon's expansion in sum-of-products form. Using the principle of duality, derive the equivalent expression in product-of-sums form.

6.11   Consider the function $f = \overline{w}_1 \overline{w}_2 + \overline{w}_2 \overline{w}_3 + w_1 w_2 w_3$. Give a circuit that implements f using the minimal number of two-input LUTs. Show the truth table implemented inside each LUT.

6.12   For the function in problem 6.11, the cost of the minimal sum-of-products expression is 14, which includes four gates and 10 inputs to the gates. Use Shannon's expansion to derive a multilevel circuit that has a lower cost and give the cost of your circuit.

6.13   Consider the function $f(w_1, w_2, w_3, w_4) = \sum m(0, 1, 3, 6, 8, 9, 14, 15)$. Derive an implementation using the minimum possible number of three-input LUTs.

6.14   Give two examples of logic functions with five inputs, $w_1, \ldots, w_5$, that can be realized using 2 four-input LUTs.

6.15 Assume that an FPGA exists in which the logic blocks are 4-LUTs. What is the minimum number of 4-LUTs needed to construct a 4-to-1 multiplexer with select inputs s_1 and s_0 and data inputs w_3, w_2, w_1, and w_0? Show two different circuits that can implement the desired multiplexer using the minimum number of 4-LUTs. Indicate the logic function implemented on the output of each LUT.

6.16 Actel Corporation manufactures an FPGA family called Act 1, which has the multiplexer-based logic block illustrated in Figure P6.1. Show how the function $f = w_2\overline{w}_3 + w_1 w_3 + \overline{w}_2 w_3$ can be implemented using only one Act 1 logic block.

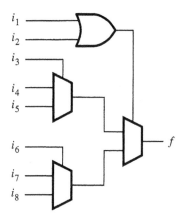

Figure P6.1   The Actel Act 1 logic block.

6.17 Show how the function $f = w_1\overline{w}_3 + \overline{w}_1 w_3 + w_2\overline{w}_3 + w_1\overline{w}_2$ can be realized using Act 1 logic blocks. Note that there are no NOT gates in the chip; hence complements of signals have to be generated using the multiplexers in the logic block.

6.18 Consider the VHDL code in Figure P6.2. What type of circuit does the code represent? Comment on whether or not the style of code used is a good choice for the circuit that it represents.

6.19 Write VHDL code that represents the function in problem 6.1, using one selected signal assignment.

6.20 Write VHDL code that represents the function in problem 6.2, using one selected signal assignment.

6.21 Using a selected signal assignment, write VHDL code for a 4-to-2 binary encoder.

6.22 Using a conditional signal assignment, write VHDL code for an 8-to-3 binary encoder.

6.23 Derive the circuit for an 8-to-3 priority encoder.

6.24 Using a conditional signal assignment, write VHDL code for an 8-to-3 priority encoder.

6.25 Repeat problem 6.24, using an if-then-else statement.

```
LIBRARY ieee ;
USE ieee.std_logic_1164.all ;

ENTITY problem IS
     PORT ( w              : IN    STD_LOGIC_VECTOR(1 DOWNTO 0) ;
            En             : IN    STD_LOGIC ;
            y0, y1, y2, y3 : OUT  STD_LOGIC ) ;
END problem ;

ARCHITECTURE Behavior OF problem IS
BEGIN
     PROCESS (w, En)
     BEGIN
         y0 <= '0' ; y1 <= '0' ; y2 <= '0' ; y3 <= '0' ;
         IF En = '1' THEN
             IF w = "00" THEN y0 <= '1' ;
             ELSIF w = "01" THEN y1 <= '1' ;
             ELSIF w = "10" THEN y2 <= '1' ;
             ELSE y3 <= '1' ;
             END IF ;
         END IF ;
     END PROCESS ;
END Behavior ;
```

Figure P6.2   Code for problem 6.17.

6.26   Create a VHDL entity named *if2to4* that represents a 2-to-4 binary decoder using an if-then-else statement. Create a second entity named *h3to8* that represents the 3-to-8 binary decoder in Figure 6.17, using two instances of the *if2to4* entity.

6.27   Create a VHDL entity named *h6to64* that represents a 6-to-64 binary decoder. Use the treelike structure in Figure 6.18, in which the 6-to-64 decoder is built using five instances of the *h3to8* decoder created in problem 6.26.

6.28   Write VHDL code that represents the circuit in Figure 6.19. Use the *dec2to4* entity in Figure 6.30 as a subcircuit in your code. Compare the circuit synthesized from your code to the circuit synthesized from the code in Figure 6.28.

6.29   Use MAX+plusII to create a schematic that represents the circuit in Figure 6.20. Use the *dec2to4* VHDL entity in Figure 6.30 as a subcircuit in your schematic. Also, create a tri-state buffer VHDL entity, named *tristate*, and use it as a subcircuit in your schematic. For the *tristate* entity, specify that the output of the buffer has the value Z when the enable is 0. Compare the circuit synthesized from your schematic to the circuit synthesized from the code in Figure 6.28. (Note: do not attempt to write hierarchical VHDL code for the circuit in Figure 6.20, rather than draw a schematic. The MAX+plusII VHDL compiler will not properly synthesize the resulting code. We discuss this issue in section 7.14.1.)

6.30 Write VHDL code for a BCD-to-7-segment code converter, using a selected signal assignment.

6.31 Derive minimal sum-of-products expressions for the outputs a, b, and c of the 7-segment display in Figure 6.25.

6.32 Derive minimal sum-of-products expressions for the outputs d, e, f, and g of the 7-segment display in Figure 6.25.

6.33 Figure 6.21 shows a block diagram of a ROM. A circuit that implements a small ROM, with four rows and four columns, is depicted in Figure P6.3. Each X in the figure represents a switch that determines whether the ROM produces a 1 or 0 when that location is read.

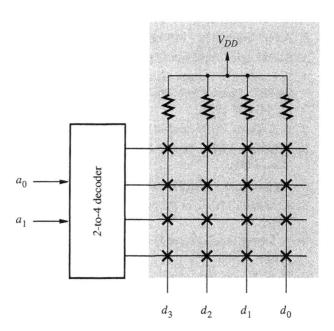

Figure P6.3   A 4 × 4 ROM circuit.

(a) Show how a switch (X) can be realized using a single NMOS transistor.

(b) Draw the complete 4×4 ROM circuit, using your switches from part (a). The ROM should be programmed to store the bits 0101 in row 0 (the top row), 1010 in row 1, 1100 in row 2, and 0011 in row 3 (the bottom row).

(c) Show how each (X) can be implemented as a programmable switch (as opposed to providing either a 1 or 0 permanently), using an EEPROM cell as shown in Figure 3.64. Briefly describe how the storage cell is used.

6.34   Show the complete circuit for a ROM using the storage cells designed in Part (*a*) of problem 6.33 that realizes the logic functions

$$d_3 = a_0 \oplus a_1$$

$$d_2 = \overline{a_0 \oplus a_1}$$

$$d_1 = a_0 a_1$$

$$d_0 = a_0 + a_1$$

REFERENCES

1. C. E. Shannon, "Symbolic Analysis of Relay and Switching Circuits," *Transactions AIEE* 57 (1938), pp. 713–723.

2. Actel Corporation, "MX FPGA Data Sheet," *http://www.actel.com.*

3. QuickLogic Corporation, "pASIC 3 FPGA Data Sheet," *http://www.quicklogic.com.*

4. R. Landers, S. Mahant-Shetti, and C. Lemonds, "A Multiplexer-Based Architecture for High-Density, Low Power Gate Arrays," *IEEE Journal of Solid-State Circuits* 30, no. 4 (April 1995).

5. D. L. Perry, *VHDL*, 2nd ed. (McGraw-Hill: New York, 1994).

6. Z. Navabi, *VHDL—Analysis and Modeling of Digital Systems* (McGraw-Hill: New York, 1993).

7. J. Bhasker, *A VHDL Primer* (Prentice-Hall: Englewood Cliffs, NJ, 1995).

8. K. Skahill, *VHDL for Programmable Logic* (Addison-Wesley: Menlo Park, CA, 1996).

9. A. Dewey, *Analysis and Design of Digital Systems with VHDL* (PWS Publishing Co.: Boston, 1997).

10. D. W. Knapp, *Behavioral Synthesis; Digital System Design Using the Synopsys Behavioral Compiler* (Prentice-Hall: Englewood Cliffs, NJ, 1996).

chapter
7

FLIP-FLOPS, REGISTERS, COUNTERS, AND A SIMPLE PROCESSOR

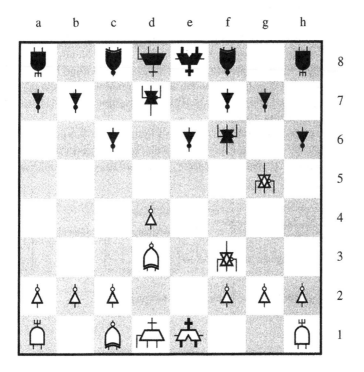

7. Ng1–f3, h7–h6

In previous chapters we considered combinational circuits where the value of each output depends solely on the values of signals applied to the inputs. There exists another class of logic circuits in which the values of the outputs depend not only on the present values of the inputs but also on the past behavior of the circuit. Such circuits include storage elements that store the values of logic signals. The contents of the storage elements are said to represent the *state* of the circuit. When the circuit's inputs change values, the new input values either leave the circuit in the same state or cause it to change into a new state. Over time the circuit changes through a sequence of states as a result of changes in the inputs. Circuits that behave in this way are referred to as *sequential circuits*.

In this chapter we will introduce circuits that can be used as storage elements. But first, we will motivate the need for such circuits by means of a simple example. Suppose that we wish to control an alarm system, as shown in Figure 7.1. The alarm mechanism responds to the control input $On/\overline{Off}$. It is turned on when $On/\overline{Off} = 1$, and it is off when $On/\overline{Off} = 0$. The desired operation is that the alarm turns on when the sensor generates a positive voltage signal, *Set*, in response to some undesirable event. Once the alarm is triggered, it must remain active even if the sensor output goes back to zero. The alarm is turned off manually by means of a *Reset* input. The circuit requires a memory element to remember that the alarm has to be active until the *Reset* signal arrives.

Figure 7.2 gives a rudimentary memory element, consisting of a loop that has two inverters. If we assume that $A = 0$, then $B = 1$. The circuit will maintain these values indefinitely. We say that the circuit is in the *state* defined by these values. If we assume that $A = 1$, then $B = 0$, and the circuit will remain in this second state indefinitely. Thus the circuit has two possible states. This circuit is not useful, because it lacks some practical means for changing its state.

A more useful circuit is shown in Figure 7.3. It includes a mechanism for changing the state of the circuit in Figure 7.2, using two transmission gates of the type discussed in section 3.9. One transmission gate, $TG1$, is used to connect the *Data* input terminal to point

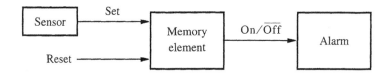

Figure 7.1   Control of an alarm system.

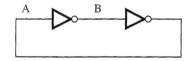

Figure 7.2   A simple memory element.

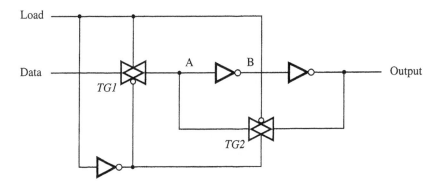

Figure 7.3   A controlled memory element.

A in the circuit. The second, *TG2*, is used as a switch in the *feedback loop* that maintains the state of the circuit. The transmission gates are controlled by the *Load* signal. If *Load* = 1, then *TG1* is on and the point *A* will have the same value as the *Data* input. Since the value presently stored at *Output* may not be the same value as *Data*, the feedback loop is broken by having *TG2* turned off when *Load* = 1. When *Load* changes to zero, then *TG1* turns off and *TG2* turns on. The feedback path is closed and the memory element will retain its state as long as *Load* = 0. This memory element cannot be applied directly to the system in Figure 7.1, but it is useful for many other applications, as we will see later.

7.1 BASIC LATCH

Instead of using the transmission gates, we can construct a similar circuit using ordinary logic gates. Figure 7.4 presents a memory element built with NOR gates. Its inputs, *Set* and *Reset*, provide the means for changing the state, Q, of the circuit. A more usual way of drawing this circuit is given in Figure 7.5a, where the two NOR gates are said to be connected in cross-coupled style. The circuit is referred to as a *basic latch*. Its behavior is described by the truth table in Figure 7.5b. When both inputs, *R* and *S*, are equal to 0 the latch maintains its existing state. This state may be either $Q_a = 0$ and $Q_b = 1$, or $Q_a = 1$ and $Q_b = 0$, which is indicated in the truth table by stating that the Q_a and Q_b outputs have values 0/1 and 1/0, respectively. Observe that Q_a and Q_b are complements of each other in this case. When $R = 0$ and $S = 1$, the latch is *set* into a state where $Q_a = 1$ and $Q_b = 0$. When $R = 1$ and $S = 0$, the latch is *reset* into a state where $Q_a = 0$ and $Q_b = 1$. The fourth possibility is to have $R = S = 1$. In this case both Q_a and Q_b will be 0.

Figure 7.5c gives a timing diagram for the latch, assuming that the propagation delay through the NOR gates is negligible. Of course, in a real circuit the changes in the waveforms would be delayed according to the propagation delays of the gates. We assume that initially $Q_a = 0$ and $Q_b = 1$. The state of the latch remains unchanged until time t_2,

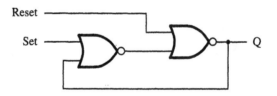

Figure 7.4   A memory element with NOR gates.

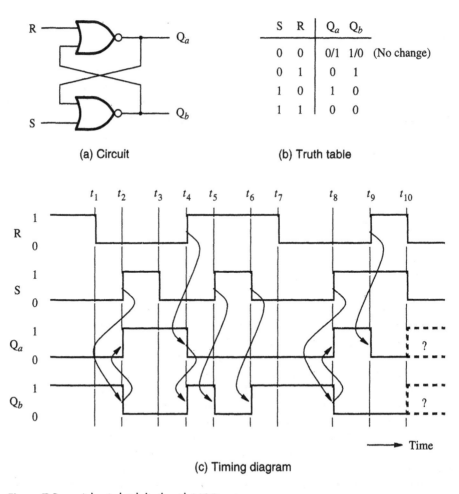

Figure 7.5   A basic latch built with NOR gates.

when S becomes equal to 1, causing Q_b to change to 0, which in turn causes Q_a to change to 1. The causality relationship is indicated by the arrows in the diagram. When S goes to 0 at t_3, there is no change in the state because both S and R are then equal to 0. At t_4 we have $R = 1$, which causes Q_a to go to 0, which in turn causes Q_b to go to 1. At t_5 both S and R are equal to 1, which forces both Q_a and Q_b to be equal to 0. As soon as S returns to 0, at t_6, Q_b becomes equal to 1 again. At t_8 we have $S = 1$ and $R = 0$, which causes $Q_b = 0$ and $Q_a = 1$. An interesting situation occurs at t_{10}. From t_9 to t_{10} we have $Q_a = Q_b = 0$ because $R = S = 1$. Now if both R and S change to 0 at t_{10}, both Q_a and Q_b will go to 1. But having both Q_a and Q_b equal to 1 will immediately force $Q_a = Q_b = 0$. There will be an oscillation between $Q_a = Q_b = 0$ and $Q_a = Q_b = 1$. If the delays through the two NOR gates are exactly the same, the oscillation will continue indefinitely. In a real circuit there will invariably be some difference in the delays through these gates, and the latch will eventually settle into one of its two stable states, but we don't know which state it will be. This uncertainty is indicated in the waveforms by dashed lines.

The oscillations discussed above illustrate that even though the basic latch is a simple circuit, careful analysis has to be done to fully appreciate its behavior. In general, any circuit that contains one or more feedback paths, such that the state of the circuit depends on the propagation delays through logic gates, has to be designed carefully. We discuss timing issues in detail in Chapter 9.

The latch in Figure 7.5a can perform the functions needed for the memory element in Figure 7.1, by connecting the *Set* signal to the S input and *Reset* to the R input. The Q_a output provides the desired $On/\overline{Off}$ signal. To initialize the operation of the alarm system, the latch is reset. Thus the alarm is off. When the sensor generates the logic value 1, the latch is set and Q_a becomes equal to 1. This turns on the alarm mechanism. If the sensor output returns to 0, the latch retains its state where $Q_a = 1$; hence the alarm remains turned on. The only way to turn off the alarm is by resetting the latch, which is accomplished by making the *Reset* input equal to 1.

7.2   GATED SR LATCH

In section 7.1 we saw that the basic SR latch can serve as a useful memory element. It remembers its state when both the S and R inputs are 0. It changes its state in response to changes in the signals on these inputs. The state changes occur at the time when the changes in the signals occur. If we cannot control the time of such changes, then we don't know when the latch may change its state.

In the alarm system of Figure 7.1, it may be desirable to be able to enable or disable the entire system by means of a control input, *Enable*. Thus when enabled, the system would function as described above. In the disabled mode, changing the *Set* input from 0 to 1 would not cause the alarm to turn on. The latch in Figure 7.5a cannot provide the desired operation. But the latch circuit can be modified to respond to the input signals S and R only when *Enable* = 1. Otherwise, it would maintain its state.

The modified circuit is depicted in Figure 7.6a. It includes two AND gates that provide the desired control. When the control signal *Clk* is equal to 0, the S' and R' inputs to the

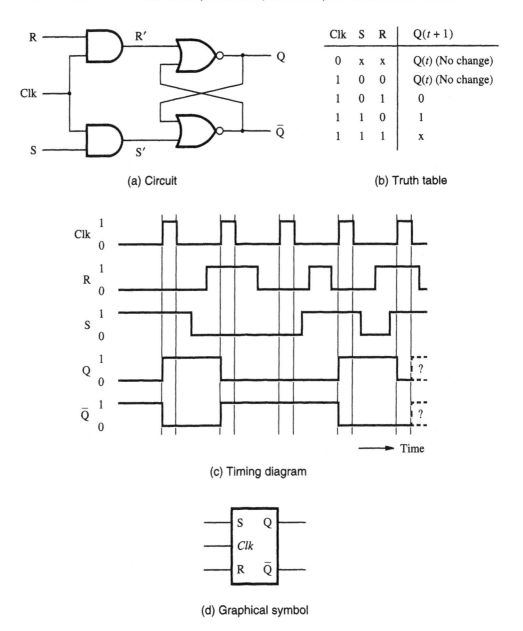

Clk	S	R	$Q(t+1)$
0	x	x	$Q(t)$ (No change)
1	0	0	$Q(t)$ (No change)
1	0	1	0
1	1	0	1
1	1	1	x

(a) Circuit

(b) Truth table

(c) Timing diagram

(d) Graphical symbol

Figure 7.6   Gated SR latch.

latch will be 0, regardless of the values of signals S and R. Hence the latch will maintain its existing state as long as $Clk = 0$. When Clk changes to 1, the S' and R' signals will be the same as the S and R signals, respectively. Therefore, in this mode the latch will behave as we described in section 7.1. Note that we have used the name Clk for the control signal that allows the latch to be set or reset, rather than call it the *Enable* signal. The reason is that such circuits are often used in digital systems where it is desirable to allow the changes in the states of memory elements to occur only at well-defined time intervals, as if they were controlled by a clock. The control signal that defines these time intervals is usually called the *clock* signal. The name *Clk* is meant to reflect this nature of the signal.

Circuits of this type, which use a control signal, are called *gated latches*. Because our circuit exhibits set and reset capability, it is called a *gated SR latch*. Figure 7.6b describes its behavior. It defines the state of the Q output at time $t + 1$, namely, $Q(t + 1)$, as a function of the inputs S, R, and *Clk*. When *Clk* = 0, the latch will remain in the state it is in at time t, that is, $Q(t)$, regardless of the values of inputs S and R. This is indicated by specifying $S = x$ and $R = x$, where x means that the signal value can be either 0 or 1. (Recall that we already used this notation in Chapter 4.) When *Clk* = 1, the circuit behaves as the basic latch in Figure 7.5. It is set by $S = 1$ and reset by $R = 1$. The last row of the truth table, where $S = R = 1$, shows that the state $Q(t + 1)$ is undefined because we don't know whether it will be 0 or 1. This corresponds to the situation described in section 7.1 in conjunction with the timing diagram in Figure 7.5 at time t_{10}. At this time both S and R inputs go from 1 to 0, which causes the oscillatory behavior that we discussed. If $S = R = 1$, this situation will occur as soon as *Clk* goes from 1 to 0. To ensure a meaningful operation of the gated SR latch, it is essential to avoid the possibility of having both the S and R inputs equal to 1 when *Clk* changes from 1 to 0.

A timing diagram for the gated SR latch is given in Figure 7.6c. It shows *Clk* as a periodic signal that is equal to 1 at regular time intervals to suggest that this is how the clock signal usually appears in a real system. The diagram presents the effect of several combinations of signal values. Observe that we have labeled one output as Q and the other as its complement $\overline{Q}$, rather than Q_a and Q_b as in Figure 7.5. Since the undefined mode, where $S = R = 1$, must be avoided in practice, the normal operation of the latch will have the outputs as complements of each other. Moreover, we will often say that the latch is *set* when $Q = 1$, and it is *reset* when $Q = 0$. A graphical symbol for the gated SR latch is given in Figure 7.6d.

7.2.1 GATED SR LATCH WITH NAND GATES

So far we have implemented the basic latch with cross-coupled NOR gates. We can also construct the latch with NAND gates. Using this approach, we can implement the gated SR latch as depicted in Figure 7.7. The behavior of this circuit is described by the truth table

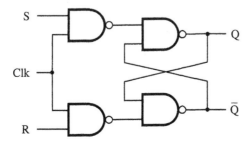

Figure 7.7   Gated SR latch with NAND gates.

in Figure 7.6*b*. Note that in this circuit, the clock is gated by NAND gates, rather than by AND gates. Note also that the *S* and *R* inputs are reversed in comparison with the circuit in Figure 7.6*a*. The circuit with NAND gates requires fewer transistors than the circuit with AND gates. We will use the circuit in Figure 7.7, in preference to the circuit in Figure 7.6*a*.

7.3 GATED D LATCH

In section 7.2 we presented the gated SR latch and showed how it can be used as the memory element in the alarm system of Figure 7.1. This latch is useful for many other applications. In this section we describe another gated latch that is even more useful in practice. It has a single data input, called *D*, and it stores the value on this input, under the control of a clock signal. It is called a *gated D latch*.

To motivate the need for a gated D latch, consider the adder/subtractor unit discussed in Chapter 5 (Figure 5.13). When we described how that circuit is used to add numbers, we did not discuss what is likely to happen with the sum bits that are produced by the adder. Adder/subtractor units are often used as part of a computer. The result of an addition or subtraction operation is often used as an operand in a subsequent operation. Therefore, it is necessary to be able to remember the values of the sum bits generated by the adder until they are needed again. We might think of using the basic latches to remember these bits, one bit per latch. In this context, instead of saying that a latch remembers the value of a bit, it is more illuminating to say that the latch *stores* the value of the bit or simply "stores the bit." We should think of the latch as a storage element.

But can we obtain the desired operation using the basic latches? We can certainly reset all latches before the addition operation begins. Then we would expect that by connecting a sum bit to the *S* input of a latch, the latch would be set to 1 if the sum bit has the value 1; otherwise, the latch would remain in the 0 state. This would work fine if all sum bits are 0 at the start of the addition operation and, after some propagation delay through the adder, some of these bits become equal to 1 to give the desired sum. Unfortunately, the propagation delays that exist in the adder circuit cause a big problem in this arrangement. Suppose that we use a ripple-carry adder. When the *X* and *Y* inputs are applied to the adder, the sum outputs may alternate between 0 and 1 a number of times as the carries ripple through the circuit. This situation was illustrated in the timing diagram in Figure 5.21. The problem is that if we connect a sum bit to the *S* input of a latch, then if the sum bit is temporarily a 1 and then settles to 0 in the final result, the latch will remain set to 1 erroneously.

The problem caused by the alternating values of the sum bits in the adder could be solved by using the gated SR latches, instead of the basic latches. Then we could arrange that the clock signal is 0 during the time needed by the adder to produce a correct sum. After allowing for the maximum propagation delay in the adder circuit, the clock should go to 1 to store the values of the sum bits in the gated latches. As soon as the values have been stored, the clock can return to 0, which ensures that the stored values will be retained until the next time the clock goes to 1. To achieve the desired operation, we would also have to reset all latches to 0 prior to loading the sum-bit values into these latches. This is an awkward way of dealing with the problem, and it is preferable to use the gated D latches instead.

Figure 7.8a shows the circuit for a gated D latch. It is based on the gated SR latch, but instead of using the S and R inputs separately, it has just one data input, D. For convenience we have labeled the points in the circuit that are equivalent to the S and R inputs. If $D = 1$, then $S = 1$ and $R = 0$, which forces the latch into the state $Q = 1$. If $D = 0$, then $S = 0$ and $R = 1$, which causes $Q = 0$. Of course, the changes in state occur only when $Clk = 1$.

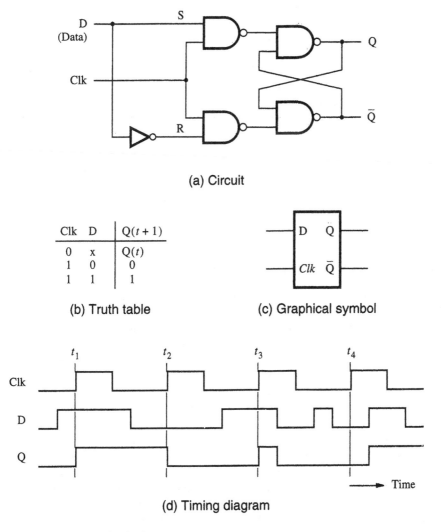

(a) Circuit

Clk	D	$Q(t + 1)$
0	x	$Q(t)$
1	0	0
1	1	1

(b) Truth table

(c) Graphical symbol

(d) Timing diagram

Figure 7.8   Gated D latch.

It is important to observe that in this circuit it is impossible to have the troublesome situation where $S = R = 1$. In the gated D latch, the output Q merely tracks the value of the input D while $Clk = 1$. As soon as Clk goes to 0, the state of the latch is frozen until the next time the clock signal goes to 1. Therefore, the gated D latch stores the value of the D input seen at the time the clock changes from 1 to 0. Figure 7.8 also gives the truth table, the graphical symbol, and the timing diagram for the gated D latch.

The timing diagram illustrates what happens if the D signal changes while $Clk = 1$. During the third clock pulse, starting at t_3, the output Q changes to 1 because $D = 1$. But midway through the pulse D goes to 0, which causes Q to go to 0. This value of Q is stored when Clk changes to 0. Now no further change in the state of the latch occurs until the next clock pulse, at t_4. The key point to observe is that as long as the clock has the value 1, the Q output follows the D input. But when the clock has the value 0, the Q output cannot change. In Chapter 3 we saw that the logic values are implemented as low and high voltage levels. Since the output of the gated D latch is controlled by the level of the clock input, the latch is said to be *level sensitive*. The circuits in Figures 7.6 through 7.8 are level sensitive. We will show in section 7.4 that it is possible to design storage elements for which the output changes only at the point in time when the clock changes from one value to the other. Such circuits are said to be *edge triggered*.

At this point we should reconsider the circuit in Figure 7.3. Careful examination of that circuit shows that it behaves in exactly the same way as the circuit in Figure 7.8a. The *Data* and *Load* inputs correspond to the D and Clk inputs, respectively. The *Output*, which has the same signal value as point A, corresponds to the Q output. Point B corresponds to $\overline{Q}$. Therefore, the circuit in Figure 7.3 is also a gated D latch. An advantage of this circuit is that it can be implemented using fewer transistors than the circuit in Figure 7.8a.

7.3.1 EFFECTS OF PROPAGATION DELAYS

In the previous discussion we ignored the effects of propagation delays. In practical circuits it is essential to take these delays into account. Consider the gated D latch in Figure 7.8a. It stores the value of the D input that is present at the time the clock signal changes from 1 to 0. It operates properly if the D signal is stable (that is, not changing) at the time Clk goes from 1 to 0. But it may lead to unpredictable results if the D signal also changes at this time. Therefore, the designer of a logic circuit that generates the D signal must ensure that this signal is stable when the critical change in the clock signal takes place.

Figure 7.9 illustrates the critical timing region. The minimum time that the D signal must be stable prior to the negative edge of the Clk signal is called the *setup time*, t_{su}, of the latch. The minimum time that the D signal must remain stable after the negative edge of the Clk signal is called the *hold time*, t_h, of the latch. The values of t_{su} and t_h depend on the technology used. Manufacturers of integrated circuit chips provide this information on the data sheets that describe their chips. Typical values for CMOS technology are $t_{su} = 3$ ns and $t_h = 2$ ns. We will give examples of how setup and hold times affect the speed of operation of circuits in section 7.13. The behavior of storage elements when setup or hold times are violated is discussed in section 10.3.3.

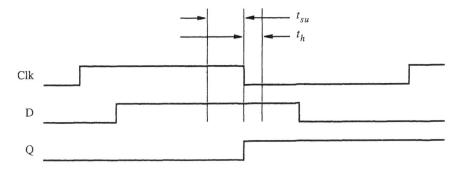

Figure 7.9   Setup and hold times.

7.4   MASTER-SLAVE AND EDGE-TRIGGERED D FLIP-FLOPS

In the level-sensitive latches, the state of the latch keeps changing according to the values of
input signals during the period when the clock signal is active (equal to 1 in our examples).
As we will see in sections 7.8 and 7.9, there is also a need for storage elements that can
change their states no more than once during one clock cycle. We will discuss two types of
circuits that exhibit such behavior.

7.4.1   MASTER-SLAVE D FLIP-FLOP

Consider the circuit given in Figure 7.10a, which consists of two gated D latches. The first,
called *master*, changes its state while $Clock = 1$. The second, called *slave*, changes its state
while $Clock = 0$. The operation of the circuit is such that when the clock is high, the master
tracks the value of the D input signal and the slave does not change. Thus the value of Q_m
follows any changes in D, and the value of Q_s remains constant. When the clock signal
changes to 0, the master stage stops following the changes in the D input. At the same time,
the slave stage responds to the value of the signal Q_m and changes state accordingly. Since
Q_m does not change while $Clock = 0$, the slave stage can undergo at most one change of
state during a clock cycle. From the external observer's point of view, namely, the circuit
connected to the output of the slave stage, the master-slave circuit changes its state at the
negative-going edge of the clock. The *negative edge* is the edge where the clock signal
changes from 1 to 0. Regardless of the number of changes in the D input to the master
stage during one clock cycle, the observer of the Q_s signal will see only the change that
corresponds to the D input at the negative edge of the clock.

   The circuit in Figure 7.10 is called a *master-slave D flip-flop*. The term *flip-flop* denotes
a storage element that changes its output state at the edge of a controlling clock signal. The
timing diagram for this flip-flop is shown in Figure 7.10b. A graphical symbol is given in
Figure 7.10c. In the symbol we use the > mark to denote that the flip-flop responds to the
"active edge" of the clock. We place a bubble on the clock input to indicate that the active
edge for this particular circuit is the negative edge.

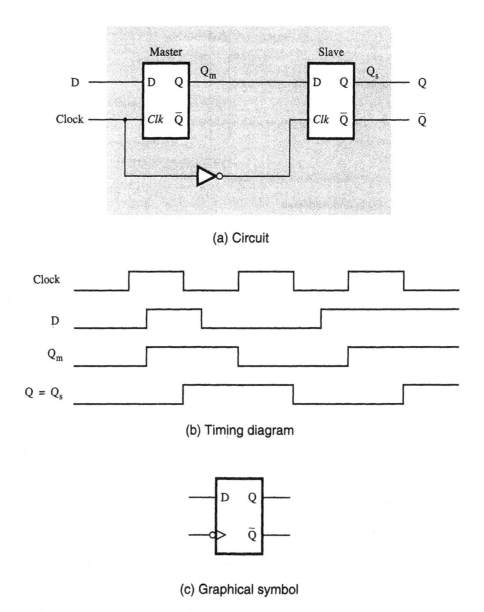

(a) Circuit

(b) Timing diagram

(c) Graphical symbol

Figure 7.10   Master-slave D flip-flop.

7.4.2 EDGE-TRIGGERED D FLIP-FLOP

The output of the master-slave D flip-flop in Figure 7.10a responds on the negative edge of the clock signal. The circuit can be changed to respond to the positive clock edge by connecting the slave stage directly to the clock and the master stage to the complement of the clock. A different circuit that accomplishes the same task is presented in Figure 7.11a.

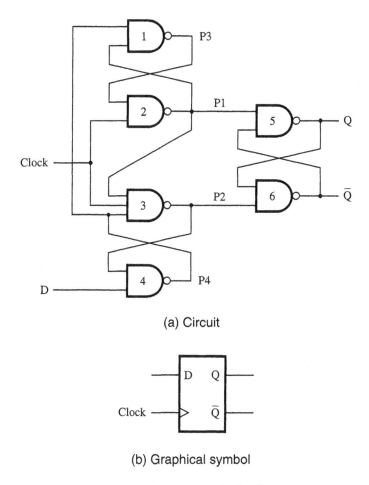

(a) Circuit

(b) Graphical symbol

Figure 7.11 A positive-edge-triggered D flip-flop.

It requires only six NAND gates and, hence, fewer transistors. The operation of the circuit is as follows. When *Clock* = 0, the outputs of gates 2 and 3 are high. Thus $P1 = P2 = 1$, which maintains the output latch, comprising gates 5 and 6, in its present state. At the same time, the signal $P3$ is equal to D, and $P4$ is equal to its complement $\overline{D}$. When *Clock* changes to 1, the following changes take place. The values of $P3$ and $P4$ are transmitted through gates 2 and 3 to cause $P1 = \overline{D}$ and $P2 = D$, which sets $Q = D$ and $\overline{Q} = \overline{D}$. To operate reliably, $P3$ and $P4$ must be stable when *Clock* changes from 0 to 1. Hence the setup time of the flip-flop is equal to the delay from the D input through gates 4 and 1 to $P3$. The hold time is given by the delay through gate 3 because once $P2$ is stable, the changes in D no longer matter.

For proper operation it is necessary to show that, after *Clock* changes to 1, any further changes in D will not affect the output latch as long as *Clock* = 1. We have to consider two cases. Suppose first that $D = 0$ at the positive edge of the clock. Then $P2 = 0$, which will keep the output of gate 4 equal to 1 as long as $Clock = 1$, regardless of the value of the D input. The second case is if $D = 1$ at the positive edge of the clock. Then $P1 = 0$, which forces the outputs of gates 1 and 3 to be equal to 1, regardless of the D input. Therefore, the flip-flop ignores changes in the D input while $Clock = 1$.

Figure 7.11b gives a graphical symbol for this flip-flop. The clock input indicates that the positive edge of the clock is the active edge. A similar circuit, constructed with NOR gates, can be used as a negative-edge-triggered flip-flop.

Level-Sensitive versus Edge-Triggered Storage Elements

Figure 7.12 shows three different types of storage elements that are driven by the same data and clock inputs. The first element is a gated D latch, which is level sensitive. The second one is a positive-edge-triggered D flip-flop, and the third one is a negative-edge-triggered D flip-flop. To accentuate the differences between these storage elements, the D input changes its values more than once during each half of the clock cycle. Observe that the gated D latch follows the D input as long as the clock is high. The positive-edge-triggered flip-flop responds only to the value of D when the clock changes from 0 to 1. The negative-edge-triggered flip-flop responds only to the value of D when the clock changes from 1 to 0.

7.4.3 D FLIP-FLOPS WITH CLEAR AND PRESET

Flip-flops are often used for implementation of circuits that can have many possible states, where the response of the circuit depends not only on the present values of the circuit's inputs but also on the particular state that the circuit is in at that time. We will discuss a general form of such circuits in Chapter 8. A simple example is a counter circuit that counts the number of occurrences of some event, perhaps passage of time. We will discuss counters in detail in section 7.9. A counter comprises a number of flip-flops, whose outputs are interpreted as a number. The counter circuit has to be able to increment or decrement the number. It is also important to be able to force the counter into a known initial state (count). Obviously, it must be possible to clear the count to zero, which means that all flip-flops must have $Q = 0$. It is equally useful to be able to preset each flip-flop to $Q = 1$, to insert some specific count as the initial value in the counter. These features can be incorporated into the circuits of Figures 7.10 and 7.11 as follows.

Figure 7.13a shows an implementation of the circuit in Figure 7.10a using NAND gates. The master stage is just the gated D latch of Figure 7.8a. Instead of using another latch of the same type for the slave stage, we can use the slightly simpler gated SR latch of Figure 7.7. This eliminates one NOT gate from the circuit.

A simple way of providing the clear and preset capability is to add an extra input to each NAND gate in the cross-coupled latches, as indicated in blue. Placing a 0 on the $Clear$ input will force the flip-flop into the state $Q = 0$. If $Clear = 1$, then this input will have no effect on the NAND gates. Similarly, $Preset = 0$ forces the flip-flop into the state $Q = 1$, while $Preset = 1$ has no effect. To denote that the $Clear$ and $Preset$ inputs are active when their value is 0, we placed an overbar on the names in the figure. We should note that the circuit that uses this flip-flop should not try to force both $Clear$ and $Preset$ to 0 at the same time. A graphical symbol for this flip-flop is shown in Figure 7.13b.

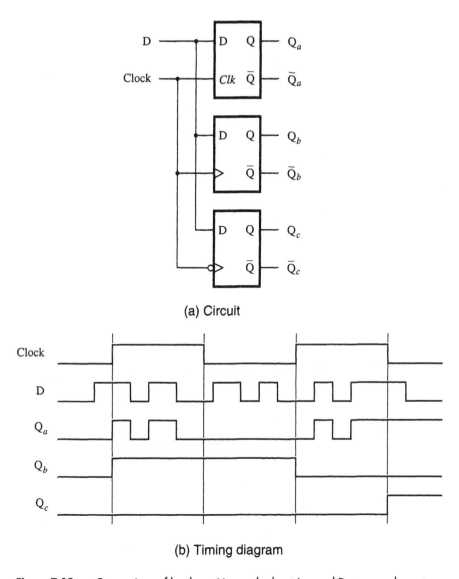

(a) Circuit

(b) Timing diagram

Figure 7.12 Comparison of level-sensitive and edge-triggered D storage elements.

A similar modification can be done on the edge-triggered flip-flop of Figure 7.11a, as indicated in Figure 7.14a. Again, both *Clear* and *Preset* inputs are active low. They do not disturb the flip-flop when they are equal to 1.

In the circuits in Figures 7.13a and 7.14a, the effect of a low signal on either the *Clear* or *Preset* input is immediate. For example, if *Clear* = 0 then the flip-flop goes into the state $Q = 0$ immediately, regardless of the value of the clock signal. In such a circuit, where the *Clear* signal is used to clear a flip-flop without regard to the clock signal, we say that the

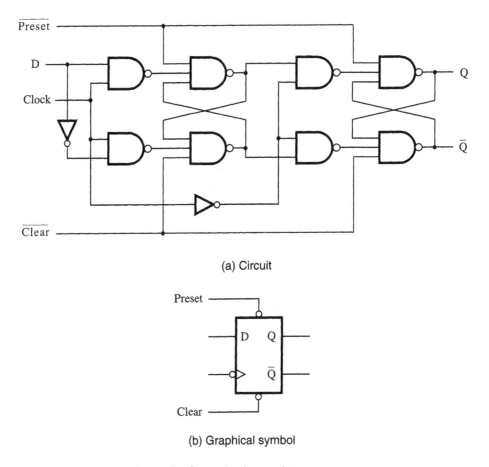

(a) Circuit

(b) Graphical symbol

Figure 7.13   Master-slave D flip-flop with *Clear* and *Preset.*

flip-flop has an *asynchronous clear*. In practice, it is often preferable to clear the flip-flops on the active edge of the clock. Such *synchronous clear* can be accomplished as shown in Figure 7.15. The flip-flop operates normally when the *Clear* input is equal to 1. But if *Clear* goes to 0, then on the next positive edge of the clock the flip-flop will be cleared to 0. We will examine the clearing of flip-flops in more detail in section 7.10.

7.5   T FLIP-FLOP

The D flip-flop is a versatile storage element that can be used for many purposes. By including some simple logic circuitry to drive its input, the D flip-flop may appear to be a different type of storage element. An interesting modification is presented in Figure 7.16*a*. This circuit uses a positive-edge-triggered D flip-flop. The *feedback* connections make the input signal D equal to either the value of Q or $\overline{Q}$ under the control of the signal that is labeled T. On each positive edge of the clock, the flip-flop may change its state Q(*t*). If

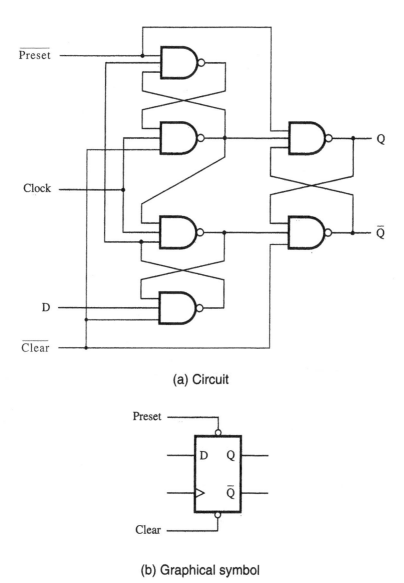

(a) Circuit

(b) Graphical symbol

Figure 7.14   Positive-edge-triggered D flip-flop with *Clear* and *Preset*.

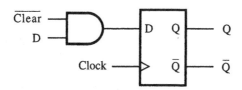

Figure 7.15   Synchronous reset for a D flip-flop.

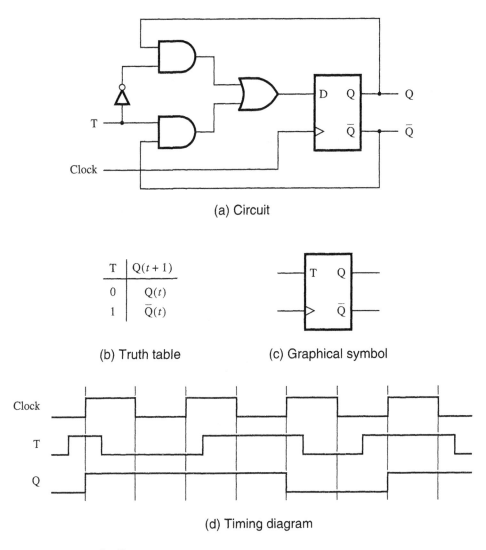

(a) Circuit

T	Q(t + 1)
0	Q(t)
1	$\overline{Q}(t)$

(b) Truth table

(c) Graphical symbol

(d) Timing diagram

Figure 7.16   T flip-flop.

$T = 0$, then $D = Q$ and the state will remain the same, that is, $Q(t + 1) = Q(t)$. But if $T = 1$, then $D = \overline{Q}$ and the new state will be $Q(t + 1) = \overline{Q}(t)$. Therefore, the overall operation of the circuit is that it retains its present state if $T = 0$, and it reverses its present state if $T = 1$.

The operation of the circuit is specified in the form of a truth table in Figure 7.16b. Any circuit that implements this truth table is called a *T flip-flop*. The name T flip-flop derives from the behavior of the circuit, which "toggles" its state when $T = 1$. The toggle feature makes the T flip-flop a useful element for building counter circuits, as we will see in section 7.9.

7.5.1   CONFIGURABLE FLIP-FLOPS

For some circuits one type of flip-flop may lead to a more efficient implementation than a different type of flip-flop. In general purpose chips like PLDs, the flip-flops that are provided are sometimes *configurable*, which means that a flip-flop circuit can be configured to be either D, T, or some other type. For example, in the MAX 7000 CPLDs the flip-flops can be configured as either D or T types (see problems 7.6 and 7.8).

7.6   JK FLIP-FLOP

Another interesting circuit can be derived from Figure 7.16a. Instead of using a single control input, T, we can use two inputs, J and K, as indicated in Figure 7.17a. For this circuit the input D is defined as

$$D = J\overline{Q} + \overline{K}Q$$

A corresponding truth table is given in Figure 7.17b. The circuit is called a *JK flip-flop*. It combines the behaviors of SR and T flip-flops in a useful way. It behaves as the SR flip-flop,

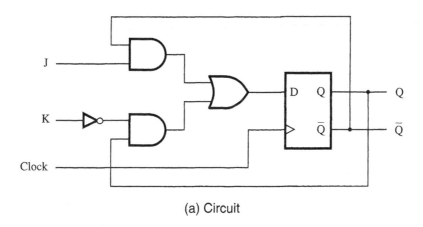

(a) Circuit

J	K	Q(t + 1)
0	0	Q(t)
0	1	0
1	0	1
1	1	$\overline{Q}(t)$

(b) Truth table   (c) Graphical symbol

Figure 7.17   JK flip-flop.

where $J = S$ and $K = R$, for all input values except $J = K = 1$. For the latter case, which has to be avoided in the SR flip-flop, the JK flip-flop toggles its state like the T flip-flop.

The JK flip-flop is a versatile circuit. It can be used for straight storage purposes, just like the D and SR flip-flops. But it can also serve as a T flip-flop by connecting the J and K inputs together.

7.7 SUMMARY OF TERMINOLOGY

We have used the terminology that is quite common. But the reader should be aware that different interpretations of the terms *latch* and *flip-flop* can be found in the literature. Our terminology can be summarized as follows:

Basic latch is a feedback connection of two NOR gates or two NAND gates, which can store one bit of information. It can be set to 1 using the S input and reset to 0 using the R input.

Gated latch is a basic latch that includes input gating and a control input signal. The latch retains its existing state when the control input is equal to 0. Its state may be changed when the control signal is equal to 1. In our discussion we referred to the control input as the clock. We considered two types of gated latches:

- **Gated SR latch** uses the S and R inputs to set the latch to 1 or reset it to 0, respectively.

- **Gated D latch** uses the D input to force the latch into a state that has the same logic value as the D input.

A **flip-flop** is a storage element based on the gated latch principle, which can have its output state changed only on the edge of the controlling clock signal. We considered two types:

- **Edge-triggered flip-flop** is affected only by the input values present when the active edge of the clock occurs.

- **Master-slave flip-flop** is built with two gated latches. The master stage is active during half of the clock cycle, and the slave stage is active during the other half. The output value of the flip-flop changes on the edge of the clock that activates the transfer into the slave stage. Master-slave flip-flops can be edge-triggered or level sensitive. If the master stage is a gated D latch, then it behaves as an edge-triggered flip-flop. If the master stage is a gated SR latch, then the flip-flop is level sensitive (see problem 7.19).

7.8 REGISTERS

A flip-flop stores one bit of information. When a set of n flip-flops is used to store n bits of information, such as an n-bit number, we refer to these flip-flops as a *register*. A common clock is used for each flip-flop in a register, and each flip-flop operates as described in the previous sections. The term register is merely a convenience for referring to *n*-bit structures consisting of flip-flops.

7.8.1 SHIFT REGISTER

In section 5.6 we explained that a given number is multiplied by 2 if its bits are shifted one bit position to the left and a 0 is inserted as the new least-significant bit. Similarly, the number is divided by 2 if the bits are shifted one bit-position to the right. A register that provides the ability to shift its contents is called a *shift register*.

Figure 7.18*a* shows a four-bit shift register that is used to shift its contents one bit-position to the right. The data bits are loaded into the shift register in a serial fashion using the *In* input. The contents of each flip-flop are transferred to the next flip-flop at each positive edge of the clock. An illustration of the transfer is given in Figure 7.18*b*, which shows what happens when the signal values at *In* during eight consecutive clock cycles are 1, 0, 1, 1, 1, 0, 0, and 0, assuming that the initial state of all flip-flops is 0.

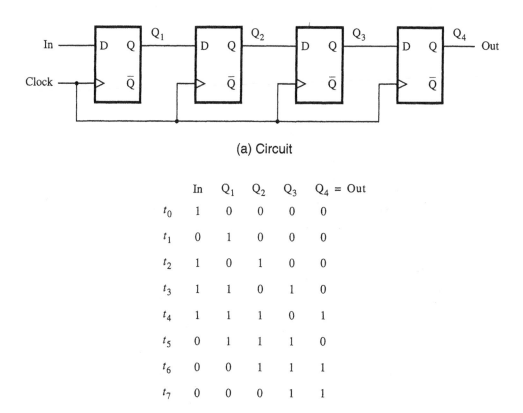

(a) Circuit

	In	Q_1	Q_2	Q_3	Q_4 = Out
t_0	1	0	0	0	0
t_1	0	1	0	0	0
t_2	1	0	1	0	0
t_3	1	1	0	1	0
t_4	1	1	1	0	1
t_5	0	1	1	1	0
t_6	0	0	1	1	1
t_7	0	0	0	1	1

(b) A sample sequence

Figure 7.18   A simple shift register.

To implement a shift register, it is necessary to use either edge-triggered or master-slave flip-flops. The level-sensitive gated latches are not suitable, because a change in the value of *In* would propagate through more than one latch during the time when the clock is equal to 1.

7.8.2 PARALLEL-ACCESS SHIFT REGISTER

In computer systems it is often necessary to transfer *n*-bit data items. This may be done by transmitting all bits at once using *n* separate wires, in which case we say that the transfer is performed in *parallel*. But it is also possible to transfer all bits using a single wire, by performing the transfer one bit at a time, in *n* consecutive clock cycles. We refer to this scheme as *serial* transfer. To transfer an *n*-bit data item serially, we can use a shift register that can be loaded with all *n* bits in parallel (in one clock cycle). Then during the next *n* clock cycles, the contents of the register can be shifted out for serial transfer. The reverse operation is also needed. If bits are received serially, then after *n* clock cycles the contents of the register can be accessed in parallel as an *n*-bit item.

Figure 7.19 shows a four-bit shift register that allows the parallel access. Instead of using the normal shift register connection, the *D* input of each flip-flop is connected to

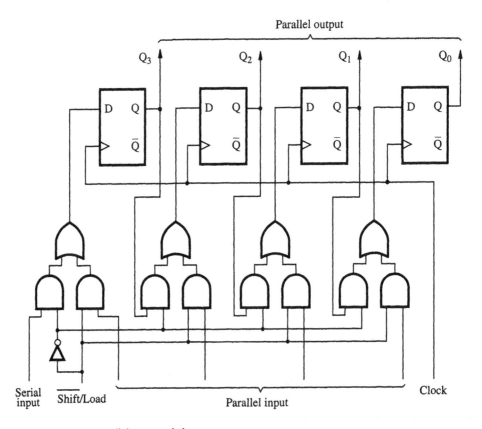

Figure 7.19   Parallel-access shift register.

two different sources. One source is the preceding flip-flop, which is needed for the shift-register operation. The other source is the external input that corresponds to the bit that is to be loaded into the flip-flop as a part of the parallel-load operation. The control signal $\overline{Shift}/Load$ is used to select the mode of operation. If $\overline{Shift}/Load = 0$, then the circuit operates as a shift register. If $\overline{Shift}/Load = 1$, then the parallel input data are loaded into the register. In both cases the action takes place on the positive edge of the clock.

In Figure 7.19 we have chosen to label the flip-flops outputs as $Q_3, \ldots, Q_0$ because shift registers are often used to hold binary numbers. The contents of the register can be accessed in parallel by observing the outputs of all flip-flops. The flip-flops can also be accessed serially, by observing the values of Q_0 during consecutive clock cycles while the contents are being shifted. A circuit in which data can be loaded in series and then accessed in parallel is called a series-to-parallel converter. Similarly, the opposite type of circuit is a parallel-to-series converter. The circuit in Figure 7.19 can perform both of these functions.

7.9 COUNTERS

In Chapter 5 we dealt with circuits that perform arithmetic operations. We showed how adder/subtractor circuits can be designed, either using a simple cascaded (ripple-carry) structure that is inexpensive but slow or using a more complex carry-lookahead structure that is both more expensive and faster. In this section we examine special types of addition and subtraction operations, which are used for the purpose of counting. In particular, we want to design circuits that can increment or decrement a count by 1. Counter circuits are used in digital systems for many purposes. They may count the number of occurrences of certain events, generate timing intervals for control of various tasks in a system, keep track of time elapsed between specific events, and so on.

Counters can be implemented using the adder/subtractor circuits discussed in Chapter 5 and the registers discussed in section 7.8. However, since we only need to change the contents of a counter by 1, it is not necessary to use such elaborate circuits. Instead, we can use much simpler circuits that have a significantly lower cost. We will show how the counter circuits can be designed using T and D flip-flops.

7.9.1 ASYNCHRONOUS COUNTERS

The simplest counter circuits can be built using T flip-flops because the toggle feature is naturally suited for the implementation of counting operation.

Up-Counter with T Flip-Flops

Figure 7.20a gives a three-bit counter capable of counting from 0 to 7. The clock inputs of the three flip-flops are connected in cascade. The T input of each flip-flop is connected to a constant 1, which means that the state of the flip-flop will be reversed (toggled) at each positive edge of its clock. We are assuming that the purpose of this circuit is to count the number of pulses that occur on the primary input called *Clock*. Thus the clock input of the first flip-flop is connected to the *Clock* line. The other two flip-flops have their clock inputs driven by the $\overline{Q}$ output of the preceding flip-flop. Therefore, they toggle their state

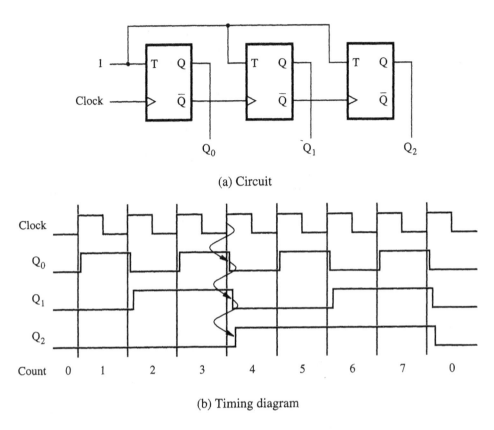

(a) Circuit

(b) Timing diagram

Figure 7.20   A three-bit up-counter.

whenever the preceding flip-flop changes its state from $Q = 1$ to $Q = 0$, which results in a positive edge of the $\overline{Q}$ signal.

Figure 7.20b shows a timing diagram for the counter. The value of Q_0 toggles once each clock cycle. The change takes place shortly after the positive edge of the *Clock* signal. The delay is caused by the propagation delay through the flip-flop. Since the second flip-flop is clocked by $\overline{Q}_0$, the value of Q_1 changes shortly after the negative edge of the Q_0 signal. Similarly, the value of Q_2 changes shortly after the negative edge of the Q_1 signal. If we look at the values $Q_2 Q_1 Q_0$ as the count, then the timing diagram indicates that the counting sequence is 0, 1, 2, 3, 4, 5, 6, 7, 0, 1, and so on. This circuit is a modulo-8 counter. Because it counts in the upward direction, we call it an *up-counter*.

The counter in Figure 7.20a has three *stages*, each comprising a single flip-flop. Only the first stage responds directly to the *Clock* signal; we say that this stage is *synchronized* to the clock. The other two stages respond after an additional delay. For example, when *Count* $= 3$, the next clock pulse will cause the *Count* to go to 4. As indicated by the arrows in the timing diagram in Figure 7.20b, this change requires the toggling of the states of all three flip-flops. The change in Q_0 is observed only after a propagation delay from the positive edge of *Clock*. The Q_1 and Q_2 flip-flops have not yet changed; hence for a brief time the count is $Q_2Q_1Q_0 = 010$. The change in Q_1 appears after a second propagation delay, at which point the count is 000. Finally, the change in Q_2 occurs after a third delay, at which point the stable state of the circuit is reached and the count is 100. This behavior is similar to the rippling of carries in the ripple-carry adder circuit of Figure 5.6. The circuit in Figure 7.20a is an *asynchronous counter*, or a *ripple counter*.

Down-Counter with T Flip-Flops

A slight modification of the circuit in Figure 7.20a is presented in Figure 7.21a. The only difference is that in Figure 7.21a the clock inputs of the second and third flip-flops are driven by the Q outputs of the preceding stages, rather than by the $\overline{Q}$ outputs. The timing diagram, given in Figure 7.21b, shows that this circuit counts in the sequence 0, 7, 6, 5, 4, 3, 2, 1, 0, 7, and so on. Because it counts in the downward direction, we say that it is a *down-counter*.

It is possible to combine the functionality of the circuits in Figures 7.20a and 7.21a to form a counter that can count either up or down. Such a counter is called an *up/down-counter*. We leave the derivation of this counter as an exercise for the reader (problem 7.16).

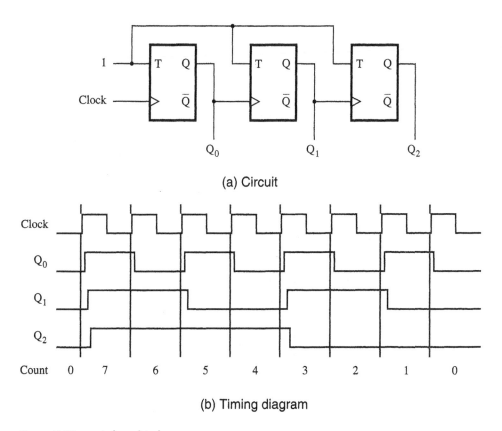

(a) Circuit

(b) Timing diagram

Figure 7.21   A three-bit down-counter.

7.9.2 SYNCHRONOUS COUNTERS

The asynchronous counters in Figures 7.20a and 7.21a are simple, but not very fast. If a counter with a larger number of bits is constructed in this manner, then the delays caused by the cascaded clocking scheme may become too long to meet the desired performance requirements. We can build a faster counter by clocking all flip-flops at the same time, using the approach described below.

Synchronous Counter with T Flip-Flops

Table 7.1 shows the contents of a three-bit up-counter for eight consecutive clock cycles, assuming that the count is initially 0. Observing the pattern of bits in each row of the table, it is apparent that bit Q_0 changes on each clock cycle. Bit Q_1 changes only when $Q_0 = 1$. Bit Q_2 changes only when both Q_1 and Q_0 are equal to 1. In general, for an n-bit up-counter, a given flip-flop changes its state only when all the preceding flip-flops are in the state $Q = 1$. Therefore, if we use T flip-flops to realize the counter, then the T inputs are defined as

$$T_0 = 1$$
$$T_1 = Q_0$$
$$T_2 = Q_0 Q_1$$
$$T_3 = Q_0 Q_1 Q_2$$

$$\cdot$$
$$\cdot$$
$$\cdot$$

$$T_n = Q_0 Q_1 \cdots Q_{n-1}$$

An example of a four-bit counter based on these expressions is given in Figure 7.22a. Instead of using AND gates of increased size for each stage, which may lead to fan-in problems, we use a factored arrangement, as shown in the figure. This arrangement does not slow down the response of the counter, because all flip-flops change their states after a

Table 7.1   Derivation of the synchronous up-counter

Clock cycle	Q_2	Q_1	Q_0
0	0	0	0
1	0	0	1
2	0	1	0
3	0	1	1
4	1	0	0
5	1	0	1
6	1	1	0
7	1	1	1
8	0	0	0

Q_1 changes
Q_2 changes

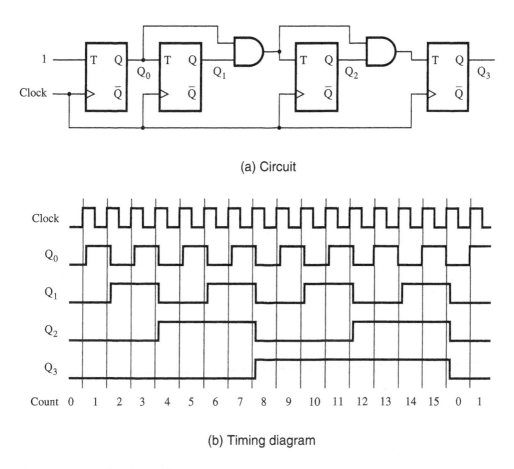

(a) Circuit

(b) Timing diagram

Figure 7.22   A four-bit synchronous up-counter.

propagation delay from the positive edge of the clock. Note that a change in the value of Q_0 may have to propagate through several AND gates to reach the flip-flops in the higher stages of the counter, which requires a certain amount of time. This time must not exceed the clock period. Actually, it must be less than the clock period minus the setup time for the flip-flops.

Figure 7.22b gives a timing diagram. It shows that the circuit behaves as a modulo-16 up-counter. Because all changes take place with the same delay after the active edge of the *Clock* signal, the circuit is called a *synchronous counter*.

Enable and Clear Capability

The counters in Figures 7.20 through 7.22 change their contents in response to each clock pulse. Often it is desirable to be able to inhibit counting, so that the count remains in its present state. This may be accomplished by including an *Enable* control signal, as indicated in Figure 7.23. The circuit is the counter of Figure 7.22, where the *Enable* signal controls directly the T input of the first flip-flop. Connecting the *Enable* also to the AND-

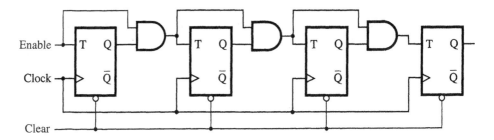

Figure 7.23   Inclusion of Enable and Clear capability.

gate chain means that if *Enable* = 0, then all *T* inputs will be equal to 0. If *Enable* = 1, then the counter operates as explained previously.

In many applications it is necessary to start with the count equal to zero. This is easily achieved if the flip-flops can be cleared, as explained in section 7.4.3. The clear inputs on all flip-flops can be tied together and driven by a *Clear* control input.

Synchronous Counter with D Flip-Flops

While the toggle feature makes T flip-flops a natural choice for the implementation of counters, it is also possible to build counters using other types of flip-flops. The JK flip-flops can be used in exactly the same way as the T flip-flops because if the *J* and *K* inputs are tied together, a JK flip-flop becomes a T flip-flop. We will now consider using D flip-flops for this purpose.

It is not obvious how D flip-flops can be used to implement a counter. We will present a formal method for deriving such circuits in Chapter 8. Here we will present a circuit structure that meets the requirements but will leave the derivation for Chapter 8. Figure 7.24 gives a four-bit up-counter that counts in the sequence 0, 1, 2, ..., 14, 15, 0, 1, and so on. The count is indicated by the flip-flop outputs $Q_3Q_2Q_1Q_0$. If we assume that *Enable* = 1, then the *D* inputs of the flip-flops are defined by the expressions

$$D_0 = \overline{Q}_0 = 1 \oplus Q_0$$
$$D_1 = Q_1 \oplus Q_0$$
$$D_2 = Q_2 \oplus Q_1Q_0$$
$$D_3 = Q_3 \oplus Q_2Q_1Q_0$$

For a larger counter the *i*th stage is defined by

$$D_i = Q_i \oplus Q_{i-1}Q_{i-2}\cdots Q_1Q_0$$

We will show how to derive these equations in Chapter 8.

We have included the *Enable* control signal so that the counter counts the clock pulses only if *Enable* = 1. In effect, the above equations are modified to implement the circuit in the figure as follows

$$D_0 = Q_0 \oplus Enable$$
$$D_1 = Q_1 \oplus Q_0 \cdot Enable$$

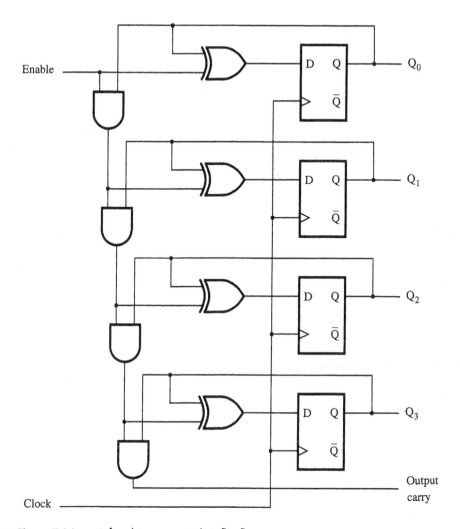

Figure 7.24 A four-bit counter with D flip-flops.

$$D_2 = Q_2 \oplus Q_1 \cdot Q_0 \cdot Enable$$
$$D_3 = Q_3 \oplus Q_2 \cdot Q_1 \cdot Q_0 \cdot Enable$$

The operation of the counter is based on our observation for Table 7.1 that the state of the flip-flop in stage i changes only if all preceding flip-flops are in the state $Q = 1$. This makes the output of the AND gate that feeds stage i equal to 1, which causes the output of the XOR gate connected to D_i to be equal to $\overline{Q}_i$. Otherwise, the output of the XOR gate provides $D_i = Q_i$, and the flip-flop remains in the same state. This resembles the carry propagation in a carry-lookahead adder circuit (see section 5.4); hence the AND-gate chain can be thought of as the *carry chain*. Even though the circuit is only a four-bit counter, we have included an extra AND that produces the "output carry." This signal makes it easy to concatenate two such four-bit counters to create an eight-bit counter.

Finally, the reader should note that the counter in Figure 7.24 is essentially the same as the circuit in Figure 7.23. We showed in Figure 7.16a that a T flip-flop can be formed from a D flip-flop by providing the extra gating that gives

$$D = Q\overline{T} + \overline{Q}T$$
$$= Q \oplus T$$

Thus in each stage in Figure 7.24, the D flip-flop and the associated XOR gate implement the functionality of a T flip-flop.

7.9.3 COUNTERS WITH PARALLEL LOAD

Often it is necessary to start counting with the initial count being equal to 0. This state can be achieved by using the capability to clear the flip-flops as indicated in Figure 7.23. But sometimes it is desirable to start with a different count. To allow this mode of operation, a counter circuit must have some inputs through which the initial count can be loaded. Using the *Clear* and *Preset* inputs for this purpose is a possibility, but a better approach is discussed below.

The circuit of Figure 7.24 can be modified to provide the parallel-load capability as shown in Figure 7.25. A two-input multiplexer is inserted before each *D* input. One input to the multiplexer is used to provide the normal counting operation. The other input is a data bit that can be loaded directly into the flip-flop. A control input, *Load*, is used to choose the mode of operation. The circuit counts when $Load = 0$. A new initial value, $D_3D_2D_1D_0$, is loaded into the counter when $Load = 1$.

7.10 RESET SYNCHRONIZATION

We have already mentioned that it is important to be able to clear, or *reset*, the contents of a counter prior to commencing a counting operation. This can be done using the clear capability of the individual flip-flops. But we may also be interested in resetting the count to 0 during the normal counting process. An n-bit up-counter functions naturally as a modulo-2^n counter. Suppose that we wish to have a counter that counts modulo some base that is not a power of 2. For example, we may want to design a modulo-6 counter, for which the counting sequence is 0, 1, 2, 3, 4, 5, 0, 1, and so on.

The most straightforward approach is to recognize when the count reaches 5 and then reset the counter. An AND gate can be used to detect the occurrence of the count of 5. Actually, it is sufficient to ascertain that $Q_2 = Q_0 = 1$, which is true only for 5 in our desired counting sequence. A circuit based on this approach is given in Figure 7.26a. It uses a three-bit synchronous counter of the type depicted in Figure 7.25. The parallel-load feature of the counter is used to reset its contents when the count reaches 5. The resetting action takes place at the positive clock edge after the count has reached 5. It involves loading $D_2D_1D_0 = 000$ into the flip-flops. As seen in the timing diagram in Figure 7.26b,

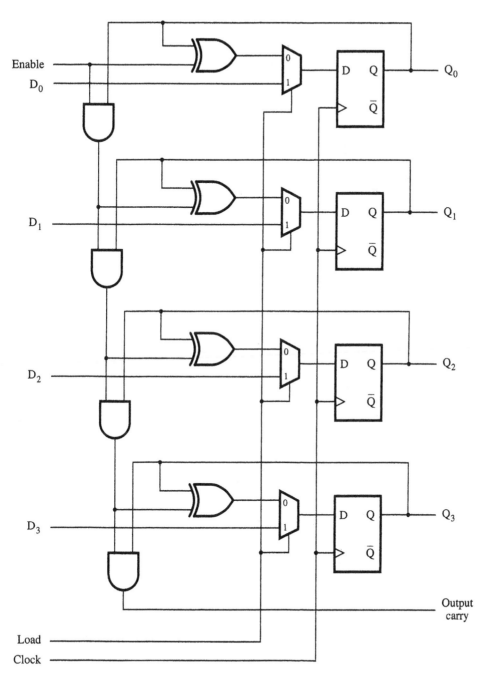

Figure 7.25   A counter with parallel-load capability.

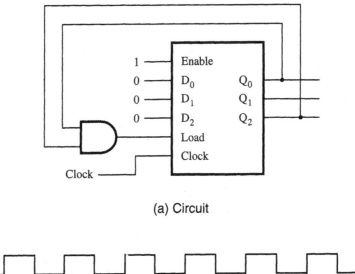

(a) Circuit

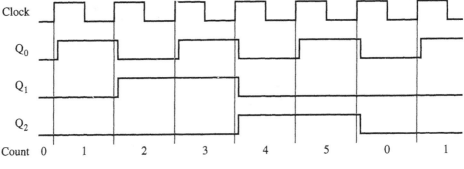

(b) Timing diagram

Figure 7.26   A modulo-6 counter with synchronous reset.

the desired counting sequence is achieved, with each value of the count being established for one full clock cycle. Because the counter is reset on the active edge of the clock, we say that this type of counter has a *synchronous reset*.

Consider now the possibility of using the clear feature of individual flip-flops, rather than the parallel-load approach. The circuit in Figure 7.27*a* illustrates one possibility. It uses the counter structure of Figure 7.22*a*. Since the clear inputs are active when low, a NAND gate is used to detect the occurrence of the count of 5 and cause the clearing of all three flip-flops. Conceptually, this seems to work fine, but closer examination reveals a potential problem. The timing diagram for this circuit is given in Figure 7.27*b*. It shows a difficulty that arises when the count is equal to 5. As soon as the count reaches this value, the NAND gate triggers the resetting action. The flip-flops are cleared to 0 a short time after the NAND gate has detected the count of 5. This time depends on the gate delays in the

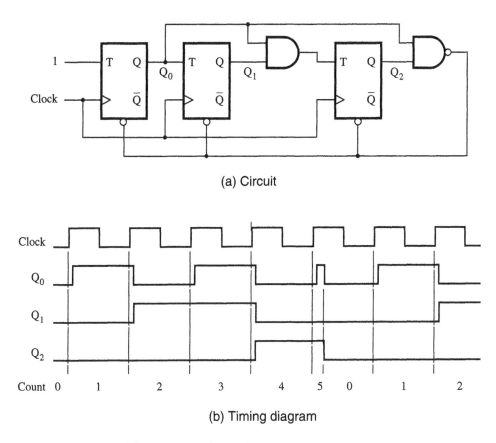

(a) Circuit

(b) Timing diagram

Figure 7.27   A modulo-6 counter with asynchronous reset.

circuit, but not on the clock. Therefore, signal values $Q_2Q_1Q_0 = 101$ are maintained for a time that is much less than a clock cycle. Depending on a particular application of such a counter, this may be adequate, but it may also be completely unacceptable. For example, if the counter is used in a digital system where all operations in the system are synchronized by the same clock, then this narrow pulse denoting *Count* = 5 would not be seen by the rest of the system. To solve this problem, we could try to use a modulo-7 counter instead, assuming that the system would ignore the short pulse that denotes the count of 6. This is not a good way of designing circuits, because undesirable pulses often cause unforeseen difficulties in practice. The approach employed in Figure 7.27a is said to use *asynchronous reset*.

The timing diagrams in Figures 7.26b and 7.27b suggest that synchronous reset is a better choice than asynchronous reset. The same observation is true if the natural counting sequence has to be broken by loading some value other than zero. The new value of the count can be established cleanly using the parallel-load feature. The alternative of using the clear and preset capability of individual flip-flops to set their states to reflect the desired count has the same problems as discussed in conjunction with the asynchronous reset.

7.15   CONCLUDING REMARKS

In this chapter we have presented circuits that serve as basic storage elements in digital systems. These elements are used to build larger units such as registers, shift registers, and counters. Many other texts that deal with this material are available [3–11]. We have illustrated how circuits with flip-flops can be described using VHDL code. More information on VHDL can be found in [12–17]. In the next chapter a more formal method for designing circuits with flip-flops will be presented.

PROBLEMS

7.1   Consider the timing diagram in Figure P7.1. Assuming that the D and *Clock* inputs shown are applied to the circuit in Figure 7.12, draw waveforms for the Q_a, Q_b, and Q_c signals.

7.2   Can the circuit in Figure 7.3 be modified to implement an SR latch? Explain your answer.

7.3   Figure 7.5 shows a latch built with NOR gates. Draw a similar latch using NAND gates. Derive its truth table and show its timing diagram.

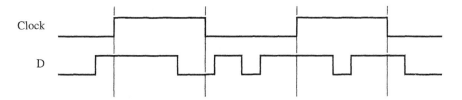

Figure P7.1   Timing diagram for problem 7.1.

7.4 Show a circuit that implements the gated SR latch using NAND gates only.

7.5 Given a 100-MHz clock signal, derive a circuit using D flip-flops to generate 50-MHz and 25-MHz clock signals. Draw a timing diagram for all three clock signals, assuming reasonable delays.

7.6 An SR flip-flop is a flip-flop that has set and reset inputs like a gated SR latch. Show how an SR flip-flop can be constructed using a D flip-flop and other logic gates.

7.7 The gated SR latch in Figure 7.6a has unpredictable behavior if the S and R inputs are both equal to 1 when the *Clk* changes to 0. One way to solve this problem is to create a *set-dominant* gated SR latch in which the condition $S = R = 1$ cause the latch to be set to 1. Design a set-dominant gated SR latch and show the circuit.

7.8 Show how a JK flip-flop can be constructed using a T flip-flop and other logic gates.

7.9 Consider the circuit in Figure P7.2. Derive a truth table for this circuit to determine its functionality. How does this circuit compare with the circuits that we discussed in this chapter?

7.10 Write VHDL code that represents a T flip-flop with an asynchronous clear input. Use behavioral code, rather than structural code.

7.11 Write VHDL code that represents a JK flip-flop. Use behavioral code, rather than structural code.

7.12 Synthesize a circuit for the code written for problem 7.11 for implementation in a CPLD. Simulate the circuit and show a timing diagram that verifies the desired functionality.

7.13 A barrel shifter is a shift register in which the data can be shifted either by one bit position, as in a normal shift register, or by multiple bit positions. Design a four-bit barrel shifter that can shift to the right by 0, 1, 2, or 3 positions.

7.14 Write VHDL code for the barrel shifter described in problem 7.13.

7.15 Design a four-bit synchronous counter with parallel load. Use T flip-flops, instead of the D flip-flops used in section 7.9.3.

7.16 Design a three-bit up/down counter using T flip-flops. It should include a control input called $\overline{Up}$/Down. If $\overline{Up}$/Down $= 0$, then the circuit should behave as an up-counter. If $\overline{Up}$/Down $= 1$, then the circuit should behave as a down-counter.

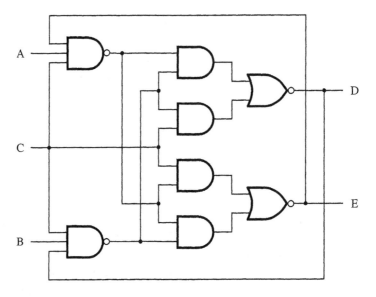

Figure P7.2   Circuit for problem 7.9.

7.17   Repeat problem 7.16 using D flip-flops.

7.18   The circuit in Figure P7.3 looks like a counter. What is the sequence that this circuit counts in?

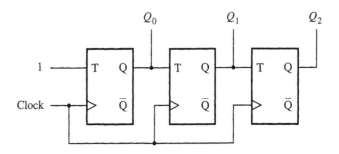

Figure P7.3   The circuit for problem 7.18.

7.19   Consider the circuit in Figure P7.4. How does this circuit compare with the circuit in Figure 7.17? Can the circuits be used for the same purposes? If not, what is the key difference between them?

7.20   Construct a NOR-gate circuit, similar to the one in Figure 7.11*a*, which implements a negative-edge-triggered D flip-flop.

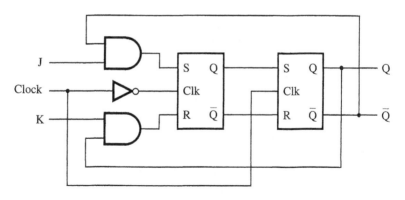

Figure P7.4   Circuit for problem 7.19.

7.21   Write behavioral VHDL code that represents a 24-bit up/down-counter with parallel load and asynchronous reset.

7.22   Modify the VHDL code in Figure 7.53 by adding a parameter that sets the number of flip-flops in the counter.

7.23   Write behavioral VHDL code that represents a modulo-12 up-counter with synchronous reset.

7.24   For the flip-flops in the counter in Figure 7.25, assume that $t_{su} = 3$ ns, $t_h = 1$ ns, and the propagation delay through a flip-flop is 1 ns. Assume that each AND gate, XOR gate, and 2-to-1 multiplexer has the propagation delay equal to 1 ns. What is the maximum clock frequency for which the circuit will operate correctly?

7.25   Write hierarchical code (structural) for the circuit in Figure 7.28. Use the counter in Figure 7.25 as a subcircuit.

7.26   Write VHDL code that represents an eight-bit Johnson counter. Implement the counter in a CPLD and give a timing simulation that shows the counting sequence.

7.27   Write behavioral VHDL code in the style shown in Figure 7.52 that represents a ring counter. Your code should have a parameter N that sets the number of flip-flops in the counter.

7.28   Write behavioral VHDL code that describes the functionality of the circuit shown in Figure 7.43.

7.29   Write structural VHDL code that instantiates the *lpm_counter* module from the LPM library. Configure the module as a 32-bit up-counter. For the counter circuit in Figure 7.24, we said that the AND-gate chain can be thought of as the carry-chain. The FLEX 10K FPGA contains special-purpose logic to implement this carry-chain such that it has minimal propagation delay. Use the MAX+plusII synthesis options to implement the *lpm_counter* in two ways: with the dedicated carry-chain used and with the dedicated carry-chain not used. Use the Timing Analyzer in MAX+plusII to determine the maximum speed of operation of the counter in both cases. See the tutorials in Appendices B, C, and D for instructions on using the appropriate features of the CAD tools.

7.30 Figure 7.66 gives VHDL code for a digital system that swaps the contents of two registers, $R1$ and $R2$, using register $R3$ for temporary storage. Create an equivalent schematic using MAX+plusII for this system. Implement the schematic in a CPLD or FPGA and perform a timing simulation.

7.31 Repeat problem 7.30 using the control circuit in Figure 7.60.

7.32 Modify the code in Figure 7.68 to use the control circuit in Figure 7.60. Implement the code in a CPLD or FPGA and perform a timing simulation.

7.33 In section 7.14 we designed a processor that performs the operations listed in Table 7.3. Design a modified circuit that performs an additional operation Swap Rx, Ry. This operation swaps the contents of registers Rx and Ry. Use three bits $f_2 f_1 f_0$ to represent the input F shown in Figure 7.72 because there are now five operations, rather than four. Add a new register, named Tmp, into the system, to be used for temporary storage during the swap operation. Show logic expressions for the outputs of the control circuit, as was done in section 7.14.

7.34 A ring oscillator is a circuit that has an odd number, n, of inverters connected in a ringlike structure, as shown in Figure P7.5. The output of each inverter is a periodic signal with a certain period.

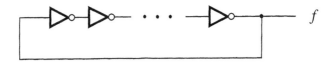

Figure P7.5   A ring oscillator.

(a) Assume that all the inverters are identical; hence they all have the same delay, called t_p. Let the output of one of the inverters be named f. Give an equation that expresses the period of the signal f in terms of n and t_p.

(b) For this part you are to design a circuit that can be used to experimentally measure the delay t_p through one of the inverters in the ring oscillator. Assume the existence of an input called *Reset* and another called *Interval*. The timing of these two signals is shown in Figure P7.6. The length of time for which *Interval* has the value 1 is known. Assume that this

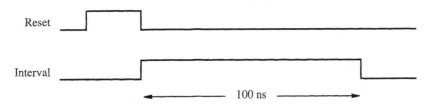

Figure P7.6   Timing of signals for problem 7.34

length of time is 100 ns. Design a circuit that uses the *Reset* and *Interval* signals and the signal *f* from part (*a*) to experimentally measure t_p. In your design you may use logic gates and subcircuits such as adders, flip-flops, counters, registers, and so on.

7.35 A circuit for a gated D latch is shown in Figure P7.7. Assume that the propagation delay through either a NAND gate or an inverter is 1 ns. Complete the timing diagram given in the figure, which shows the signal values with 1 ns resolution.

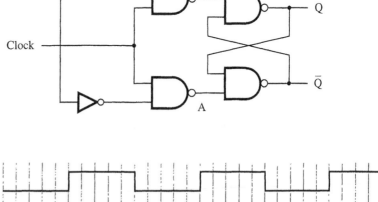

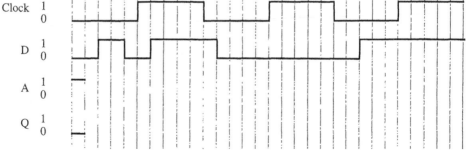

Figure P7.7 Circuit and timing diagram for problem 7.35.

7.36 A logic circuit has two inputs, *Clock* and *Start*, and two outputs, *f* and *g*. The behavior of the circuit is described by the timing diagram in Figure P7.8. When a pulse is received on the *Start* input, the circuit produces pulses on the *f* and *g* outputs as shown in the timing diagram. Design a suitable circuit using only the following components: a three-bit resettable positive-edge-triggered synchronous counter and basic logic gates. For your answer assume that the delays through all logic gates and the counter are negligible.

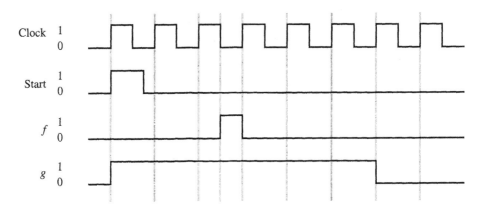

Figure P7.8   Timing diagram for problem 7.36.

REFERENCES

1. V. C. Hamacher, Z. G. Vranesic, and S. G. Zaky, *Computer Organization*, 4th ed., (McGraw-Hill: New York, 1996).

2. D. A. Patterson and J. L. Hennessy, *Computer Organization and Design—The Hardware/Software Interface*, 2nd ed., (Morgan Kaufmann: San Francisco, Ca., 1998).

3. D. D. Gajski, *Principles of Digital Design*, (Prentice-Hall: Upper Saddle River, N.J., 1997).

4. M. M. Mano and C. R. Kime, *Logic and Computer Design Fundamentals*, (Prentice-Hall: Upper Saddle River, N.J., 1997).

5. J. P. Daniels, *Digital Design from Zero to One*, (Wiley: New York, 1996).

6. V. P. Nelson, H. T. Nagle, B. D. Carroll, and J. D. Irwin, *Digital Logic Circuit Analysis and Design*, (Prentice-Hall: Englewood Cliffs, N.J., 1995).

7. R. H. Katz, *Contemporary Logic Design*, (Benjamin/Cummings: Redwood City, Ca., 1994).

8. J. P. Hayes, *Introduction to Logic Design*, (Addison-Wesley: Reading, Ma., 1993).

9. C. H. Roth Jr., *Fundamentals of Logic Design*, 4th ed., (West: St. Paul, Mn., 1993).

10. J. F. Wakerly, *Digital Design Principles and Practices*, (Prentice-Hall: Englewood Cliffs, N.J., 1990).

11. E. J. McCluskey, *Logic Design Principles*, (Prentice-Hall: Englewood Cliffs, N.J., 1986).

12. Institute of Electrical and Electronics Engineers, "1076-1993 IEEE Standard VHDL Language Reference Manual," 1993.

13. D. L. Perry, *VHDL*, 3rd ed., (McGraw-Hill: New York, 1998).

14. Z. Navabi, *VHDL—Analysis and Modeling of Digital Systems*, (McGraw-Hill: New York, 1993).

15. J. Bhasker, *A VHDL Primer*, (Prentice-Hall: Englewood Cliffs, N.J., 1995).

16. K. Skahill, *VHDL for Programmable Logic*, (Addison-Wesley: Menlo Park, Ca., 1996).

17. A. Dewey, *Analysis and Design of Digital Systems with VHDL*, (PWS Publishing Co.: Boston, Ma., 1997).

chapter
8

SYNCHRONOUS SEQUENTIAL CIRCUITS

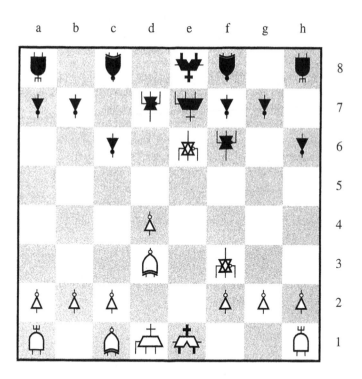

8. Ng5xe6, Qd8–e7

In preceding chapters we considered combinational logic circuits in which outputs are determined fully by the present values of inputs. We also discussed how simple storage elements can be implemented in the form of flip-flops. The output of a flip-flop depends on the state of the flip-flop rather than the value of its inputs at any given time; the inputs cause changes in the state.

In this chapter we deal with a general class of circuits in which the outputs depend on the past behavior of the circuit, as well as on the present values of inputs. They are called *sequential circuits*. In most cases a clock signal is used to control the operation of a sequential circuit; such a circuit is called a *synchronous sequential circuit*. The alternative, in which no clock signal is used, is called an *asynchronous sequential circuit*. Synchronous circuits are easier to design and are used in a vast majority of practical applications; they are the topic of this chapter. Asynchronous circuits will be discussed in Chapter 9.

Synchronous sequential circuits are realized using combinational logic and one or more flip-flops. The general structure of such a circuit is shown in Figure 8.1. The circuit has a set of primary inputs, W, and produces a set of outputs, Z. The values of the outputs of the flip-flops are referred to as the *state*, Q, of the circuit. Under control of the clock signal, the flip-flop outputs change their state as determined by the combinational logic that feeds the inputs of these flip-flops. Thus the circuit moves from one state to another. To ensure that only one transition from one state to another takes place during one clock cycle, the flip-flops have to be of the edge-triggered type. They can be triggered either by the positive (0 to 1 transition) or by the negative (1 to 0 transition) edge of the clock. We will use the term *active clock edge* to refer to the clock edge that causes the change in state.

The combinational logic that provides the input signals to the flip-flops derives its inputs from two sources: the primary inputs, W, and the present (current) outputs of the flip-flops, Q. Thus changes in state depend on both the present state and the values of the primary inputs.

Figure 8.1 indicates that the outputs of the sequential circuit are generated by another combinational circuit, such that the outputs are a function of the present state of the flip-flops and of the primary inputs. Although the outputs always depend on the present state, they do not necessarily have to depend directly on the primary inputs. Thus the connection shown in blue in the figure may or may not exist. To distinguish between these two possibilities, it is customary to say that sequential circuits whose outputs depend only on the state of the circuit are of *Moore* type, while those whose outputs depend on both the state and the primary inputs are of *Mealy* type. These names are in honor of Edward Moore and George Mealy, who investigated the behavior of such circuits in the 1950s.

Sequential circuits are also called *finite state machines (FSMs)*, which is a more formal name that is often found in technical literature. The name derives from the fact that the functional behavior of these circuits can be represented using a finite number of states. In this chapter we will often use the term *finite state machine*, or simply *machine*, when referring to sequential circuits.

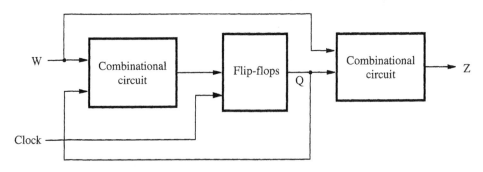

Figure 8.1   The general form of a sequential circuit.

8.1 BASIC DESIGN STEPS

We will introduce the techniques for designing sequential circuits by means of a simple example. Suppose that we wish to design a circuit that meets the following specification:

1. The circuit has one input, w, and one output, z.
2. All changes in the circuit occur on the positive edge of a clock signal.
3. The output z is equal to 1 if during two immediately preceding clock cycles the input w was equal to 1. Otherwise, the value of z is equal to 0.

From this specification it is apparent that the output z cannot depend solely on the present value of w. To illustrate this, consider the sequence of values of the w and z signals during 11 clock cycles, as shown in Figure 8.2. The values of w are assumed arbitrarily; the values of z correspond to our specification. These sequences of input and output values indicate that for a given input value the output may be either 0 or 1. For example, $w = 0$ during clock cycles t_2 and t_5, but $z = 0$ during t_2 and $z = 1$ during t_5. Similarly, $w = 1$ during t_1 and t_8, but $z = 0$ during t_1 and $z = 1$ during t_8. This means that z is not determined only by the present value of w, so there must exist different states in the circuit that determine the value of z.

8.1.1 STATE DIAGRAM

The first step in designing a finite state machine is to determine how many states are needed and which transitions are possible from one state to another. There is no set procedure for this task. The designer must think carefully about what the machine has to accomplish. A good way to begin is to select one particular state as a *starting* state; this is the state that the circuit should enter when power is first turned on or when a *reset* signal is applied. For our example let us assume that the starting state is called state A. As long as the input w is 0, the circuit need not do anything, and so each active clock edge should result in the circuit remaining in state A. When w becomes equal to 1, the machine should recognize this, and move to a different state, which we will call state B. This transition takes place on the next active clock edge after w has become equal to 1. In state B, as in state A, the circuit should keep the value of output z at 0, because it has not yet seen $w = 1$ for two consecutive clock cycles. When in state B, if w is 0 at the next active clock edge, the circuit should move back to state A. However, if $w = 1$ when in state B, the circuit should change to a third state, called C, and it should then generate an output $z = 1$. The circuit should remain in state C as long as $w = 1$ and should continue to maintain $z = 1$. When w becomes 0, the machine should move back to state A. Since the preceding description handles all possible values

Clock cycle:	t_0	t_1	t_2	t_3	t_4	t_5	t_6	t_7	t_8	t_9	t_{10}
w:	0	1	0	1	1	0	1	1	1	0	1
z:	0	0	0	0	0	1	0	0	1	1	0

Figure 8.2 Sequences of input and output signals.

of input w that the machine can encounter in its various states, we can conclude that three states are needed to implement the desired machine.

Now that we have determined in an informal way the possible transitions between states, we will describe a more formal procedure that can be used to design the corresponding sequential circuit. Behavior of a sequential circuit can be described in several different ways. The conceptually simplest method is to use a pictorial representation in the form of a *state diagram*, which is a graph that depicts states of the circuit as nodes (circles) and transitions between states as directed arcs. The state diagram in Figure 8.3 defines the behavior that corresponds to our specification. States A, B, and C appear as nodes in the diagram. Node A represents the starting state, and it is also the state that the circuit will reach *after* an input $w = 0$ is applied. In this state the output z should be 0, which is indicated as $A/z=0$ in the node. The circuit should remain in state A as long as $w = 0$, which is indicated by an arc with a label $w = 0$ that originates and terminates at this node. The first occurrence of $w = 1$ (following the condition $w = 0$) is recorded by moving from state A to state B. This transition is indicated on the graph by an arc originating at A and terminating at B. The label $w = 1$ on this arc denotes the input value that causes the transition. In state B the output remains at 0, which is indicated as $B/z=0$ in the node.

When the circuit is in state B, it will change to state C if w is still equal to 1 at the next active clock edge. In state C the output z becomes equal to 1. If w stays at 1 during subsequent clock cycles, the circuit will remain in state C maintaining $z = 1$. However, if w becomes 0 when the circuit is either in state B or in state C, the next active clock edge will cause a transition to state A to take place.

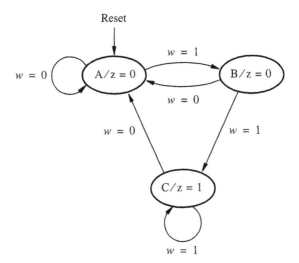

Figure 8.3   State diagram of a simple sequential circuit.

8.1.2 STATE TABLE

Although the state diagram provides a description of the behavior of a sequential circuit that is easy to understand, to proceed with the implementation of the circuit, it is convenient to translate the information contained in the state diagram into a tabular form. Figure 8.4 shows the *state table* for our sequential circuit. The table indicates all transitions from each *present state* to the *next state* for different values of the input signal. Note that the output z is specified with respect to the present state, namely, the state that the circuit is in at present time.

We now show the design steps that will produce the final circuit. To explain the basic design concepts, we first go through a traditional process of manually performing each design step. This is followed by a discussion of automated design techniques that use modern computer aided design (CAD) tools.

8.1.3 STATE ASSIGNMENT

The state table in Figure 8.4 defines the three states in terms of letters A, B, and C. When implemented in a logic circuit, each state is represented by a particular valuation (combination of values) of *state variables*. Each state variable may be implemented in the form of a flip-flop. Since three states have to be realized, it is sufficient to use two state variables. Let these variables be y_1 and y_2.

Now we can adapt the general block diagram in Figure 8.1 to our example as shown in Figure 8.5, to indicate the structure of the circuit that implements the required finite state machine. Two flip-flops represent the state variables. In the figure we have not specified the type of flip-flops to be used; this issue is addressed in the next subsection. From the specification in Figures 8.3 and 8.4, the output z is determined only by the present state of the circuit. Thus the block diagram in Figure 8.5 shows that z is a function of only y_1 and y_2; our design is of Moore type. We need to design a combinational circuit that uses y_1 and y_2 as input signals and generates a correct output signal z for all possible valuations of these inputs.

The signals y_1 and y_2 are also fed back to the combinational circuit that determines the next state of the FSM. This circuit also uses the primary input signal w. Its outputs are two signals, Y_1 and Y_2, which are used to set the state of the flip-flops. Each active edge of the clock will cause the flip-flops to change their state to the values of Y_1 and Y_2 at that

Present state	Next state		Output z
	$w = 0$	$w = 1$	
A	A	B	0
B	A	C	0
C	A	C	1

Figure 8.4   State table for the sequential circuit in Figure 8.3.

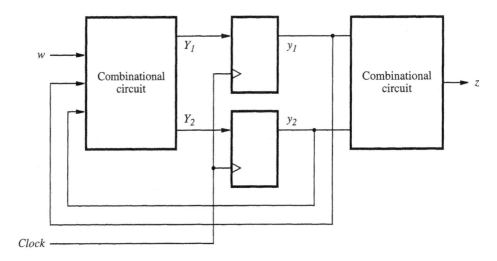

Figure 8.5   A general sequential circuit with input w, output z, and two state flip-flops.

time. Therefore, Y_1 and Y_2 are called the *next-state variables*, and y_1 and y_2 are called the *present-state variables*. We need to design a combinational circuit with inputs w, y_1, and y_2, such that for all valuations of these inputs the outputs Y_1 and Y_2 will cause the machine to move to the next state that satisfies our specification. The next step in the design process is to create a truth table that defines this circuit, as well as the circuit that generates z.

To produce the desired truth table, we assign a specific valuation of variables y_1 and y_2 to each state. One possible assignment is given in Figure 8.6, where the states A, B, and C are represented by $y_2y_1 = 00$, 01, and 10, respectively. The fourth valuation, $y_2y_1 = 11$, is not needed in this case.

The type of table given in Figure 8.6 is usually called a *state-assigned table*. This table can serve directly as a truth table for the output z with the inputs y_1 and y_2. Although for the next-state functions Y_1 and Y_2 the table does not have the appearance of a normal truth

	Present state	Next state		Output
		$w = 0$	$w = 1$	z
	y_2y_1	Y_2Y_1	Y_2Y_1	
A	00	00	01	0
B	01	00	10	0
C	10	00	10	1
	11	dd	dd	d

Figure 8.6   State-assigned table for the sequential circuit in Figure 8.4.

table, because there are two separate columns in the table for each value of w, it is obvious that the table includes all of the information that defines the next-state functions in terms of valuations of inputs w, y_1, and y_2.

8.1.4 CHOICE OF FLIP-FLOPS AND DERIVATION OF NEXT-STATE AND OUTPUT EXPRESSIONS

From the state-assigned table in Figure 8.6, we can derive the logic expressions for the next-state and output functions. But first we have to decide on the type of flip-flops that will be used in the circuit. The most straightforward choice is to use D-type flip-flops, because in this case the values of Y_1 and Y_2 are simply clocked into the flip-flops to become the new values of y_1 and y_2. In other words, if the inputs to the flip-flops are called D_1 and D_2, then these signals are the same as Y_1 and Y_2. Note that the diagram in Figure 8.5 corresponds exactly to this use of D-type flip-flops. For other types of flip-flops, such as JK type, the relationship between the next-state variable and inputs to a flip-flop is not as straightforward; we will consider this situation in section 8.7.

The required logic expressions can be derived as shown in Figure 8.7. We use Karnaugh maps to make it easy for the reader to verify the validity of the expressions. Recall that

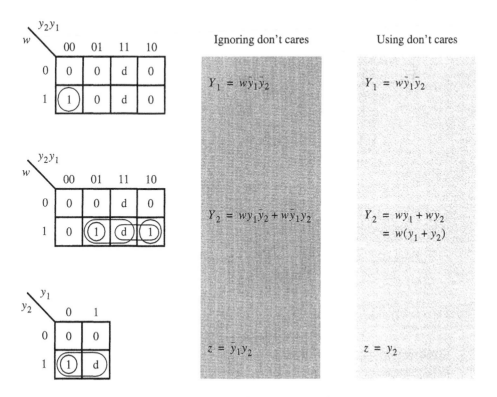

Figure 8.7   Derivation of logic expressions for the sequential circuit in Figure 8.6.

in Figure 8.6 we needed only three of the four possible binary valuations to represent the states. The fourth valuation, $y_2y_1 = 11$, should never occur in the circuit because the circuit is constrained to move only within states A, B, and C; therefore, we may choose to treat this valuation as a don't-care condition. The resulting don't-care squares in the Karnaugh maps are denoted by d's. Using the don't cares to simplify the expressions, we obtain

$$Y_1 = w\bar{y}_1\bar{y}_2$$
$$Y_2 = w(y_1 + y_2)$$
$$z = y_2$$

If we do not use don't cares, then the resulting expressions are slightly more complex; they are shown in the gray-shaded area of Figure 8.7. The reader may wonder why we have derived these expressions, since they lead to a more expensive circuit. We will give a rationale for possibly ignoring don't-care cases in section 8.4.2.

Since $D_1 = Y_1$ and $D_2 = Y_2$, the logic circuit that corresponds to the preceding expressions is implemented as shown in Figure 8.8. Observe that a clock signal is included, and the circuit is provided with an active-low reset capability. Connecting the clear input on the

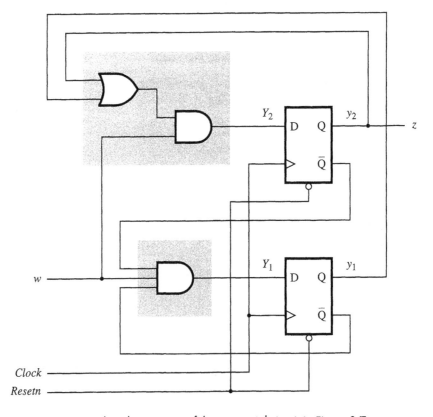

Figure 8.8   Final implementation of the sequential circuit in Figure 8.7.

flip-flops to an external *Resetn* signal, as shown in the figure, provides a simple means for forcing the circuit into a known state. If we apply the signal *Resetn* = *0* to the circuit, then both flip-flops will be cleared to 0, placing the FSM into the state $y_2y_1 = 00$.

8.1.5 TIMING DIAGRAM

To understand fully the operation of the circuit in Figure 8.8, let us consider its timing diagram presented in Figure 8.9. The diagram depicts the signal waveforms that correspond to the sequences of values in Figure 8.2.

Because we are using positive-edge-triggered flip-flops, all changes in the signals occur shortly after the positive edge of the clock. The amount of delay from the clock edge depends on the propagation delays through the flip-flops. Note that the input signal w is also shown to change slightly after the active edge of the clock. This is a good assumption because in a typical digital system an input such as w would be just an output of another circuit that is synchronized by the same clock. We discuss the synchronization of input signals with the clock signal in section 10.3.

A key point to observe is that even though w changes slightly after the active clock edge, and thus the value of w is equal to 1 (or 0) for almost the entire clock cycle, no change in the circuit will occur until the beginning of the next clock cycle when the positive edge causes the flip-flops to change their state. Thus the value of w must be equal to 1 for two clock cycles if the circuit is to reach state C and generate the output $z = 1$.

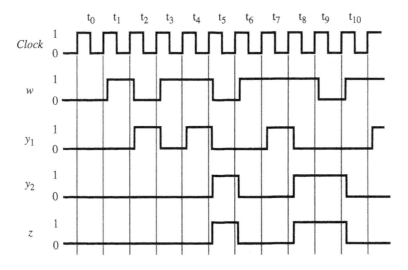

Figure 8.9   Timing diagram for the circuit in Figure 8.8.

8.1.6 SUMMARY OF DESIGN STEPS

We can summarize the steps involved in designing a synchronous sequential circuit as follows:

1. Obtain the specification of the desired circuit.

2. Derive the states for the machine by first selecting a starting state. Then, given the specification of the circuit, consider all valuations of the inputs to the circuit and create new states as needed for the machine to respond to these inputs. To keep track of the states as they are visited, create a state diagram. When completed, the state diagram shows all states in the machine and gives the conditions under which the circuit moves from one state to another.

3. Create a state table from the state diagram. Alternatively, it may be convenient to directly create the state table in step 2, rather than first creating a state diagram.

4. In our sequential circuit example, there were only three states; hence it was a simple matter to create the state table that does not contain more states than necessary. However, in practice it is common to deal with circuits that have a large number of states. In such cases it is unlikely that the first attempt at deriving a state table will produce optimal results. Almost certainly we will have more states than is really necessary. This can be corrected by a procedure that minimizes the number of states. We will discuss the process of state minimization in section 8.6.

5. Decide on the number of state variables needed to represent all states and perform the state assignment. There are many different state assignments possible for a given sequential circuit. Some assignments may be better than others. In the preceding example we used what seemed to be a natural state assignment. We will return to this example in section 8.2 and show that a different assignment may lead to a simpler circuit.

6. Choose the type of flip-flops to be used in the circuit. Derive the next-state logic expressions to control the inputs to all flip-flops and then derive logic expressions for the outputs of the circuit. So far we have used only D-type flip-flops. We will consider other types of flip-flops in section 8.7.

7. Implement the circuit as indicated by the logic expressions.

Example 8.1   We have illustrated the design steps using a very simple sequential circuit. From the reader's point of view, a circuit that detects that an input signal was high for two consecutive clock pulses may not have much practical significance. We will now consider an example that is closely tied to practical application.

Section 7.14 introduced the concept of a bus and showed the connections that have to be made to allow the contents of a register to be transferred into another register. The circuit in Figure 7.56 shows how tri-state buffers can be used to place the contents of a selected register onto the bus and how the data on the bus can be loaded into a register. Figure 7.58 shows how a control mechanism that swaps the contents of registers $R1$ and $R2$ can be realized using a shift register. We will now design the desired control mechanism, using the finite state machine approach.

The contents of registers $R1$ and $R2$ can be swapped using register $R3$ as a temporary storage location as follows: The contents of $R2$ are first loaded into $R3$, using the control signals $R2_{out} = 1$ and $R3_{in} = 1$. Then the contents of $R1$ are transferred into $R2$, using $R1_{out} = 1$ and $R2_{in} = 1$. Finally, the contents of $R3$ (which are the previous contents of $R2$) are transferred into $R1$, using $R3_{out} = 1$ and $R1_{in} = 1$. Since this step completes the required swap, we will indicate that the task is completed by setting the signal $Done = 1$. Assume that the swapping is performed in response to a pulse on an input signal called w, which has a duration of one clock cycle. Figure 8.10 indicates the external signals involved in the desired control circuit. Figure 8.11 gives a state diagram for a sequential circuit that generates the output control signals in the required sequence. Note that to keep the diagram simple, we have indicated the output signals only when they are equal to 1. In all other cases the output signals are equal to 0.

In the starting state, A, no transfer is indicated, and all output signals are 0. The circuit remains in this state until a request to swap arrives in the form of w changing to 1. In state B the signals required to transfer the contents of $R2$ into $R3$ are asserted. The next active clock edge places these contents into $R3$. It also causes the circuit to change to state C, regardless of whether w is equal to 0 or 1. In this state the signals for transferring $R1$ into $R2$ are asserted. The transfer takes place at the next active clock edge, and the circuit changes to state D regardless of the value of w. The final transfer, from $R3$ to $R1$, is performed on the clock edge that leaves state D, which also causes the circuit to return to state A.

Figure 8.12 presents the same information in a state table. Since there are four states, it is necessary to use two state variables, y_2 and y_1. A straightforward state assignment where the states A, B, C, and D are assigned the valuations $y_2y_1 = 00, 01, 10$, and 11, respectively, leads to the state-assigned table in Figure 8.13. Using this assignment and D-type flip-flops, the next-state expressions can be derived as shown in Figure 8.14. They are

$$Y_1 = w\bar{y}_1 + \bar{y}_1 y_2$$
$$Y_2 = y_1 \bar{y}_2 + \bar{y}_1 y_2$$

The output control signals are derived as

$$R1_{out} = R2_{in} = \bar{y}_1 y_2$$
$$R1_{in} = R3_{out} = Done = y_1 y_2$$
$$R2_{out} = R3_{in} = y_1 \bar{y}_2$$

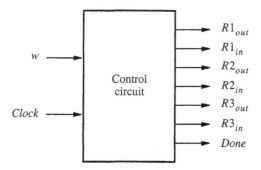

Figure 8.10   Signals needed in Example 8.1.

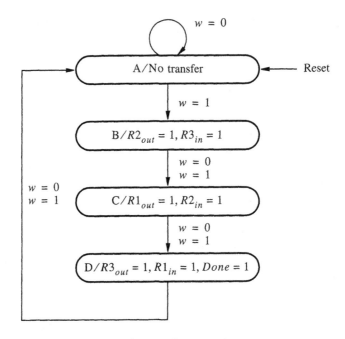

Figure 8.11   State diagram for Example 8.1.

Present	Next state		Outputs						
state	$w = 0$	$w = 1$	$R1_{out}$	$R1_{in}$	$R2_{out}$	$R2_{in}$	$R3_{out}$	$R3_{in}$	Done
A	A	B	0	0	0	0	0	0	0
B	C	C	0	0	1	0	0	1	0
C	D	D	1	0	0	1	0	0	0
D	A	A	0	1	0	0	1	0	1

Figure 8.12   State table for Example 8.1.

	Present	Next state		Outputs						
	state	$w = 0$	$w = 1$							
	$y_2 y_1$	$Y_2 Y_1$	$Y_2 Y_1$	$R1_{out}$	$R1_{in}$	$R2_{out}$	$R2_{in}$	$R3_{out}$	$R3_{in}$	Done
A	0 0	0 0	0 1	0	0	0	0	0	0	0
B	0 1	1 0	1 0	0	0	1	0	0	1	0
C	1 0	1 1	1 1	1	0	0	1	0	0	0
D	1 1	0 0	0 0	0	1	0	0	1	0	1

Figure 8.13   State-assigned table for the sequential circuit in Figure 8.12.

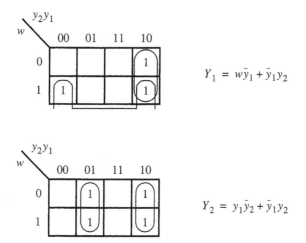

$$Y_1 = w\bar{y}_1 + \bar{y}_1 y_2$$

$$Y_2 = y_1\bar{y}_2 + \bar{y}_1 y_2$$

Figure 8.14 Derivation of next-state expressions for the sequential circuit in Figure 8.13.

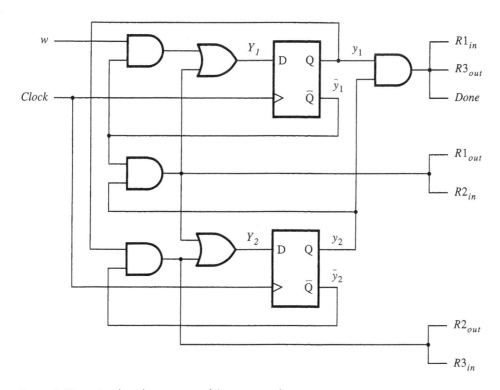

Figure 8.15 Final implementation of the sequential circuit in Figure 8.13.

These expressions lead to the circuit in Figure 8.15. This circuit appears more complex than the shift register in Figure 7.58, but it has only two flip-flops, rather than three.

8.2 STATE-ASSIGNMENT PROBLEM

Having introduced the basic concepts involved in the design of sequential circuits, we should revisit some details where alternative choices are possible. In section 8.1.6 we suggested that some state assignments may be better than others. To illustrate this we can reconsider the example in Figure 8.4. We already know that the state assignment in Figure 8.6 leads to a simple-looking circuit in Figure 8.8. But can the FSM of Figure 8.4 be implemented with an even simpler circuit by using a different state assignment?

Figure 8.16 gives one possible alternative. In this case we represent the states A, B, and C with the valuations $y_2y_1 = 00$, 01, and 11, respectively. The remaining valuation, $y_2y_1 = 10$, is not needed, and we will treat it as a don't-care condition. If we again choose to implement the circuit using D-type flip-flops, the next-state and output expressions derived from the figure will be

$$Y_1 = D_1 = w$$
$$Y_2 = D_2 = wy_1$$
$$z = y_2$$

These expressions define the circuit shown in Figure 8.17. Comparing this circuit with the one in Figure 8.8, we see that the cost of the new circuit is lower because it requires fewer gates.

In general, circuits are much larger than our example, and different state assignments can have a substantial effect on the cost of the final implementation. While highly desirable, it is often impossible to find the best state assignment for a large circuit. The exhaustive approach of trying all possible state assignments is not practical because the number of available state assignments is huge. CAD tools usually perform the state assignment using heuristic techniques. These techniques are usually proprietary, and their details are seldom published.

Present state y_2y_1	Next state $w = 0$ Y_2Y_1	Next state $w = 1$ Y_2Y_1	Output z
A 00	00	01	0
B 01	00	11	0
C 11	00	11	1
10	dd	dd	d

Figure 8.16   Improved state assignment for the sequential circuit in Figure 8.4.

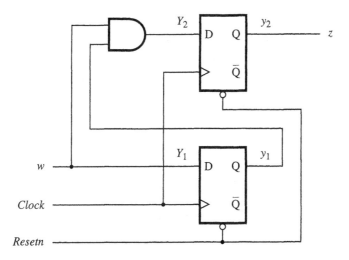

Figure 8.17 Final circuit for the improved state assignment in Figure 8.16.

In Figure 8.13 we used a straightforward state assignment for the sequential circuit in Figure 8.12. Consider now the effect of interchanging the valuations assigned to states C and D, as shown in Figure 8.18. Then the next-state expressions are

$$Y_1 = w\bar{y}_2 + y_1\bar{y}_2$$
$$Y_2 = y_1$$

Example 8.2

as derived in Figure 8.19. The output expressions are

$$R1_{out} = R2_{in} = y_1y_2$$
$$R1_{in} = R3_{out} = Done = \bar{y}_1y_2$$
$$R2_{out} = R3_{in} = y_1\bar{y}_2$$

These expressions lead to a slightly simpler circuit than the one given in Figure 8.15.

Present state	Next state		Outputs						
	$w = 0$	$w = 1$							
y_2y_1	Y_2Y_1	Y_2Y_1	$R1_{out}$	$R1_{in}$	$R2_{out}$	$R2_{in}$	$R3_{out}$	$R3_{in}$	$Done$
A 0 0	0 0	0 1	0	0	0	0	0	0	0
B 0 1	1 1	1 1	0	0	1	0	0	1	0
C 1 1	1 0	1 0	1	0	0	1	0	0	0
D 1 0	0 0	0 0	0	1	0	0	1	0	1

Figure 8.18 Improved state assignment for the sequential circuit in Figure 8.12.

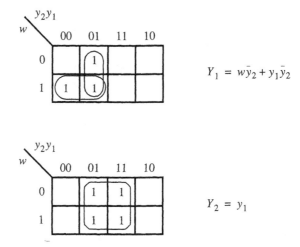

$$Y_1 = w\bar{y}_2 + y_1\bar{y}_2$$

$$Y_2 = y_1$$

Figure 8.19   Derivation of next-state expressions for the sequential circuit in Figure 8.18.

8.2.1 ONE-HOT ENCODING

Another interesting possibility is to use as many state variables as there are states in a sequential circuit. In this method, for each state all but one of the state variables are equal to 0. The variable whose value is 1 is deemed to be "hot." The approach is known as the *one-hot encoding* method.

Figure 8.20 shows how one-hot state assignment can be applied to the sequential circuit of Figure 8.4. Because there are three states, it is necessary to use three state variables. The chosen assignment is to represent the states A, B, and C using the valuations $y_3y_2y_1 = 001$, 010, and 100, respectively. The remaining five valuations of the state variables are not used. They can be treated as don't cares in the derivation of the next-state and output expressions. Using this assignment, the resulting expressions are

$$Y_1 = \bar{w}$$
$$Y_2 = wy_1$$
$$Y_3 = w\bar{y}_1$$
$$z = y_3$$

These expressions are not simpler than those obtained using the state assignment in Figure 8.16. Although in this case the one-hot assignment is not advantageous, there are many cases where this approach is attractive.

Example 8.3   The one-hot state assignment can be applied to the sequential circuit of Figure 8.12 as indicated in Figure 8.21. Four state variables are needed, and the states A, B, C, and D are

Present state	Next state		Output
	$w = 0$	$w = 1$	z
$y_3 y_2 y_1$	$Y_3 Y_2 Y_1$	$Y_3 Y_2 Y_1$	
A 001	001	010	0
B 010	001	100	0
C 100	001	100	1

Figure 8.20 One-hot state assignment for the sequential circuit in Figure 8.4.

encoded as $y_4 y_3 y_2 y_1 = 0001, 0010, 0100$, and 1000, respectively. Treating the remaining 12 valuations of the state variables as don't cares, the next-state expressions are

$$Y_1 = \overline{w} y_1 + y_4$$
$$Y_2 = w y_1$$
$$Y_3 = y_2$$
$$Y_4 = y_3$$

It is instructive to note that we can derive these expressions simply by inspecting the state diagram in Figure 8.11. Flip-flop y_1 should be set to 1 if the FSM is in state A and $w = 0$, or if the FSM is in state D; hence $Y_1 = \overline{w} y_1 + y_4$. Flip-flop y_2 should be set to 1 if the present state is A and $w = 1$; hence $Y_2 = w y_1$. Flip-flops y_3 and y_4 should be set to 1 if the FSM is presently in state B or C, respectively; hence $Y_3 = y_2$ and $Y_4 = y_3$.

The output expressions are just the outputs of the flip-flops, such that

$$R1_{out} = R2_{in} = y_3$$
$$R1_{in} = R3_{out} = Done = y_4$$
$$R2_{out} = R3_{in} = y_2$$

These expressions are simpler than those derived in Example 8.2, but four flip-flops are needed, rather than two.

Present state	Next state		Outputs						
	$w = 0$	$w = 1$							
$y_4 y_3 y_2 y_1$	$Y_4 Y_3 Y_2 Y_1$	$Y_4 Y_3 Y_2 Y_1$	$R1_{out}$	$R1_{in}$	$R2_{out}$	$R2_{in}$	$R3_{out}$	$R3_{in}$	$Done$
A 0001	0001	0010	0	0	0	0	0	0	0
B 0010	0100	0100	0	0	1	0	0	1	0
C 0100	1000	1000	1	0	0	1	0	0	0
D 1000	0001	0001	0	1	0	0	1	0	1

Figure 8.21 One-hot state assignment for the sequential circuit in Figure 8.12.

An important feature of the one-hot state assignment is that it often leads to simpler output expressions than do assignments with the minimal number of state variables. Simpler output expressions may lead to a faster circuit. For instance, if the outputs of the sequential circuit are just the outputs of the flip-flops, as is the case in our example, then these output signals are valid as soon as the flip-flops change their states. If more complex output expressions are involved, then the propagation delay through the gates that implement these expressions must be taken into account. We will consider this issue in section 8.8.2.

The examples considered to this point show that there are many ways to implement a given finite state machine as a sequential circuit. Each implementation is likely to have a different cost and different timing characteristics. In the next section we introduce another way of modeling FSMs that leads to even more possibilities.

8.3 MEALY STATE MODEL

Our introductory examples were sequential circuits in which each state had specific values of the output signals associated with it. As we explained at the beginning of the chapter, such finite state machines are said to be of Moore type. We will now explore the concept of Mealy-type machines in which the output values are generated based on both the state of the circuit and the present values of its inputs. This provides additional flexibility in the design of sequential circuits. We will introduce the Mealy-type machines, using a slightly altered version of a previous example.

The essence of the first sequential circuit in section 8.1 is to generate an output $z = 1$ whenever a second occurrence of the input $w = 1$ is detected in consecutive clock cycles. The specification requires that the output z be equal to 1 in the clock cycle that follows the detection of the second occurrence of $w = 1$. Suppose now that we eliminate this latter requirement and specify instead that the output z should be equal to 1 in the same clock cycle when the second occurrence of $w = 1$ is detected. Then a suitable input-output sequence may be as shown in Figure 8.22. To see how we can realize the behavior given in this table, we begin by selecting a starting state, A. As long as $w = 0$, the machine should remain in state A, producing an output $z = 0$. When $w = 1$, the machine has to move to a new state, B, to record the fact that an input of 1 has occurred. If w remains equal to 1 when the machine is in state B, which happens if $w = 1$ for at least two consecutive clock cycles, the machine should remain in state B and produce an output $z = 1$. As soon as w becomes 0, z should immediately become 0 and the machine should move back to state A at the next

Clock cycle:	t_0	t_1	t_2	t_3	t_4	t_5	t_6	t_7	t_8	t_9	t_{10}
w:	0	1	0	1	1	0	1	1	1	0	1
z:	0	0	0	0	1	0	0	1	1	0	0

Figure 8.22   Sequences of input and output signals.

active edge of the clock. Thus the behavior specified in Figure 8.22 can be achieved with a two-state machine, which has a state diagram shown in Figure 8.23. Only two states are needed because we have allowed the output value to depend on the present value of the input as well as the present state of the machine. The diagram indicates that if the machine is in state A, it will remain in state A if $w = 0$ and the output will be 0. This is indicated by an arc with the label $w = 0/z = 0$. When w becomes 1, the output stays at 0 until the machine moves to state B at the next active clock edge. This is denoted by the arc from A to B with the label $w = 1/z = 0$. In state B the output will be 1 if $w = 1$, and the machine will remain in state B, as indicated by the label $w=1/z=1$ on the corresponding arc. However, if $w = 0$ in state B, then the output will be 0 and a transition to state A will take place at the next active clock edge. A key point to understand is that during the present clock cycle the output value corresponds to the label on the arc emanating from the present-state node.

We can implement the FSM in Figure 8.23, using the same design steps as in section 8.1. The state table is shown in Figure 8.24. The table shows that the output z depends on the present value of input w and not just on the present state. Figure 8.25 gives the state-assigned table. Because there are only two states, it is sufficient to use a single state variable, y. Assuming that y is realized as a D-type flip-flop, the required next-state and output expressions are

$$Y = D = w$$

$$z = wy$$

The resulting circuit is presented in Figure 8.26 along with a timing diagram. The timing diagram corresponds to the input-output sequences in Figure 8.22.

The greater flexibility of Mealy-type FSMs often leads to simpler circuit realizations. This certainly seems to be the case in our examples that produced the circuits in Figures 8.8, 8.17, and 8.26, assuming that the design requirement is only to detect two consecutive occurrences of input w being equal to 1. We should note, however, that the circuit in Figure 8.26 is not the same in terms of output behavior as the circuits in Figures 8.8 and 8.17. The difference is a shift of one clock cycle in the output signal in Figure 8.26b. If we wanted to produce exactly the same output behavior using the Mealy approach, we could modify the circuit in Figure 8.26a by adding another flip-flop as shown in Figure 8.27. This flip-flop merely delays the output signal, Z, by one clock cycle with respect to z, as indicated in the timing diagram. By making this change, we effectively turn the Mealy-type circuit into

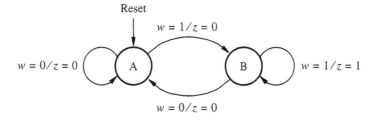

Figure 8.23   State diagram of an FSM that realizes the task in Figure 8.22.

Present state	Next state		Output z	
	$w = 0$	$w = 1$	$w = 0$	$w = 1$
A	A	B	0	0
B	A	B	0	1

Figure 8.24   State table for the FSM in Figure 8.23.

	Present state	Next state		Output	
		$w = 0$	$w = 1$	$w = 0$	$w = 1$
	y	Y	Y	z	z
A	0	0	1	0	0
B	1	0	1	0	1

Figure 8.25   State-assigned table for the FSM in Figure 8.24.

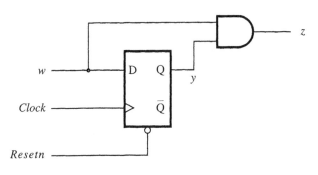

(a) Circuit

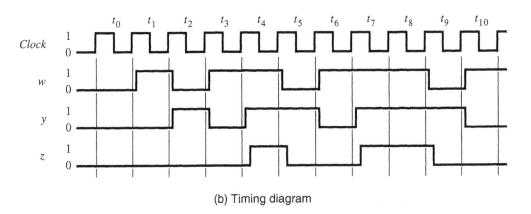

(b) Timing diagram

Figure 8.26   Implementation of FSM in Figure 8.25.

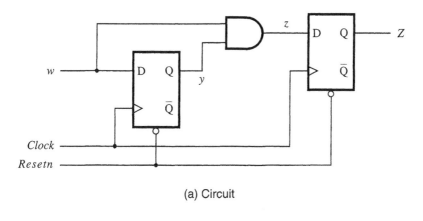

(a) Circuit

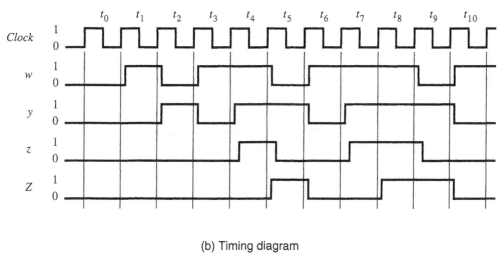

(b) Timing diagram

Figure 8.27   Circuit that implements the specification in Figure 8.2.

a Moore-type circuit with output Z. Note that the circuit in Figure 8.27 is essentially the same as the circuit in Figure 8.17.

In Example 8.1 we considered the control circuit needed to swap the contents of two registers, implemented as a Moore-type finite state machine. The same task can be achieved using a Mealy-type FSM, as indicated in Figure 8.28. State A still serves as the reset state. But as soon as w changes from 0 to 1, the output control signals $R2_{out}$ and $R3_{in}$ are asserted. They remain asserted until the beginning of the next clock cycle, when the circuit will leave state A and change to B. In state B the outputs $R1_{out}$ and $R2_{in}$ are asserted for both $w = 0$ and $w = 1$. Finally, in state C the swap is completed by asserting $R3_{out}$ and $R1_{in}$.

   The Mealy-type realization of the control circuit requires three states. This does not necessarily imply a simpler circuit because two flip-flops are still needed to implement

Example 8.4

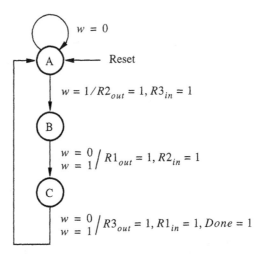

Figure 8.28   State diagram for Example 8.4.

the state variables. The most important difference in comparison with the Moore-type realization is the timing of output signals. A circuit that implements the FSM in Figure 8.28 generates the output control signals one clock cycle sooner than the circuits derived in Examples 8.1 and 8.2.

Note also that using the FSM in Figure 8.28, the entire process of swapping the contents of $R1$ and $R2$ takes three clock cycles, starting and finishing in state A. Using the Moore-type FSM in Example 8.1, the swapping process involves four clock cycles before the circuit returns to state A.

Suppose that we wish to implement this FSM using one-hot encoding. Then three flip-flops are needed, and the states A, B, and C may be assigned the valuations $y_3 y_2 y_1 = 001, 010$, and 100, respectively. Examining the state diagram in Figure 8.28, we can derive the next-state equations by inspection. The input to flip-flop y_1 should have the value 1 if the FSM is in state A and $w = 0$ or if the FSM is in state C; hence $Y_1 = \overline{w}y_1 + y_3$. Flip-flop y_2 should be set to 1 if the FSM is in state A and $w = 1$; hence $Y_2 = wy_1$. Flip-flop y_3 should be set to 1 if the present state is B; hence $Y_3 = y_2$. The derivation of the output expressions, which we leave as an exercise for the reader, can also be done by inspection. The corresponding circuit is shown in Figure 7.59, in section 7.14, where it was derived using an ad hoc approach.

The preceding discussion deals with the basic principles involved in the design of sequential circuits. Although it is essential to understand these principles, the manual approach used in the examples is difficult and tedious when large circuits are involved. We will now show how CAD tools are used to greatly simplify the design task.

8.5 SERIAL ADDER EXAMPLE

We will now present another simple example that illustrates the complete design process. In Chapter 5 we discussed the addition of binary numbers in detail. We explained several schemes that can be used to add two n-bit numbers in parallel, ranging from carry-ripple to carry-lookahead adders. In these schemes the speed of the adder unit is an important design parameter. Fast adders are more complex and thus more expensive. If speed is not of great importance, then a cost-effective option is to use a *serial adder*, in which bits are added a pair at a time.

8.5.1 MEALY-TYPE FSM FOR SERIAL ADDER

Let $A = a_{n-1}a_{n-2} \ldots a_0$ and $B = b_{n-1}b_{n-2} \ldots b_0$ be two unsigned numbers that have to be added to produce $Sum = s_{n-1}s_{n-2} \ldots s_0$. Our task is to design a circuit that will perform serial addition, dealing with a pair of bits in one clock cycle. The process starts by adding bits a_0 and b_0. In the next clock cycle, bits a_1 and b_1 are added, including a possible carry from the bit-position 0, and so on. Figure 8.39 shows a block diagram of a possible implementation. It includes three shift registers that are used to hold A, B, and Sum as the computation proceeds. Assuming that the input shift registers have parallel-load capability, as depicted in Figure 7.19, the addition task begins by loading the values of A and B into these registers. Then in each clock cycle, a pair of bits is added by the adder FSM, and at the end of the cycle the resulting sum bit is shifted into the *Sum* register. We will use positive-edge-triggered flip-flops in which case all changes take place soon after the positive edge of the clock, depending on the propagation delays within the various flip-flops. At this time the contents of all three shift registers are shifted to the right; this shifts the existing sum bit into *Sum*, and it presents the next pair of input bits a_i and b_i to the adder FSM.

Now we are ready to design the required FSM. This cannot be a combinational circuit because different actions will have to be taken, depending on the value of the carry from the previous bit position. Hence two states are needed: let G and H denote the states where the

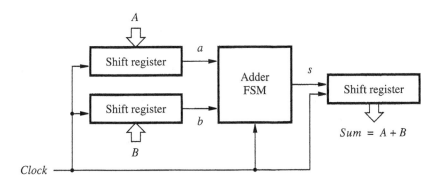

Figure 8.39 Block diagram for the serial adder.

carry-in values are 0 and 1, respectively. Figure 8.40 gives a suitable state diagram, defined as a Mealy model. The output value, s, depends on both the state and the present value of the inputs a and b. Each transition is labeled using the notation ab/s, which indicates the value of s for a given valuation ab. In state G the input valuation 00 will produce $s = 0$, and the FSM will remain in the same state. For input valuations 01 and 10, the output will be $s = 1$, and the FSM will remain in G. But for 11, $s = 0$ is generated, and the machine moves to state H. In state H valuations 01 and 10 cause $s = 0$, while 11 causes $s = 1$. In all three of these cases, the machine remains in H. However, when the valuation 00 occurs, the output of 1 is produced and a change into state G takes place.

The corresponding state table is presented in Figure 8.41. A single flip-flop is needed to represent the two states. The state assignment can be done as indicated in Figure 8.42. This assignment leads to the following next-state and output equations

$$Y = ab + ay + by$$
$$s = a \oplus b \oplus y$$

Comparing these expressions with those for the full-adder in section 5.2, it is obvious that y is the carry-in, Y is the carry-out, and s is the sum of the full-adder. Therefore, the adder FSM box in Figure 8.39 consists of the circuit shown in Figure 8.43. The flip-flop can be cleared by the *Reset* signal at the start of the addition operation.

The serial adder is a simple circuit that can be used to add numbers of any length. The structure in Figure 8.39 is limited in length only by the size of the shift registers.

8.5.2 MOORE-TYPE FSM FOR SERIAL ADDER

In the preceding example we saw that a Mealy-type FSM nicely meets the requirement for implementing the serial adder. Now we will try to achieve the same objective using a Moore-type FSM. A good starting point is the state diagram in Figure 8.40. In a Moore-type FSM, the output must depend only on the state of the machine. Since in both states, G and H, it is possible to produce two different outputs depending on the valuations of the inputs a and b, a Moore-type FSM will need more than two states. We can derive a suitable state diagram by splitting both G and H into two states. Instead of G, we will use G_0 and G_1 to

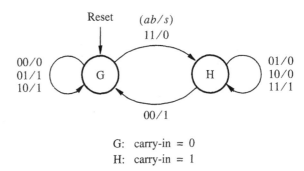

Figure 8.40   State diagram for the serial adder FSM.

Present state	Next state				Output s			
	ab = 00	01	10	11	00	01	10	11
G	G	G	G	H	0	1	1	0
H	G	H	H	H	1	0	0	1

Figure 8.41   State table for the serial adder FSM.

denote the fact that the carry is 0 and that the sum is either 0 or 1, respectively. Similarly, instead of H, we will use H_0 and H_1. Then the information in Figure 8.40 can be mapped into the Moore-type state diagram in Figure 8.44 in a straightforward manner.

The corresponding state table is given in Figure 8.45 and the state-assigned table in Figure 8.46. The next-state and output expressions are

$$Y_1 = a \oplus b \oplus y_2$$
$$Y_2 = ab + ay_2 + by_2$$
$$s = y_1$$

The expressions for Y_1 and Y_2 correspond to the sum and carry-out expressions in the full-adder circuit. The FSM is implemented as shown in Figure 8.47. It is interesting to observe that this circuit is very similar to the circuit in Figure 8.43. The only difference is that in the Moore-type circuit, the output signal, s, is passed through an extra flip-flop and thus delayed by one clock cycle with respect to the Mealy-type sequential circuit. Recall that we observed the same difference in our previous example, as depicted in Figures 8.26 and 8.27.

A key difference between the Mealy and Moore types of FSMs is that in the former a change in inputs reflects itself immediately in the outputs, while in the latter the outputs do not change until the change in inputs forces the machine into a new state, which takes place one clock cycle later. We encourage the reader to draw the timing diagrams for the circuits in Figures 8.43 and 8.47, which will exemplify further this key difference between the two types of FSMs.

Present state	Next state				Output			
y	ab = 00	01	10	11	00	01	10	11
		Y				s		
0	0	0	0	1	0	1	1	0
1	0	1	1	1	1	0	0	1

Figure 8.42   State-assigned table for Figure 8.41.

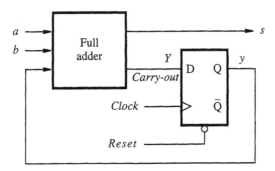

Figure 8.43   Circuit for the adder FSM in Figure 8.39.

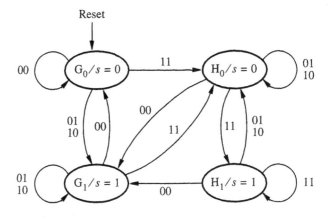

Figure 8.44   State diagram for the Moore-type serial adder FSM.

Present	Next state				Output
state	$ab = 00$	01	10	11	s
G_0	G_0	G_1	G_1	H_0	0
G_1	G_0	G_1	G_1	H_0	1
H_0	G_1	H_0	H_0	H_1	0
H_1	G_1	H_0	H_0	H_1	1

Figure 8.45   State table for the Moore-type serial adder FSM.

Present state y_2y_1	Next state $ab = 00 \quad 01 \quad 10 \quad 11$ Y_2Y_1				Output s
0 0	0 0	0 1	0 1	1 0	0
0 1	0 0	0 1	0 1	1 0	1
1 0	0 1	1 0	1 0	1 1	0
1 1	0 1	1 0	1 0	1 1	1

Figure 8.46   State-assigned table for Figure 8.45.

8.7   DESIGN OF A COUNTER USING THE SEQUENTIAL CIRCUIT APPROACH

In this section we discuss the design of a counter circuit using the general approach for designing sequential circuits. From Chapter 7 we already know that counters can be realized as cascaded stages of flip-flops and some gating logic, where each stage divides the number of incoming pulses by two. To keep our example simple, we choose a counter of small size but also show how the design can be extended to larger sizes. The specification for the counter is

- The counting sequence is 0, 1, 2, ..., 6, 7, 0, 1, ...

- There exists an input signal w. The value of this signal is considered during each clock cycle. If $w = 0$, the present count remains the same; if $w = 1$, the count is incremented.

The counter can be designed as a synchronous sequential circuit using the design techniques introduced in the previous sections. We show first the classical manual approach to designing the counter, which illustrates the basic concepts involved in the design process. After that we show how the design task is accomplished using CAD tools, which is much easier to do and indicates how the task would be tackled in practice.

8.7.1   STATE DIAGRAM AND STATE TABLE FOR A MODULO-8 COUNTER

Figure 8.60 gives a state diagram for the desired counter. There is a state associated with each count. In the diagram state A corresponds to count 0, state B to count 1, and so on. We show the transitions between the states needed to implement the counting sequence. Note that the output signals are specified as depending only on the state of the counter at a given time, which is the Moore model of sequential circuits.

The state diagram may be represented in the state-table form as shown in Figure 8.61.

8.7.2   STATE ASSIGNMENT

Three state variables are needed to represent the eight states. Let these variables, denoting the present state, be called y_2, y_1, and y_0. Let Y_2, Y_1, and Y_0 denote the corresponding next-state functions. The most convenient (and simplest) state assignment is to encode

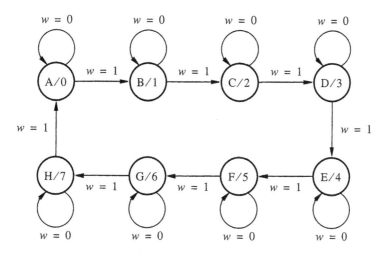

Figure 8.60 State diagram for the counter.

each state with the binary number that the counter should give as output in that state. Then the required output signals will be the same as the signals that represent the state variables. This leads to the state-assigned table in Figure 8.62.

The final step in the design is to choose the type of flip-flops and derive the expressions that control the flip-flop inputs. The most straightforward choice is to use D-type flip-flops. We pursue this approach first. Then we show the alternative of using JK-type flip-flops. In either case the flip-flops must be edge triggered to ensure that only one transition takes place during a single clock cycle.

Present state	Next state		Output
	$w = 0$	$w = 1$	
A	A	B	0
B	B	C	1
C	C	D	2
D	D	E	3
E	E	F	4
F	F	G	5
G	G	H	6
H	H	A	7

Figure 8.61 State table for the counter.

Present state $y_2 y_1 y_0$	Next state		Count $z_2 z_1 z_0$
	$w = 0$ $Y_2 Y_1 Y_0$	$w = 1$ $Y_2 Y_1 Y_0$	
A 000	000	001	000
B 001	001	010	001
C 010	010	011	010
D 011	011	100	011
E 100	100	101	100
F 101	101	110	101
G 110	110	111	110
H 111	111	000	111

Figure 8.62   State-assigned table for the counter.

8.7.3 IMPLEMENTATION USING D-TYPE FLIP-FLOPS

When using D-type flip-flops to realize the finite state machine, each next-state function, Y_i, is connected to the D input of the flip-flop that implements the state variable y_i. The next-state functions are derived from the information in Figure 8.62. Using Karnaugh maps in Figure 8.63, we obtain the following implementation

$$D_0 = Y_0 = \overline{w}y_0 + w\overline{y}_0$$
$$D_1 = Y_1 = \overline{w}y_1 + y_1\overline{y}_0 + wy_0\overline{y}_1$$
$$D_2 = Y_2 = \overline{w}y_2 + \overline{y}_0 y_2 + \overline{y}_1 y_2 + wy_0 y_1 \overline{y}_2$$

The resulting circuit is given in Figure 8.64. It is not obvious how to extend this circuit to implement a larger counter, because no clear pattern is discernible in the expressions for D_0, D_1, and D_2. However, we can rewrite these expressions as follows

$$D_0 = \overline{w}y_0 + w\overline{y}_0$$
$$= w \oplus y_0$$
$$D_1 = \overline{w}y_1 + y_1\overline{y}_0 + wy_0\overline{y}_1$$
$$= (\overline{w} + \overline{y}_0)y_1 + wy_0\overline{y}_1$$
$$= \overline{w y_0} y_1 + wy_0\overline{y}_1$$
$$= wy_0 \oplus y_1$$
$$D_2 = \overline{w}y_2 + \overline{y}_0 y_2 + \overline{y}_1 y_2 + wy_0 y_1 \overline{y}_2$$
$$= (\overline{w} + \overline{y}_0 + \overline{y}_1)y_2 + wy_0 y_1 \overline{y}_2$$
$$= \overline{w y_0 y_1} y_2 + wy_0 y_1 \overline{y}_2$$
$$= wy_0 y_1 \oplus y_2$$

Then an obvious pattern emerges, which leads to the circuit in Figure 7.24.

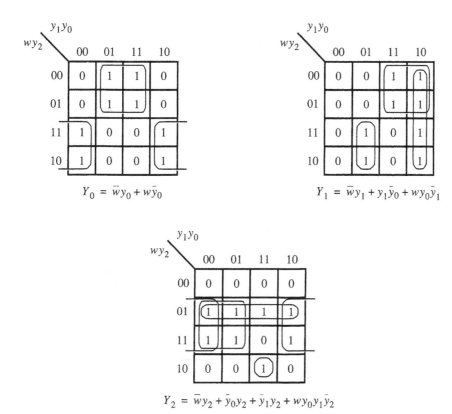

$$Y_0 = \bar{w}y_0 + w\bar{y}_0$$

$$Y_1 = \bar{w}y_1 + y_1\bar{y}_0 + wy_0\bar{y}_1$$

$$Y_2 = \bar{w}y_2 + \bar{y}_0y_2 + \bar{y}_1y_2 + wy_0y_1\bar{y}_2$$

Figure 8.63   Karnaugh maps for D flip-flops for the counter.

8.7.4 IMPLEMENTATION USING JK-TYPE FLIP-FLOPS

JK-type flip-flops provide an attractive alternative. Using these flip-flops to implement the sequential circuit specified in Figure 8.62 requires derivation of J and K inputs for each flip-flop. The following control is needed:

- If a flip-flop in state 0 is to remain in state 0, then $J = 0$ and $K = d$ (where d means that K can be equal to either 0 or 1).

- If a flip-flop in state 0 is to change to state 1, then $J = 1$ and $K = d$.

- If a flip-flop in state 1 is to remain in state 1, then $J = d$ and $K = 0$.

- If a flip-flop in state 1 is to change to state 0, then $J = d$ and $K = 1$.

Following these guidelines, we can create a truth table that specifies the required values of the J and K inputs for the three flip-flops in our design. Figure 8.65 shows a modified version of the state-assigned table in Figure 8.62, with the J and K input functions included. To see how this table is derived, consider the first row in which the present state is $y_2y_1y_0 = 000$. If $w = 0$, then the next state is also $Y_2Y_1Y_0 = 000$. Thus the present value of each

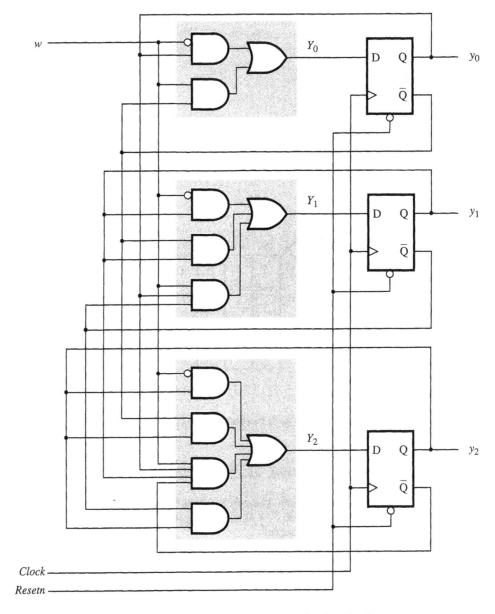

Figure 8.64   Circuit diagram for the counter implemented with D flip-flops.

flip-flop is 0, and it should remain 0. This implies the control $J = 0$ and $K = d$ for all three flip-flops. Continuing with the first row, if $w = 1$, the next state will be $Y_2 Y_1 Y_0 = 001$. Thus flip-flops y_2 and y_1 still remain at 0 and have the control $J = 0$ and $K = d$. However, flip-flop y_0 must change from 0 to 1, which is accomplished with $J = 1$ and $K = d$. The

Present state $y_2y_1y_0$	Flip-flop inputs								Count $z_2z_1z_0$
	$w = 0$				$w = 1$				
	$Y_2Y_1Y_0$	J_2K_2	J_1K_1	J_0K_0	$Y_2Y_1Y_0$	J_2K_2	J_1K_1	J_0K_0	
A 000	000	0d	0d	0d	001	0d	0d	1d	000
B 001	001	0d	0d	d0	010	0d	1d	d1	001
C 010	010	0d	d0	0d	011	0d	d0	1d	010
D 011	011	0d	d0	d0	100	1d	d1	d1	011
E 100	100	d0	0d	0d	101	d0	0d	1d	100
F 101	101	d0	0d	d0	110	d0	1d	d1	101
G 110	110	d0	d0	0d	111	d0	d0	1d	110
H 111	111	d0	d0	d0	000	d1	d1	d1	111

Figure 8.65   Excitation table for the counter with JK flip-flops.

rest of the table is derived in the same manner by considering each present state $y_2y_1y_0$ and providing the necessary control signals to reach the new state $Y_2Y_1Y_0$.

A state-assigned table is essentially the state table in which each state is encoded using the state variables. When D flip-flops are used to implement an FSM, the next-state entries in the state-assigned table correspond directly to the signals that must be applied to the D inputs. This is not the case if some other type of flip-flops is used. A table that gives the state information in the form of the flip-flop inputs that must be "excited" to cause the transitions to the next states is usually called an *excitation table*. The excitation table in Figure 8.65 indicates how JK flip-flops can be used. In many books the term excitation table is used even when D flip-flops are involved, in which case it is synonymous with the state-assigned table.

Once the table in Figure 8.65 has been derived, it provides a truth table with inputs y_2, y_1, y_0, and w, and outputs J_2, K_2, J_1, K_1, J_0, and K_0. We can then derive expressions for these outputs as shown in Figure 8.66. The resulting expressions are

$$J_0 = K_0 = w$$
$$J_1 = K_1 = wy_0$$
$$J_2 = K_2 = wy_0y_1$$

This leads to the circuit shown in Figure 8.67. It is apparent that this design can be extended easily to larger counters. The pattern $J_n = K_n = wy_0y_1 \cdots y_{n-1}$ defines the circuit for each stage in the counter. Note that the size of the AND gate that implements the product term $y_0y_1 \cdots y_{n-1}$ grows with successive stages. A circuit with a more regular structure can be obtained by factoring out the previously needed terms as we progress through the stages of the counter. This gives

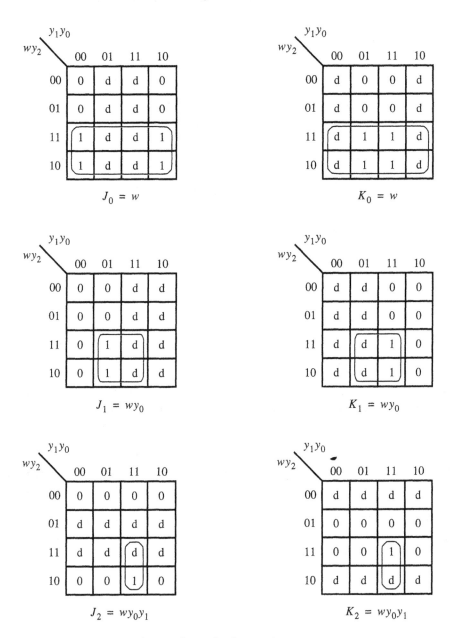

Figure 8.66   Karnaugh maps for JK flip-flops in the counter.

$$J_2 = K_2 = (wy_0)y_1 \qquad\qquad = J_1y_1$$
$$J_n = K_n = (wy_0 \cdots y_{n-2})y_{n-1} = J_{n-1}y_{n-1}$$

Using the factored form, the counter circuit can be realized as indicated in Figure 8.68. In this circuit all stages (except the first) look the same. Note that this circuit has the same structure as the circuit in Figure 7.23 because connecting the J and K inputs of a flip-flop together turns the flip-flop into a T flip-flop.

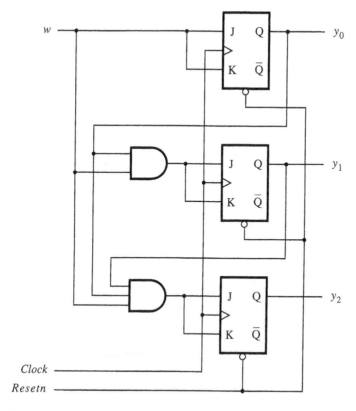

Figure 8.67   Circuit diagram using JK flip-flops.

8.7.5 EXAMPLE—A DIFFERENT COUNTER

Having considered the design of an ordinary counter, we will now apply this knowledge to design a slightly different counterlike circuit. Suppose that we wish to derive a three-bit counter that counts the pulses on an input line, w. But instead of displaying the count as $0, 1, 2, 3, 4, 5, 6, 7, 0, 1, \ldots$, this counter must display the count in the sequence $0, 4, 2, 6, 1, 5, 3, 7, 0, 4$, and so on. The count is to be represented directly by the flip-flop values themselves, without using any extra gates. Namely, Count $= Q_2 Q_1 Q_0$.

Since we wish to count the pulses on the input line w, it makes sense to use w as the clock input to the flip-flops. Thus the counter circuit should always be enabled, and it should change its state whenever the next pulse on the w line appears. The desired counter can be designed in a straightforward manner using the FSM approach. Figures 8.69 and 8.70 give the required state table and a suitable state assignment. Using D flip-flops, we obtain the next-state equations

$$D_2 = Y_2 = \bar{y}_2$$
$$D_1 = Y_1 = y_1 \oplus y_2$$

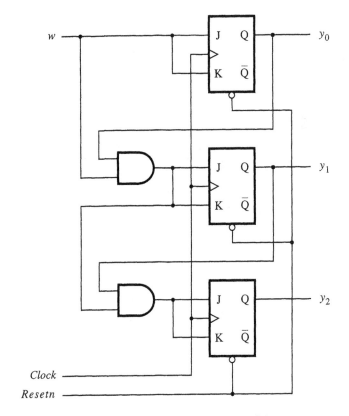

Figure 8.68   Factored-form implementation of the counter.

Present state	Next state	Output $z_2 z_1 z_0$
A	B	0 0 0
B	C	1 0 0
C	D	0 1 0
D	E	1 1 0
E	F	0 0 1
F	G	1 0 1
G	H	0 1 1
H	A	1 1 1

Figure 8.69   State table for counterlike example.

$$D_0 = Y_0 = y_0\bar{y}_1 + y_0\bar{y}_2 + \bar{y}_0 y_1 y_2$$
$$= y_0(\bar{y}_1 + \bar{y}_2) + \bar{y}_0 y_1 y_2$$
$$= y_0 \oplus y_1 y_2$$

This leads to the circuit in Figure 8.71.

Present state	Next state	Output
$y_2 y_1 y_0$	$Y_2 Y_1 Y_0$	$z_2 z_1 z_0$
0 0 0	1 0 0	0 0 0
1 0 0	0 1 0	1 0 0
0 1 0	1 1 0	0 1 0
1 1 0	0 0 1	1 1 0
0 0 1	1 0 1	0 0 1
1 0 1	0 1 1	1 0 1
0 1 1	1 1 1	0 1 1
1 1 1	0 0 0	1 1 1

Figure 8.70   State-assigned table for Figure 8.69.

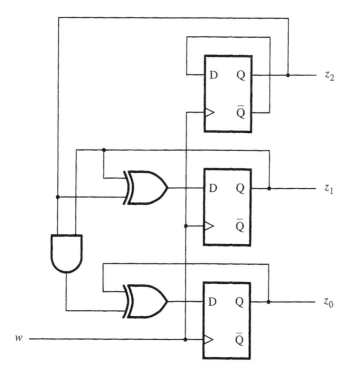

Figure 8.71   Circuit for Figure 8.70.

The reader should compare this circuit with the normal up-counter in Figure 7.24. Take the first three stages of that counter, set the *Enable* input to 1, and let *Clock* = *w*. Then the two circuits are essentially the same with one small difference in the order of bits in the count. In Figure 7.24 the top flip-flop corresponds to the least-significant bit of the count, whereas in Figure 8.71 the top flip-flop corresponds to the most-significant bit of the count. This is not just a coincidence. In Figure 8.70 the required count is defined as $Count = y_2y_1y_0$. However, if the bit patterns that define the states are viewed in the reverse order and interpreted as binary numbers, such that $Count = y_0y_1y_2$, then the states $A, B, C, \ldots, H$ have the values $0, 1, 2, \ldots, 7$. These values are the same as the values that are associated with the normal three-bit up-counter.

8.9   ANALYSIS OF SYNCHRONOUS SEQUENTIAL CIRCUITS

In addition to knowing how to design a synchronous sequential circuit, the designer has to be able to analyze the behavior of an existing circuit. The analysis task is much simpler than the synthesis task. In this section we will show how analysis may be performed.

To analyze a circuit, we simply reverse the steps of the synthesis process. The outputs of the flip-flops represent the present-state variables. Their inputs determine the next state that the circuit will enter. From this information we can construct the state-assigned table for the circuit. This table leads to a state table and the corresponding state diagram by giving a name to each state. The type of flip-flops used in the circuit is a factor, as we will see in the examples that follow.

Example 8.8   **D-TYPE FLIP-FLOPS**   Figure 8.80 gives an FSM that has two D flip-flops. Let y_1 and y_2 be the present-state variables and Y_1 and Y_2 the next-state variables. The next-state and output expressions are

$$Y_1 = w\bar{y}_1 + wy_2$$
$$Y_2 = wy_1 + wy_2$$
$$z = y_1y_2$$

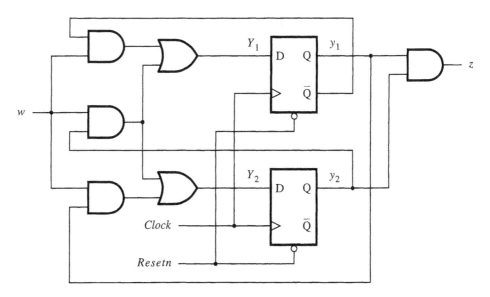

Figure 8.80   Circuit for Example 8.8.

Since there are two flip-flops, the FSM has four states. A good starting point in the analysis is to assume an initial state of the flip-flops such as $y_1 = y_2 = 0$. From the expressions for Y_1 and Y_2, we can derive the state-assigned table in Figure 8.81a. For example, in the first row of the table $y_1 = y_2 = 0$. Then $w = 0$ causes $Y_1 = Y_2 = 0$, and $w = 1$ causes $Y_1 = 1$ and $Y_2 = 0$. The output for this state is $z = 0$. The other rows are derived in the same manner. Labeling the states as A, B, C, and D yields the state table in Figure 8.81b. From this table it is apparent that following the reset condition the FSM produces the output $z = 1$ whenever three consecutive 1s occur on the input w. Therefore, the FSM acts as a sequence detector for this pattern.

JK-TYPE FLIP-FLOPS   Now consider the circuit in Figure 8.82, which has two JK flip-flops.   **Example 8.9**
The expressions for the inputs to the flip-flops are

$$J_1 = w$$
$$K_1 = \overline{w} + \overline{y}_2$$

Present state $y_2 y_1$	Next State $w = 0$ $Y_2 Y_1$	Next State $w = 1$ $Y_2 Y_1$	Output z
0 0	0 0	0 1	0
0 1	0 0	1 0	0
1 0	0 0	1 1	0
1 1	0 0	1 1	1

(a) State-assigned table

Present state	Next state $w = 0$	Next state $w = 1$	Output z
A	A	B	0
B	A	C	0
C	A	D	0
D	A	D	1

(b) State table

Figure 8.81   Tables for the circuit in Figure 8.80.

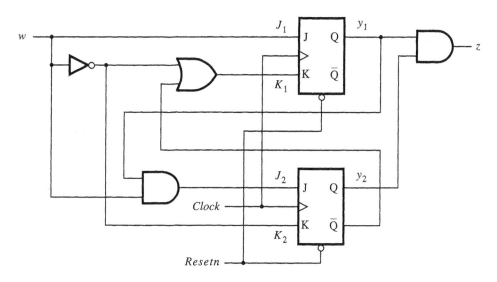

Figure 8.82 Circuit for Example 8.9.

$$J_2 = wy_1$$
$$K_2 = \overline{w}$$

The output is given by $z = y_1y_2$.

From these expressions we can derive the excitation table in Figure 8.83. Interpreting the entries in this table, we can construct the state-assigned table. For example, consider $y_2y_1 = 00$ and $w = 0$. Then, since $J_2 = J_1 = 0$ and $K_2 = K_1 = 1$, both flip-flops will remain in the 0 state; hence $Y_2 = Y_1 = 0$. If $y_2y_1 = 00$ and $w = 1$, then $J_2 = K_2 = 0$ and $J_1 = K_1 = 1$, which leaves the y_2 flip-flop unchanged and sets the y_1 flip-flop to 1; hence $Y_2 = 0$ and $Y_1 = 1$. If $y_2y_1 = 01$ and $w = 0$, then $J_2 = J_1 = 0$ and $K_2 = K_1 = 1$, which resets the y_1 flip-flop and results in the state $y_2y_1 = 00$; hence $Y_2 = Y_1 = 0$. Similarly, if $y_2y_1 = 01$ and $w = 1$, then $J_2 = 1$ and $K_2 = 0$ sets y_2 to 1; hence $Y_2 = 1$, while

Present state	Flip-flop inputs				Output
	$w = 0$		$w = 1$		
y_2y_1	J_2K_2	J_1K_1	J_2K_2	J_1K_1	z
0 0	0 1	0 1	0 0	1 1	0
0 1	0 1	0 1	1 0	1 1	0
1 0	0 1	0 1	0 0	1 0	0
1 1	0 1	0 1	1 0	1 0	1

Figure 8.83 The excitation table for the circuit in Figure 8.82.

$J_1 = K_1 = 1$ toggles y_1; hence $Y_1 = 0$. This leads to the state $y_2y_1 = 10$. Completing this process, we find that the resulting state-assigned table is the same as the one in Figure 8.81a. The conclusion is that the circuits in Figures 8.80 and 8.82 implement the same FSM.

MIXED FLIP-FLOPS   There is no reason why one cannot use a mixture of flip-flop types in one circuit. Figure 8.84 shows a circuit with one D and one T flip-flop. The expressions for this circuit are **Example 8.10**

$$D_1 = w(\bar{y}_1 + y_2)$$
$$T_2 = \bar{w}y_2 + wy_1\bar{y}_2$$
$$z = y_1y_2$$

From these expressions we derive the excitation table in Figure 8.85. Since it is a T flip-flop, y_2 changes its state only when $T_2 = 1$. Thus if $y_2y_1 = 00$ and $w = 0$, then because $T_2 = D_1 = 0$ the state of the circuit will not change. An example of where $T_2 = 1$ is when $y_2y_1 = 01$ and $w = 1$, which causes y_2 to change to 1; $D_1 = 0$ makes $y_1 = 0$, hence $Y_2 = 1$ and $Y_1 = 0$. The other cases where $T_2 = 1$ occur when $w = 0$ and $y_2y_1 = 10$ or 11. In both of these cases $D_1 = 0$. Hence the T flip-flop changes its state from 1 to 0, while the D flip-flop is cleared, which means that the next state is $Y_2Y_1 = 00$. Completing this analysis we again obtain the state-assigned table in Figure 8.81a. Thus this circuit is yet another implementation of the FSM represented by the state table in Figure 8.81b.

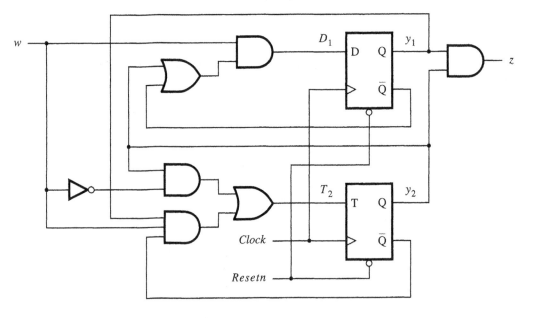

Figure 8.84   Circuit for Example 8.10.

Present state y_2y_1	Flip-flop inputs		Output z
	$w = 0$ T_2D_1	$w = 1$ T_2D_1	
0 0	0 0	0 1	0
0 1	0 0	1 0	0
1 0	1 0	0 1	0
1 1	1 0	0 1	1

Figure 8.85   The excitation table for the circuit in Figure 8.84.

8.12   CONCLUDING REMARKS

The existence of closed loops and delays in a sequential circuit leads to a behavior that is characterized by the set of states that the circuit can reach. The present values of the inputs are not the sole determining factor in this behavior, because a given valuation of inputs may cause the circuit to behave differently in different states.

The propagation delays through a sequential circuit must be taken into account. The design techniques presented in this chapter are based on the assumption that all changes in the circuit are triggered by the active edge of a clock signal. Such circuits work correctly only if all internal signals are stable when the clock signal arrives. Thus the clock period must be longer than the longest propagation delay in the circuit.

Synchronous sequential circuits are used extensively in practical designs. They are supported by the commonly used CAD tools. All textbooks on the design of logic circuits devote considerable space to synchronous sequential circuits. Some of the more notable references are [1–14].

In the next chapter we will present a different class of sequential circuits, which do not use flip-flops to represent the states of the circuit and do not use clock pulses to trigger changes in the states.

PROBLEMS

8.1   An FSM is defined by the state-assigned table in Figure P8.1. Derive a circuit that realizes this FSM using D flip-flops.

8.2   Derive a circuit that realizes the FSM defined by the state-assigned table in Figure P8.1 using JK flip-flops.

Present	Next state		Output
state	$w = 0$	$w = 1$	
y_2y_1	Y_2Y_1	Y_2Y_1	z
0 0	1 0	1 1	0
0 1	0 1	0 0	0
1 0	1 1	0 0	0
1 1	1 0	0 1	1

Figure P8.1   State-assigned table for problems 8.1 and 8.2.

8.3   Derive the state diagram for an FSM that has an input w and an output z. The machine has to generate $z = 1$ when the previous four values of w were 1001 or 1111; otherwise, $z = 0$. Overlapping input patterns are allowed. An example of the desired behavior is

$$w : 0101111001100111111$$
$$z : 0000001001000010011$$

8.4   Write VHDL code for the FSM described in problem 8.3.

8.5   Derive a minimal state table for a single-input and single-output Moore-type FSM that produces an output of 1 if in the input sequence it detects either 110 or 101 patterns. Overlapping sequences should be detected.

8.6   Repeat problem 8.5 for a Mealy-type FSM.

8.7   Derive the circuits that implement the state tables in Figures 8.51 and 8.52. What is the effect of state minimization on the cost of implementation?

8.8   Derive the circuits that implement the state tables in Figures 8.55 and 8.56. Compare the costs of these circuits.

8.9   A sequential circuit has two inputs, w_1 and w_2, and an output, z. Its function is to compare the input sequences on the two inputs. If $w_1 = w_2$ during any four consecutive clock cycles, the circuit produces $z = 1$; otherwise, $z = 0$. For example

$$w_1 : 0110111000110$$
$$w_2 : 1110101000111$$
$$z : 0000100001110$$

Derive a suitable circuit.

8.10   Write VHDL code for the FSM described in problem 8.9.

8.11   A given FSM has an input, w, and an output, z. During four consecutive clock pulses, a sequence of four values of the w signal is applied. Derive a state table for the FSM that produces $z = 1$ when it detects that either the sequence $w : 0010$ or $w : 1110$ has been applied; otherwise, $z = 0$. After the fourth clock pulse, the machine has to be again in the reset state, ready for the next sequence. Minimize the number of states needed.

8.12   Derive a minimal state table for an FSM that acts as a three-bit parity generator. For every three bits that are observed on the input w during three consecutive clock cycles, the FSM generates the parity bit $p = 1$ if and only if the number of 1s in the three-bit sequence is odd.

8.13   Write VHDL code for the FSM described in problem 8.12.

8.14   Draw timing diagrams for the circuits in Figures 8.43 and 8.47, assuming the same changes in a and b signals for both circuits. Account for propagation delays.

8.15   Show a state table for the state-assigned table in Figure P8.1, using A, B, C, D for the four rows in the table. Give a new state-assigned table using a one-hot encoding. For A use the code $y_4y_3y_2y_1 = 0001$. For states B, C, D use the codes 0010, 0100, and 1000, respectively. Synthesize a circuit using D flip-flops.

8.16   Show how the circuit derived in problem 8.15 can be modified such that the code $y_4y_3y_2y_1 = 0000$ is used for the reset state, A, and the other codes for state B, C, D are changed as needed. (Hint: you do not have to resynthesize the circuit!)

8.17   In Figure 8.59 assume that the unspecified outputs in states B and G are 0 and 1, respectively. Derive the minimized state table for this FSM.

8.18   In Figure 8.59 assume that the unspecified outputs in states B and G are 1 and 0, respectively. Derive the minimized state table for this FSM.

8.19   Derive circuits that implement the FSMs defined in Figures 8.57 and 8.58. Can you draw any conclusions about the complexity of circuits that implement Moore and Mealy types of machines?

8.20   Design a counter that counts pulses on line w and displays the count in the sequence $0, 2, 1, 3, 0, 2, \ldots$. Use D flip-flops in your circuit.

8.21   Repeat problem 8.20 using JK flip-flops.

8.22   Repeat problem 8.20 using T flip-flops.

8.23   Design a modulo-6 counter, which counts in the sequence $0, 1, 2, 3, 4, 5, 0, 1, \ldots$. The counter counts the clock pulses if its enable input, w, is equal to 1. Use D flip-flops in your circuit.

8.24   Repeat problem 8.23 using JK flip-flops.

8.25   Repeat problem 8.23 using T flip-flops.

8.26   Design a three-bit counterlike circuit controlled by the input w. If $w = 1$, then the counter adds 2 to its contents, wrapping around if the count reaches 8 or 9. Thus if the present state is 8 or 9, then the next state becomes 0 or 1, respectively. If $w = 0$, then the counter subtracts 1 from its contents, acting as a normal down-counter. Use D flip-flops in your circuit.

8.27   Repeat problem 8.26 using JK flip-flops.

8.28   Repeat problem 8.26 using T flip-flops.

8.29   Derive the state table for the circuit in Figure P8.2. What sequence of input values on wire w is detected by this circuit?

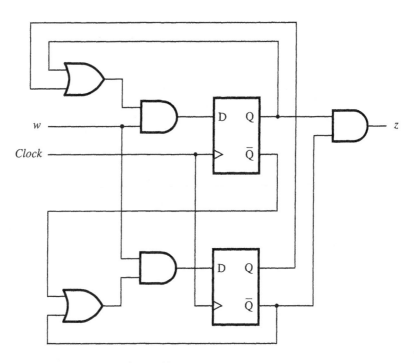

Figure P8.2   Circuit for problem 8.29.

8.30   Write VHDL code for the FSM shown in Figure 8.57, using the style of code in Figure 8.29.

8.31   Repeat problem 8.30, using the style of code in Figure 8.33.

8.32   Write VHDL code for the FSM shown in Figure 8.58, using the style of code in Figure 8.29.

8.33   Repeat problem 8.32, using the style of code in Figure 8.33.

8.34   Write VHDL code for the FSM shown in Figure P8.1. Use the method of state assignment shown in Figure 8.34.

8.35   Repeat problem 8.34, using the method of state assignment shown in Figure 8.35.

8.36   Represent the FSM in Figure 8.57 in form of an ASM chart.

8.37   Represent the FSM in Figure 8.58 in form of an ASM chart.

8.38   The arbiter FSM defined in section 8.8 (Figure 8.72) may cause device 3 to never get serviced if devices 1 and 2 continuously keep raising requests, so that in the Idle state it always happens that either device 1 or device 2 has an outstanding request. Modify the proposed FSM to ensure that device 3 will get serviced, such that if it raises a request, the devices 1 and 2 will be serviced only once before the device 3 is granted its request.

8.39   Write VHDL code for the FSM designed in problem 8.38.

8.40   Consider a more general version of the task presented in Example 8.1. Assume that there are four n-bit registers connected to a bus in a processor. The contents of register R are placed on the bus by asserting the control signal R_{out}. The data on the bus are loaded into register R on the active edge of the clock signal if the control signal R_{in} is asserted. Assume that three of the registers, called $R1$, $R2$, and $R3$, are used as normal registers. The fourth register, called *TEMP*, is used for temporary storage in special cases.

We want to realize an operation SWAP Ri,Rj, which swaps the contents of registers Ri and Rj. This is accomplished by the following sequence of steps (each performed in one clock cycle)

$$
\begin{aligned}
TEMP &\leftarrow [Rj] \\
Rj &\leftarrow [Ri] \\
Ri &\leftarrow [TEMP]
\end{aligned}
$$

Two input signals, w_1 and w_2, are used to indicate that two registers have to be swapped as follows

If $w_2 w_1 = 01$, then swap $R1$ and $R2$.
If $w_2 w_1 = 10$, then swap $R1$ and $R3$.
If $w_2 w_1 = 11$, then swap $R2$ and $R3$.

An input valuation that specifies a swap is present for three clock cycles. Design a circuit that generates the required control signals: $R1_{out}$, $R1_{in}$, $R2_{out}$, $R2_{in}$, $R3_{out}$, $R3_{in}$, $TEMP_{out}$, and $TEMP_{in}$. Derive the next-state and output expressions for this circuit, trying to minimize the cost.

REFERENCES

1. A. Dewey, *Analysis and Design of Digital Systems with VHDL*, (PWS Publishing Co.: 1997).

2. D. D. Gajski, *Principles of Digital Design*, (Prentice-Hall: Upper Saddle River, N.J., 1997).

3. M. M. Mano and C. R. Kime, *Logic and Computer Design Fundamentals*, (Prentice-Hall: Upper Saddle River, N.J., 1997).

4. J. P. Daniels, *Digital Design from Zero to One*, (Wiley: New York, 1996).

5. V. P. Nelson, H. T. Nagle, B. D. Carroll, and J. D. Irwin, *Digital Logic Circuit Analysis and Design*, (Prentice-Hall: Englewood Cliffs, N.J., 1995).

6. R. H. Katz, *Contemporary Logic Design*, (Benjamin/Cummings: Redwood City, Ca., 1994).

7. F. J. Hill and G. R. Peterson, *Computer Aided Logical Design with Emphasis on VLSI*, 4th ed., (Wiley: New York, 1993).

8. J. P. Hayes, *Introduction to Logic Design*, (Addison-Wesley: Reading, Ma., 1993).

9. C. H. Roth Jr., *Fundamentals of Logic Design*, 4th ed., (West: St. Paul, Mn., 1993).

10. J. F. Wakerly, *Digital Design Principles and Practices*, (Prentice-Hall: Engelwood Cliffs, N.J., 1990).

11. E. J. McCluskey, *Logic Design Principles*, (Prentice-Hall: Englewood Cliffs, N.J., 1986).

12. T. L. Booth, *Digital Networks and Computer Systems*, (Wiley: New York, 1971).

13. Z. Kohavi, *Switching and Finite Automata Theory*, (McGraw-Hill: New York, 1970).

14. J. Hartmanis and R. E. Stearns, *Algebraic Structure Theory of Sequential Machines*, (Prentice-Hall: Englewood Cliffs, N.J, 1966).

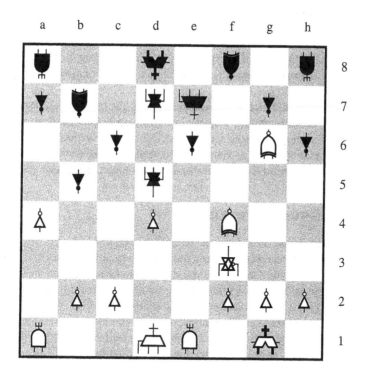

13. Rf1–e1, Nf6–d5

MAX+plusII is one of the most sophisticated and easiest to use CAD systems available on the market. In this tutorial we introduce the design of logic circuits using MAX+plusII. Step-by-step instructions are presented for performing design entry with three methods: using schematic capture, writing VHDL code, and using a truth table. The tutorial also illustrates functional simulation.

B.1　INTRODUCTION

This tutorial assumes that the reader has access to a computer on which MAX+plusII is installed. Instructions for installing the copy of MAX+plusII provided with the book are included with the CD-ROM. The MAX+plusII software will run on several different types of computer systems. For this tutorial a computer running a Microsoft operating systems (Windows95, Windows98, or WindowsNT) is assumed. Although MAX+plusII operates similarly on all of the supported types of computers, there are some minor differences. A reader who is not using a Microsoft Windows operating system may experience some slight discrepancies from this tutorial. Examples of potential differences are the locations of files in the computer's file system and the exact appearance of windows displayed by the software. All such discrepancies are minor and will not affect the reader's ability to follow the tutorial.

This tutorial does not describe how to use the operating system provided on the computer. We assume that the reader already knows how to perform actions such as running programs, operating a mouse, moving, resizing, minimizing and maximizing windows, creating directories (folders) and files, and the like. A reader who is not familiar with these procedures will need to learn how to use the computer's operating system before proceeding.

B.1.1　GETTING STARTED

Each logic circuit, or subcircuit, being designed in MAX+plusII is called a *project*. The software works on one project at a time and keeps all information for that project in a single directory in the file system (we use the traditional term *directory* for a location in the file system, but in Microsoft Windows the term *folder* is used). To begin a new logic circuit design, the first step is to create a directory to hold its files. As part of the installation of the MAX+plusII software, a few sample projects are placed into a directory called *max2work*. To hold the design files for this tutorial, we created the subdirectory *max2work**tutorial1*. The location and name of the directory is not important; hence the reader may use any valid directory.

To create a directory to work in, use the normal utilities provided by the computer's operating system. MAX+plusII is not involved in this step. After the directory has been created, start the MAX+plusII software. You should see a window similar to the one in Figure B.1. This window is called the *MAX+plusII Manager*. It provides access to all the features of MAX+plusII, which the user selects with the computer mouse.

Most of the commands provided by MAX+plusII are accessed by using a set of menus that are located in the Manager window below the title bar. For example, in Figure B.1

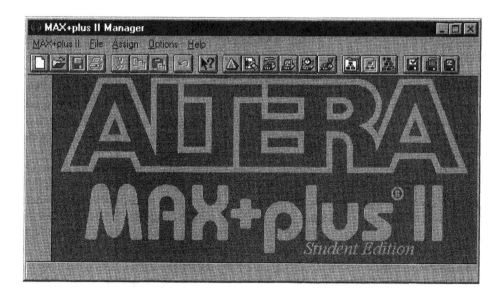

Figure B.1   The MAX+plusII Manager window.

clicking the left mouse button on the menu named File opens the menu shown in Figure B.2. Clicking the left mouse button on the entry Exit MAX+plusII Alt+F4 exits from MAX+plusII. In general, whenever the mouse is used to select something, the *left* button is used. Hence we will not normally specify which button to use. In the few cases when it is necessary to use the *right* mouse button, it will be specified explicitly. We should note that the Alt+F4 part of

Figure B.2   The File menu in the Manager window.

the menu item indicates a keyboard shortcut; instead of using the mouse, the command can alternatively be invoked by the holding down the Alt key on the keyboard and pressing the F4 function key. Keyboard shortcuts are available for a few of the MAX+plusII commands, but commands are usually invoked using the mouse. For some commands it is necessary to access two or more menus in sequence. We use the convention Menu1 | Menu2 | Item to indicate that to select the desired command the user should first click the left mouse button on Menu1, then within this menu click on Menu2, and then within Menu2 click on Item. For example, File | Exit MAX+plusII describes how to use the mouse to exit from the MAX+plusII system.

The MAX+plusII system includes 11 main software modules, called *applications*. They can be accessed in two different ways. First, all the applications can be invoked via the MAX+plusII menu in the Manager window, as illustrated in Figure B.3. Second, some of the applications can be invoked using the small icons that appear below the Manager title bar. (If no icons are visible under the Manager title bar, select Options | Preferences to open the Preferences dialog box. Then use the mouse to place a check mark beside the entry for Show Toolbar and click OK.) To see which applications in Figure B.3 a particular icon is associated with, place the mouse pointer on top of the icon; the Manager displays a message near the bottom of the window that gives the name of the application.

The applications introduced in this tutorial include the Graphic Editor, Text Editor, Waveform Editor, Compiler, Simulator, Message Processor, and Hierarchy Display. The others are introduced in Tutorial 2.

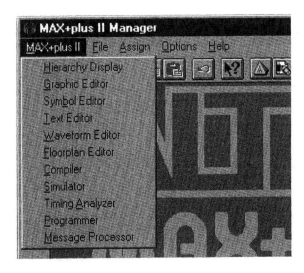

Figure B.3   The MAX+plus II menu in the Manager window.

MAX+plusII On-Line Help

MAX+plusII provides comprehensive on-line documentation that answers most of the questions that may arise when using the software. The documentation is accessed from the Help menu in the Manager window. To get some idea of the extent of documentation provided, it is worthwhile for the reader to browse through the Help menu. For instance, selecting Help | MAX+plusII Table of Contents shows all the categories of documentation available.

The user can quickly search through the Help topics by selecting Help | Search for Help on, which opens a dialog box into which keywords can be entered. The available Help topics that match the keywords are automatically displayed. Two other methods are provided for quickly finding documentation for specific topics. First, while using any application, pressing the F1 function key on the keyboard opens a Help display that shows the commands available for that application. Second, in some instances holding down the Shift key and pressing the F1 key changes the mouse pointer into a *help* pointer. This feature is available when using the schematic capture tool provided in MAX+plusII. Clicking the help pointer on any circuit element in a schematic automatically displays any documentation that is available for that circuit element.

B.2   DESIGN ENTRY USING SCHEMATIC CAPTURE

In Chapter 2 we introduced three types of design entry methods: truth tables, schematic capture, and VHDL. This section illustrates the process of using the schematic capture tool provided in MAX+plusII, which is called the Graphic Editor. As a simple example, we will draw a schematic for the logic function $f = x_1x_2 + \bar{x}_2x_3$. A circuit diagram for f was shown in Figure 2.26 and is reproduced as Figure B.4a. The truth table for f is given in Figure B.4b. Chapter 2 also introduced functional simulation. After creating the schematic, we show how to use the functional simulator in MAX+plusII to verify the schematic's functionality.

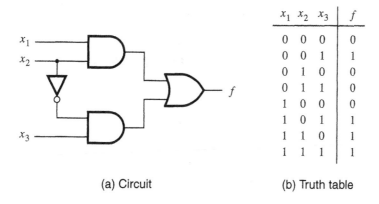

x_1	x_2	x_3	f
0	0	0	0
0	0	1	1
0	1	0	0
0	1	1	0
1	0	0	0
1	0	1	1
1	1	0	1
1	1	1	1

(a) Circuit   (b) Truth table

Figure B.4   The logic function of Figure 2.26.

B.2.1   Specifying the Project Name

As a first step we will specify the name of the design project. In the Manager window select File | Project | Name to open the pop-up box illustrated in Figure B.5. It is necessary to specify the location of the directory where MAX+plusII will store any files created for the project. For this example the directory used is named d:*max2work\tutorial1*. The disk drive designation, d:, is selected using the Drives pull-down menu shown in Figure B.5. The directory name is selected using the box labeled Directories. Use the mouse to double-click on the directory names displayed in the box until the proper directory is selected; the selected directory appears next to the words Directory is, as illustrated in the figure. In the box labeled Project Name, type *graphic1* as the name for this project and then click OK. Observe that the name of the project is displayed in the title bar of the Manager window.

B.2.2   Using the Graphic Editor

The next step is to draw the schematic. In the Manager window select MAX+plusII | Graphic Editor. The Graphic Editor window appears inside the Manager window. It may be helpful to move or resize the Graphic Editor window and to increase the size of the Manager window to provide more work space. In the screen capture in Figure B.6, the Graphic Editor window is maximized so that it fills the entire Manager window.

The title bar in Figure B.6 includes some menu names and icons that did not appear in Figure B.1. This is because the Manager window always indicates the features available in whatever application is currently being used. A number of icons that are used to invoke Graphic Editor features also appear along the left edge of the window. To see a description of the Graphic Editor feature associated with each icon, position the mouse on top of the icon; a message is displayed near the bottom of the window. Two of the most useful icons

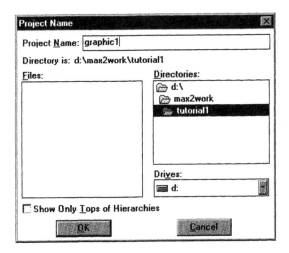

Figure B.5   Specifying the name and working directory for a project.

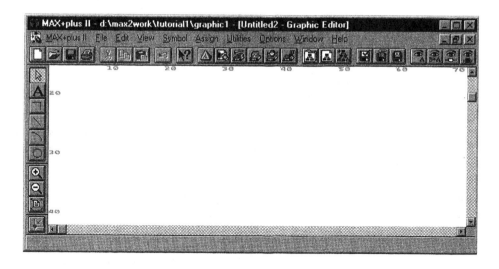

Figure B.6   The Graphic Editor display.

are the ones that look like a magnifying glass. These icons are used to see a larger or smaller view of the schematic.

Naming the Schematic

The schematic being created must be given a name. Select File | Save As to open the pop-up box depicted in Figure B.7. The directory that we chose for the project is already selected in the pop-up box. The Graphic Editor will create a separate file for the schematic and store it in the project's directory. In the box labeled File Name, type *graphic1.gdf*.

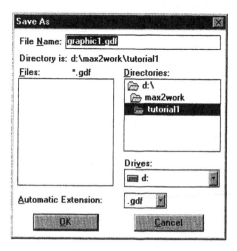

Figure B.7   Specifying the name of a schematic.

You must use exactly this name. The name *graphic1* must match the name of the project, and the filename extension *gdf*, which stands for *graphic design file*, must be used for all schematics. Click OK to return to the Graphic Editor.

Importing Logic-Gate Symbols

The Graphic Editor provides several libraries which contain circuit elements that can be imported into a schematic. For our simple example we will use a library called *Primitives*, which contains basic logic gates. To access the library, double-click on the blank space in the middle of the Graphic Editor display to open the pop-up box in Figure B.8 (another way to open this box is to select Symbol | Enter Symbol). The box labeled Symbol Libraries lists several available libraries, including the Primitives library. To open it, double-click on the line that ends with the word *prim*. A list of the logic gates in the library is automatically displayed in the Symbol Files box. Double-click on the *and2* symbol to import it into the schematic (you can alternatively click on *and2* and then click OK). A two-input AND-gate symbol now appears in the Graphic Editor window.

Any symbol in a schematic can be selected using the mouse. Position the mouse pointer on top of the AND-gate symbol in the schematic and click the mouse to select it. The symbol is highlighted in red. To move a symbol, select it and, while continuing to press the mouse button, drag the mouse to move the symbol. To make it easier to position the graphical symbols, a grid of guidelines can be displayed in the Graphic Editor window by selecting Options | Show Guidelines. Spacing between grid lines can be adjusted using Options | Guideline Spacing.

The logic function *f* requires a second two-input AND gate, a two-input OR gate, and a NOT gate. Use the following steps to import them into the schematic.

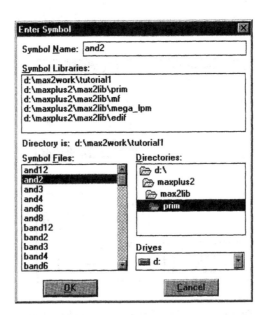

Figure B.8   Importing a logic gate from the Primitives library.

Position the mouse pointer over the AND-gate symbol that has already been imported. Press and hold down the Ctrl keyboard key and click and drag the mouse away from the AND-gate symbol. The Graphic Editor automatically imports a second instance of the AND-gate symbol. This shortcut procedure for making a copy of a circuit element is convenient when you need many instances of the same element in a schematic. Of course, an alternative approach is to import each instance of the symbol by opening the Primitives library as described above.

To import the OR-gate symbol, again double-click on a blank space in the Graphic Editor and then double-click on the Primitives library. In the box labeled Symbol Files, use the scroll bar to scroll down through the list of gates to find the symbol named *or2*. Import this symbol into the schematic. Next import the NOT gate using the same procedure. To orient the NOT gate so that it points downward, as depicted in Figure B.4*a*, select the NOT-gate symbol and then use the command Edit | Rotate | 270 to rotate the symbol 270 degrees counterclockwise. The symbols in the schematic can be moved by selecting them and dragging the mouse, as explained above. More than one symbol can be selected at the same time by clicking the mouse and dragging an outline around the symbols. The selected symbols are moved together by clicking on any one of them and moving it. Experiment with this procedure. Arrange the symbols so that the schematic appears similar to the one in Figure B.9.

Importing Input and Output Symbols

Now that the logic-gate symbols have been entered, it is necessary to import symbols to represent the input and output ports of the circuit. Open the Primitives library again. Click the mouse anywhere in the box labeled Symbol Files and then type the letter "i" to jump ahead in the list of symbols to those whose names begin with *i*. This shortcut can be used in addition to the scroll bars provided on the Symbol Files box. Import the symbol

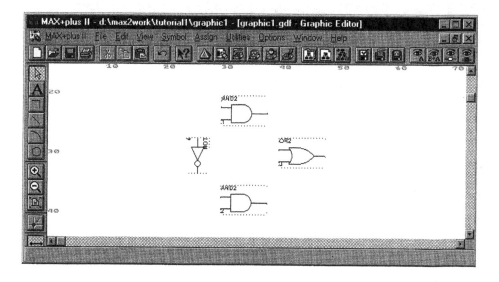

Figure B.9   A partially completed schematic for the circuit in Figure B.4.

named *input* into the schematic. Import two additional instances of the input symbol. To represent the output of the circuit, open the Primitives library and import the symbol named output. Arrange the symbols to appear as illustrated in Figure B.10.

Assigning Names to Input and Output Symbols

Point to the word PIN_NAME on the input pin symbol in the upper-left corner of the schematic and double-click the mouse. The pin name is selected, allowing a new pin name to be typed. Type $x1$ as the pin name. Hitting carriage return immediately after typing the pin name causes the mouse focus to move to the pin directly below the one currently being named. This method can be used to name any number of pins. Assign the names $x2$ and $x3$ to the middle and bottom input pins, respectively. Finally, assign the name f to the output pin.

Connecting Nodes with Wires

The next step is to draw lines (wires) to connect the symbols in the schematic together. Click on the icon that looks like an arrowhead along the left edge of the Manager window. This icon is called the **Selection** tool, and it allows the Graphic Editor to change automatically between the modes of selecting a symbol on the screen or drawing wires to interconnect symbols. The appropriate mode is chosen depending on where the mouse is pointing.

Move the mouse pointer on top of the $x1$ input symbol. The mouse pointer appears as an arrowhead when pointing anywhere on the symbol except at the right edge. The arrowhead means that the symbol will be selected if the mouse button is pressed. Move the mouse to point to the small line, called a *pinstub*, on the right edge of the $x1$ input symbol. The mouse pointer changes to a crosshair, which allows a wire to be drawn to connect the

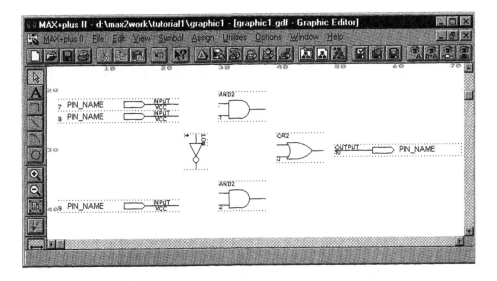

Figure B.10   Input and output symbols added to the schematic in Figure B.9.

pinstub to another location in the schematic. A connection between two or more pinstubs in a schematic is called a *node*. The name derives from electrical terminology, where the term *node* refers to any number of points in a circuit that are connected together by wires and thus have the same voltage.

Connect the input symbol for $x1$ to the AND gate at the top of the schematic as follows. While the mouse is pointing at the pinstub on the $x1$ symbol, click and hold the mouse button. Drag the mouse to the right until the line (wire) that is drawn reaches the pinstub on the top input of the AND gate; then release the button. The two pinstubs are now connected and represent a single node in the circuit.

Use the same procedure to draw a wire from the pinstub on the $x2$ input symbol to the other input on the AND gate. Then draw a wire from the pinstub on the input of the NOT gate upward until it reaches the wire connecting $x2$ to the AND gate. Release the mouse button and observe that a connecting dot is drawn automatically. The three pinstubs corresponding to the $x2$ input symbol, the AND-gate input, and the NOT-gate input now represent a single node in the circuit. Figure B.11 shows a magnified view of the part of the schematic that contains the connections drawn so far. To increase or decrease the portion of the schematic displayed on the screen, use the icons that look like magnifying glasses on the left side of the Manager window.

To complete the schematic, connect the output of the NOT gate to the lower AND gate and connect the input symbol for $x3$ to that AND gate as well. Connect the outputs of the two AND gates to the OR gate and connect the OR gate to the f output symbol. If any mistakes are made while connecting the symbols, erroneous wires can be selected with the mouse and then removed by pressing the Delete key or by selecting Edit | Delete. The finished schematic is depicted in Figure B.12. Save the schematic using File | Save.

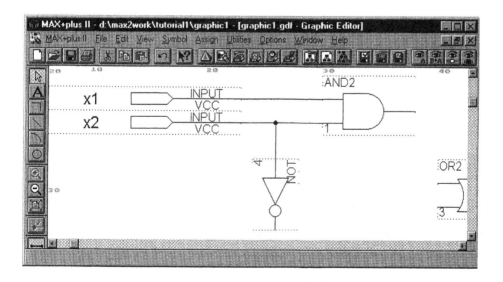

Figure B.11   Connecting the symbols in the schematic from Figure B.10.

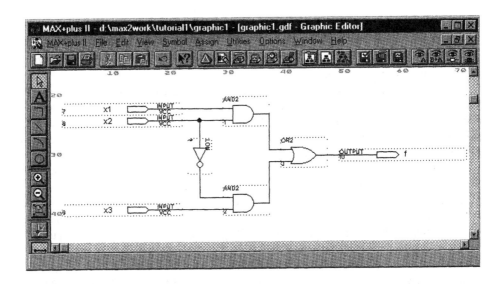

Figure B.12   The completed schematic for the circuit in Figure B.4.

Since our example schematic is quite simple, it is easy to draw all the wires in the circuit without producing a messy diagram. However, in larger schematics some nodes that have to be connected may be far apart, in which case it is awkward to draw wires between them. In such cases the nodes are connected by assigning labels to them, instead of drawing wires. We will illustrate this method of connecting nodes in section D.3.1.

B.2.3   Synthesizing a Circuit from the Schematic

As we explained in section 2.8.2, after a schematic is entered into a CAD system, it is processed by initial synthesis tools. These tools analyze the schematic and generate a Boolean equation for each logic function in the circuit. In MAX+plusII the synthesis tools are controlled by the application program called the *Compiler.*

Using the Compiler

To open the Compiler window, click the mouse on the Compiler icon (it looks like a factory with a smoke stack) below the Manager window title bar or select MAX+plusII | Compiler.

For this tutorial we will use only the tools that are needed to allow us to perform a functional simulation of the schematic. To tell the Compiler to use these tools, select Processing | Functional SNF Extractor. The Compiler window should appear as shown in Figure B.13. The window shows three software modules that are invoked in sequence by the Compiler. The Compiler Netlist Extractor and Database Builder represent the initial synthesis tools. The module called Functional SNF Extractor creates a file, called a *simulator netlist file (SNF),* which describes the functionality of the circuit and is used by the functional simulator.

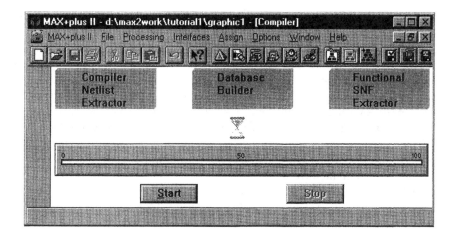

Figure B.13   The Compiler display.

Click the mouse on the Start button in the Compiler window. The Compiler indicates its progress by displaying a red progress bar and by placing an icon under each of the three software modules as they are executed. When the Compiler is finished, a window should be displayed that indicates zero warnings and zero errors. Click OK in this window to return to the Compiler window.

If the Compiler does not specify zero warnings and zero errors, then at least one mistake has been made when entering the schematic. In this case the Compiler opens a window called the **Message Processor**, which displays a message concerning each warning or error generated. An example showing how the Message Processor can be used to quickly locate and fix errors in a schematic is given in section B.2.5.

To close the Compiler window, use the *Close button* (it is an X) located in the top-right corner of its window.

B.2.4 PERFORMING FUNCTIONAL SIMULATION

Before the schematic can be simulated, it is necessary to create the desired waveforms, called *test vectors*, to represent the input signals. For this tutorial we will use the MAX+plusII Waveform Editor to draw test vectors, but it is also possible to use a text editor to create test vectors in a plain text (ASCII) file. Documentation pertaining to ASCII test vectors can be opened by selecting Help | MAX+plusII Table of Contents. Click on Simulator, then click on Basic Tools, and finally click on Vector File (.vec).

Using the Waveform Editor

Open the Waveform Editor window by selecting MAX+plusII | Waveform Editor. Because the Waveform Editor has many uses, it is necessary to indicate that we wish to enter test vectors for simulation purposes. Select File | Save As and type (if not already there) *graphic1.scf* in the box labeled File Name. A file with *scf* extension stores the waveforms that will be used as simulation test vectors.

Select Node | Enter Nodes from SNF to open the pop-up box shown in Figure B.14. Click on the List button in the upper-right corner of this box to display the names of the nodes in the current project in the box labeled Available Nodes & Groups. Click the mouse on the name $x3$ to highlight it. Click on the button labeled => to copy $x3$ into the box labeled Selected Nodes & Groups. Use the same procedure to select each of the other signals and copy them into the Selected Nodes & Groups box. It is also possible to select multiple nodes at the same time, by dragging the mouse upward or downward inside the Available Nodes & Groups box. Click OK to return to the Waveform Editor. The nodes $x1$, $x2$, $x3$, and f are now shown in the waveform display.

We will now specify the logic values to be used for the input signals during functional simulation. The logic values at the output f will be generated automatically by the simulator.

Select File | End Time to specify the total amount of time for which the circuit will be simulated. In the box labeled Time, type *160ns* to set the total simulation time to 160 nanoseconds. This amount of time is rather arbitrary because functional simulation does not include any timing delays, as discussed in section 2.8.3. The concept of *simulation time* will become more significant in Tutorial 2 when timing simulation is introduced. Click OK to return to the Waveform Editor. Select View | Fit in Window so that the entire time range from 0 to 160 ns is visible in the Waveform Editor display. In the Options menu make sure that Show Grid has a check mark next to it so that the Waveform Editor displays light vertical guidelines in the waveform area of the display. The guidelines provide a visual aid for positioning the mouse when drawing waveforms. Select Options | Grid Size and type *20ns* in the box labeled Grid Size. Click the mouse when pointing to any of the guidelines and observe that a vertical reference line is drawn at that point. We will use the reference line in Tutorial 2. Figure B.15 shows how the Waveform Editor window should look at this

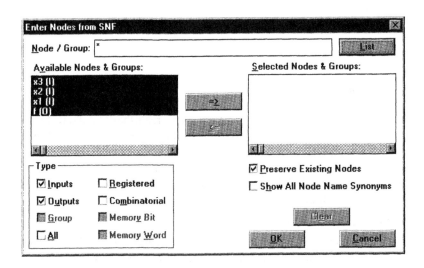

Figure B.14   Selecting nodes for simulation.

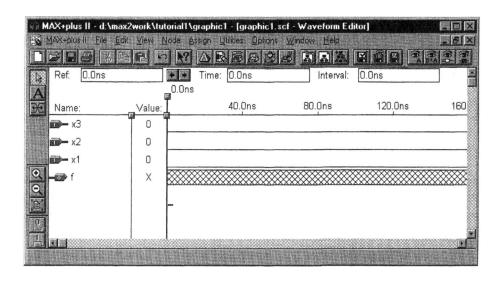

Figure B.15 The Waveform Editor display.

point. The input waveforms are set to logic value 0, and the output is shown as a hashed-line pattern that indicates that the logic value has not yet been determined.

To thoroughly test the circuit during simulation, it is desirable to use as many different values of the input signals as possible. For our small example, there are only eight different valuations, and so it is easy to include all of them. To make all eight valuations fit in the 160 ns simulation time, the signal valuations have to change every 20 ns. To create the waveforms for the input signals, do the following.

Activate the *Waveform Editing* tool by pressing its icon on the left edge of the window. The icon is shown in the top-left corner of Figure B.16; it looks like two arrows pointing left and right. Position the mouse pointer over the waveform for input $x3$ at the 20 ns grid line. Press and drag the mouse to the right to highlight the section of the $x3$ waveform from 20 ns to 40 ns, as illustrated in Figure B.16. The Waveform Editing Tool automatically

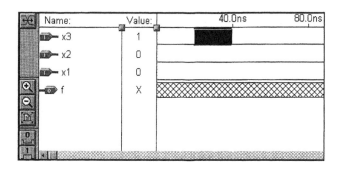

Figure B.16 Editing the waveform for $x3$ from Figure B.15.

changes the selected portion of the waveform from its present value 0 to the value 1. Next select the section of the waveform for $x3$ between 60 ns and 80 ns to set it to 1. Continue in this manner to set every second 20 ns section of $x3$ to 1.

An alternative way to draw waveforms is to use the Selection tool, which is activated by selecting the icon that looks like an arrowhead along the left edge of the window. Using the Selection tool, the procedure for drawing a waveform is to first select a section of the waveform by dragging the mouse over it. The highlighted section can be set to 1 by selecting Edit | Overwrite | High. The highlighted section can also be changed by using the buttons labeled 0 or 1 along the left edge of the window.

Use the Waveform Editing tool to set the waveform for $x2$ to 1 in the range from 40 ns to 80 ns, as well as from 120 ns to 160 ns. Also, set the waveform for $x1$ to 1 in the range from 80 ns to 160 ns. The waveforms drawn, as illustrated in Figure B.17, now include all eight input valuations. Select File | Save to save the waveforms in the *graphic1.scf* file.

Performing the Simulation

To open the Simulator window, shown in Figure B.18, click on its icon (it looks like a computer with a waveform on the screen) or Select MAX+plusII | Simulator. MAX+plusII provides both functional simulation and timing simulation. The type of simulation used by the Simulator application is determined automatically by the settings used in the Compiler application. The Simulator will perform a functional simulation in this case because we instructed the Compiler to generate information for functional simulation, as discussed for Figure B.13.

Observe in Figure B.18 that the Simulator specifies that it will use the file called *graphic1.scf* as the simulator input and will perform the simulation for the time range from 0 to 160 ns. Click the Start button to perform the simulation. The Simulator displays a message indicating that no errors were generated. Click OK to return to the Simulator window. The simulator stores the results of the simulation in the *graphic1.scf* file. To view the file, click on the Open SCF button in the simulator window, which automatically opens the Waveform Editor window and displays the file. As illustrated in Figure B.19, the Simulator creates a waveform for the output f. The reader should verify that the generated waveform corresponds to the truth table for f given in Figure B.4b. The Waveform Editor and Simulator windows can now be closed.

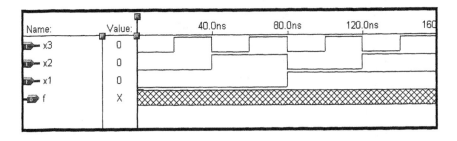

Figure B.17   The completed waveforms for $x1$, $x2$, and $x3$.

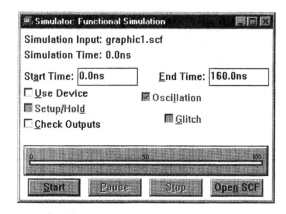

Figure B.18   The Simulator display.

B.2.5   USING THE MESSAGE PROCESSOR TO LOCATE AND FIX ERRORS

In the description in section B.2.3 of how the Compiler is used to synthesize a circuit from
the schematic, we said that the Compiler should produce a message stating that no warnings
or errors were generated. In this section we illustrate what happens when there is an error
in the schematic. To insert an error in the schematic created for f, reopen the schematic by
selecting File | Open to open the pop-up box shown in Figure B.20. In the box labeled Show
in Files List, click on Graphic Editor Files. Then in the box labeled Files, click on the name

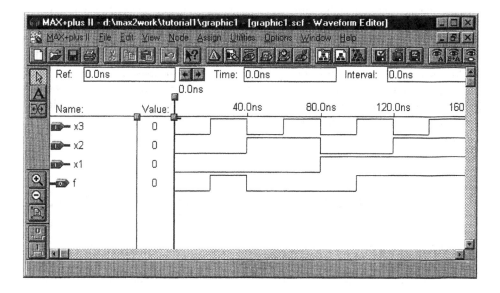

Figure B.19   Functional simulation results for the waveforms in Figure B.17.

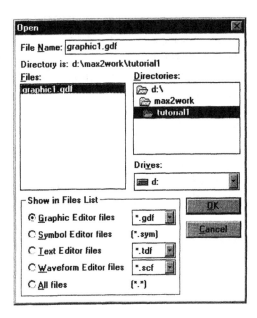

Figure B.20   The dialog box used to reopen the schematic.

graphic1.gdf to put this name in the box labeled File Name. Alternatively, *graphic1.gdf* can be typed into the box rather than using the mouse to select it from the list of files. Click OK to open the file inside the Graphic Editor.

Use the mouse to select the wire that connects the output of the OR gate to the *f* output symbol. Delete the wire by pressing the Delete key; then save the schematic file. Open the Compiler window and run the synthesis tools again. The Compiler should produce a message stating that one warning and one error were found. Click OK. A window, called the Message Processor, is automatically opened to display the messages generated by the Compiler, as illustrated in Figure B.21. If the Message Processor window is obscured by some other window, select MAX+plusII | Message Processor to bring the Message Processor window to the foreground.

The warning message is produced because the OR-gate output is not connected to any other node in the schematic. The error message states that the *f* output symbol is

Figure B.21   The Message Processor display.

not connected to anything. Although it is clear how to fix the error, since we created it purposely, in general some of the messages displayed by the Compiler when synthesizing larger circuits may not be obvious. In such cases it is possible to select a message with the mouse and then click on the Help on Message button in the Message Processor window; documentation that explains the message is automatically opened. Experiment with this feature for both the warning and error messages in Figure B.21.

Another convenient feature of the Message Processor is the Locate button in the lower-left corner of the window. It can be used to automatically display the section of the schematic where the error exists. Select the warning message and then click the Locate button. Observe that the Graphic Editor is automatically displayed with the OR gate highlighted. Next select the error message in the Message Processor window and then click the Locate button again. The *f* output symbol becomes highlighted in the Graphic Editor.

Use the Graphic Editor to redraw the missing wire between the OR-gate output and the *f* output symbol. Save the schematic and then use the Compiler to run the synthesis tools to see that the error is fixed. We have now completed our introduction to design using schematic capture. If any application windows are still open, close them to return to the Manager window.

INDEX